The Epistles
of John

The Epistles
of John

by
Oliver B. Greene

The Gospel Hour, Inc., Oliver B. Greene, Director
P. O. Box 2024, Greenville, South Carolina

First printing, March 1966—10,000 copies
Second printing, January 1967—10,000 copies
Third printing, January 1968—15,000 copies
Fourth printing, July 1969—15,000 copies
Fifth printing, May 1970—15,000 copies
Sixth printing, April 1973—15,000 copies
Seventh printing, November 1973—15,000 copies

$5.00

Contents

The First Epistle
of John

THE FIRST EPISTLE OF JOHN

Introduction

I love all of the Word of God, but I learned to love and appreciate the First Epistle of John very early in my Christian experience. I memorized the five chapters while I was in Bible school at the beginning of my ministry.

We owe much to the pen of John the Beloved. Imagine what would happen to our Bible if the books dictated to him by the Holy Spirit were removed from the Holy Scriptures. We are indebted to John for the Gospel that bears his name, for his three epistles, and also for *Revelation*, the last book in our Bible.

It is interesting to note that God intrusted to John "the salvation book": "And many other signs truly did Jesus in the presence of His disciples, which are not written in this book: *But these are written, that ye might believe that Jesus is the Christ, the Son of God; and that believing ye might have life through His name*" (John 20:30, 31).

This first epistle of John is "the joy book": "*And these things write we unto you, that your joy may be full*" (I John 1:4).

And to this same beloved disciple God intrusted His last revelation to man. John was exiled to the Isle of Patmos for his testimony, and there God gave him the twenty-two chapters that make up the last book in our Bible — *The Revelation*.

Most Bible scholars believe that this first epistle was written about 90 A.D. At that time, John was the only surviving apostle: the others had sealed their testimony with their life's blood. First John is a wonderful epistle — its words are simple, a child can understand them; but the truths it reveals are extremely deep and unsearchably rich. The epistle is direct and very plain; it contains no supposition at all, but every sentence is bursting with deep spiritual truth that makes possible the believer's "full joy."

In the epistles of Paul and Peter we find the different parts to be so clearly distinguishable that they can be outlined and set off in sections; but such is not true in the first epistle of John, because from the first word to the last, tremendous truths and precious promises are interwoven, welded together. It is a *family* epistle.

I am not suggesting that we cannot outline or divide the chapters — we *can,* but not in the marked, distinct way that the epistles of Paul and Peter can be outlined or divided. There are certain distinguishable breaks and divisions in First John. For example, the words *"light"* and *"darkness"* occur only in the first twenty-one verses. *The Holy Spirit,* is not mentioned until chapter 3, verse 24. He is mentioned seven times after that, in contrast to five references to *other* spirits. But these divisions are not such as to break specific lines of thought which run from the first of the epistle to the very last verse.

There are five main themes in this first epistle of John, themes that are connected like links in a chain:
1. Mutual love among believers.
2. The believer's abiding in Christ, and in God the Father.
3. How the believer may know and distinguish truth from error.
4. The true traits of a born again, blood washed believer.
5. The believer and his relationship to this present world.

Seven Contrasts

In this first epistle of John we find seven successive contrasts:
1. Contrast between the true Light, and darkness (ch. 1, v.5 through ch. 2, v.11).
2. Contrast between the true heavenly Father and the world (ch.2, vv.12 through 17).
3. Christ in contrast to the counterfeit christ — *Antichrist* (ch. 2, vv.18 through 28).
4. Good works of the true believer in contrast to the evil works of unbelievers and antichrists (ch. 2, v. 29 through ch. 3, v. 24).
5. The Holy Spirit in contrast to error (ch. 4, vv. 1 through 6).
6. The pure love of God in the heart of the believer in contrast to pious pretense — or hypocritical love (ch. 4 vv.7 through 21).
7. Truly born again, blood washed believers in contrast to others who are *not* truly born again (ch. 5, vv.1 through 21).
These contrasts reveal the central theme of the epistle —

Truth versus error — and how to *know* the truth and abide in Christ. Throughout the entire epistle we read such phrases as "hereby we know . . . hereby shall we know . . . by this we know." "*We*" refers to the born again believer. These clauses are like the red traffic lights along our streets — they cause us to stop and search for the truth set forth either preceding or following these "Bible red lights." God gave this epistle to John for the Church — that body of Christ made up of all truly born again people — that we may KNOW, that we may be able to distinguish between truth and error, that we may be able to know true Christian love as apart from counterfeit love; and that, *knowing* the truth, the believer may "ABIDE" in truth and in pure Christian love. The key clause in these seven contrasts between pure truth and gross error is "*hereby we KNOW.*"

A thorough study of these contrasts will readily point out to the believer seven heart-searching tests:

In number 1 — the acid test of true profession.
In number 2 — a desire.
In number 3 — the test of true doctrine.
In number 4 — the test of conduct.
In number 5 — the acid test of discernment.
In number 6 — the test of motive.
In number 7 — the new birth (the birth from above).

In this epistle we do not find such expressions as "In my opinion . . . As it were . . . The way I see it. . . ." With John the Beloved, writing under inspiration of God, light is *light*, truth is *truth*, and error is *error*. There is no "twilight," no half-truth. We might refer to this epistle as "*the book of no compromise!!*" There is no haze, no fog, over its message. It is crystal clear.

Fundamentals Set Forth in First John

From this epistle we learn that the all-inclusive commandments are just two: "Believe on Jesus Christ," and "Love one another" (ch. 3, v. 23).

We also learn that love professed with the lips but not manifested in service to those in need is not *true* love; it is false, hypocritical (ch. 3, vv.17, 18). God the Father set the example when He sacrificed His only begotten Son, the Son of His love;

and since God loved us while we were yet sinners, *enemies,* and made such sacrifice for us, then surely we should love one another (ch. 4, vv.10, 11).

In this epistle is declared the tremendous spiritual fundamental of the faith that brings unshakeable peace; and the secret of such peace is, *"perfect love casteth out fear"* (ch. 4, v.18).

A basic fundamental of "THE *FAITH"* having to do with eternal life is found in chapter 5, verses 10 through 13: "He that believeth on the Son of God hath the witness in himself: he that believeth not God hath made Him a liar; because he believeth not the record that God gave of His Son. And this is the record, that God hath given to us eternal life, and this life is in His Son. He that hath the Son hath life; and he that hath not the Son of God hath not life. These things have I written unto you that believe on the name of the Son of God; that ye may KNOW that ye have eternal life, and that ye may believe on the name of the Son of God."

The Errorists

Even in the days of John the Beloved there were false teachers. There were two main errors being taught:
1. That Christ was entirely too Divine to have been really human. They accepted Him as very God, but denied that He was just as truly man.
2. That Christ was entirely too human to have been really Divine. They taught that Jesus could not have been God in flesh.

We have both errors today. Christian Science goes along with the first, Unitarian teaching goes along with the second. In this first epistle of John, the Holy Spirit strikes quickly and powerfully at both of these errors. They are not named, but listen:

"That which was from the beginning, which we have heard, which we have seen with our eyes, which we have looked upon, and our hands have handled, of the Word of life; (For the life was manifested, and we have seen it, and bear witness, and shew unto you that eternal life, which was with the Father, and was manifested unto us;) That which we have seen and heard declare we unto you, that ye also may have fellowship with us:

12

and truly our fellowship is with the Father, and with His Son Jesus Christ" (ch. 1, vv. 1-3).

The Holy Spirit wanted us to know that what John wrote down for the Church was not only inspired of God, but that John had firsthand information. He had personally witnessed these well-proven facts. There was no mystery-mongering in the words penned down by this beloved disciple. Jesus was "the Word," He was "the Life."

In I John 2:20, 27 we have the assurance that believers shall not be confounded, confused, or led astray by teachers of error:

"But ye have an unction from the Holy One, and ye know all things. . . . But the anointing which ye have received of Him abideth in you, and ye need not that any man teach you: but as the same anointing teacheth you of all things, and is truth, and is no lie, and even as it hath taught you, ye shall abide in Him."

Seven Traits of the True Believer

These seven traits of the true believer should be studied carefully:

1. "If ye know that He is righteous, ye know that every one that doeth righteousness is born of Him" (ch. 2, v. 29).
2. "Whosoever is born of God doth not commit sin; for His seed remaineth in him: and he cannot sin, because he is born of God" (ch. 3, v. 9).
3. "Beloved, let us love one another: for love is of God; and every one that loveth is born of God, and knoweth God" (ch. 4, v. 7).
4. "Whosoever believeth that Jesus is the Christ is born of God: and every one that loveth Him that begat loveth Him also that is begotten of Him" (ch. 5, v. 1).
5. If we love Jesus the Son we love God the Father of the Son. We cannot love one without loving both (ch. 5, v. 1).
6. "For whatsoever is born of God overcometh the world: and this is the victory that overcometh the world, even our faith" (ch. 5, v. 4).
7. "We know that whosoever is born of God sinneth not; but he that is begotten of God keepeth himself, and that wicked one toucheth him not" (ch. 5, v. 18).

Seven Definite Reasons Why This
Epistle Was Given for the Church

1. "That which we have seen and heard declare we unto you, that ye also may have fellowship with us: and truly our fellowship is with the Father, and with His Son Jesus Christ" (ch. 1, v. 3).

2. "And these things write we unto you, that your joy may be full" (ch. 1, v. 4).

3. "My little children, these things write I unto you, that ye sin not. And if any man sin, we have an Advocate with the Father, Jesus Christ the righteous" (ch. 2, v. 1).

4. "I write unto you, fathers, because ye have known Him that is from the beginning. I write unto you, young men, because ye have overcome the wicked one. I write unto you, little children, because ye have known the Father. I have written unto you, fathers, because ye have known Him that is from the beginning. I have written unto you, young men, because ye are strong, and the word of God abideth in you, and ye have overcome the wicked one. Love not the world, neither the things that are IN the world. If any man love the world, the love of the Father is not in him. For all that is in the world, the lust of the flesh, and the lust of the eyes, and the pride of life, is not of the Father, but is of the world. And the world passeth away, and the lust thereof: but he that doeth the will of God abideth for ever" (ch. 2, vv. 13-17).

5. "I have not written unto you because ye know not the truth, but because ye know it, and that no lie is of the truth. Who is a liar but he that denieth that Jesus is the Christ? He is antichrist, that denieth the Father and the Son. Whosoever denieth the Son, the same hath not the Father: but he that acknowledgeth the Son hath the Father also. Let that therefore abide in you which ye have heard from the beginning. If that which ye have heard from the beginning shall remain in you, ye also shall continue in the Son, and in the Father" (ch. 2, vv. 21-24).

6. "These things have I written unto you concerning them that seduce you" (ch. 2, v. 26).

7. "These things have I written unto you that believe on the name of the Son of God; that ye may know that ye have eternal life, and that ye may believe on the name of the Son of God" (ch. 5, v. 13).

Seven Decisive, Divine Tests of Genuine Christianity

1. "If we say that we have fellowship with Him, and walk in darkness, we lie, and do not the truth" (ch. 1, v. 6).
2. "If we say that we have no sin, we deceive ourselves, and the truth is not in us" (ch. 1, v. 8).
3. "If we say that we have not sinned, we make Him a liar, and His Word is not in us" (ch. 1, v. 10).
4. "He that saith, I know Him, and keepeth not His commandments, is a liar, and the truth is not in him" (ch. 2, v. 4).
5. "He that saith he abideth in Him ought himself also so to walk, even as He walked" (ch. 2, v. 6).
6. "He that saith he is in the light, and hateth his brother, is in darkness even until now" (ch. 2, v. 9).
7. "If a man say, I love God, and hateth his brother, he is a liar: for he that loveth not his brother whom he hath seen, how can he love God whom he hath not seen?" (ch. 4, v. 20).

Seven Tests of Honesty

Last but not least, let me point out the seven "if we say," or "he that saith." These are tests of honesty and reality, and in each instance we have the mark by which hypocrisy (or the lie) is exposed:

1. *False fellowship*: "IF WE SAY that we have fellowship with Him, and walk in darkness, we lie, and do not the truth" (ch. 1, v. 6).
2. *False sanctity*: "IF WE SAY that we have no sin, we deceive ourselves, and the truth is not in us" (ch. 1, v. 8).
3. *False righteousness*: "IF WE SAY that we have not sinned, we make Him a liar, and His Word is not in us" (ch. 1, v. 10).
4. *False allegiance*: "HE THAT SAITH, I know Him, and keepeth not His commandments, is a liar, and the truth is not in him" (ch. 2, v. 4).
5. *False behavior*: "HE THAT SAITH he abideth in Him ought himself also so to walk, even as He walked" (ch. 2 v.6).

6. *False holiness*: "HE THAT SAITH he is in the light, and hateth his brother, is in darkness even until now" (ch. 2, v.9).

7. *False (hypocritical) love to God*: "IF A MAN SAY, I love God, and hateth his brother, he is a liar: for he that loveth not his brother whom he hath seen, how can he love God whom he hath not seen?" (ch. 4, v. 20).

As we study each of these verses carefully we notice that the religious "professor" — he who has not been born again — *is living a lie* having to do with others and with himself. He is not honest with his fellowman, he refuses to be honest with his own heart. But we notice also that he is living a lie as having to do with *God*, and as having to do with Jesus Christ. He is living a lie as having to do with the *world*, and as having to do with the true Christian. As a matter of fact, he is actually living a lie *throughout*, because his *entire life* is false — in things concerning himself, concerning God and concerning his fellowman.

The number-one desire of the devil is to damn your soul in the lake of fire; but if he fails (if you believe on the Lord Jesus and are truly saved) he does not give up. He knows he cannot steal a soul covered with the precious blood of the Lamb, but it IS possible for him to rob you of your spiritual birthright of "life abundant" and a "full reward."

In John's Gospel 20:31 we read, "These are written, that ye might believe that Jesus is the Christ, the Son of God; and believing ye might have life through His name." In John 5:13 we read, "These things have I written unto you that believe on the name of the Son of God; that ye may know that ye have eternal life, and that ye may believe on the name of the Son of God." Comparing these two verses, we see that the *Gospel of John* and the *first epistle of John* are complimentary one to the other. *The Gospel of John* was written specifically that men might believe on the Lord Jesus Christ, and believing, have life. *The first epistle* was given to the Church, that true believers might *know* that they have life, and that this eternal life is in Christ Jesus. In the Gospel of John we see Divine life as revealed in Christ Jesus, the Son of God. In the first epistle we see the same Divine life *realized* in the true, born again, blood washed believer. In the Gospel of John we discover the WAY of eternal life — through the Incarnate Son of God, the Way, the Truth, the Life. There is no other way, no other truth, no other life. In the first epistle we see unfolded the *nature* of eternal life now possessed by the true believer.

As we sincerely and seriously study every word in the five chapters of this, the "joy book," may we allow the Holy Spirit to open our eyes, humble our hearts, bless us, and make us vessels meet for the Master's use. May we see the true Light as never before, may we appreciate the true Life and the true Love of God as never before.

I pray that in spite of my limitations and shortcomings, the God of all grace will use this study to bless every believer who reads these lines, and to lead unbelievers to know Jesus as this commentary is passed from the hand of the believer to the hand of the unbeliever. This is my prayer in the name of Christ Jesus, Saviour and soon coming King!

I JOHN — Chapter 1

1. That which was from the beginning, which we have heard, which we have seen with our eyes, which we have looked upon, and our hands have handled, of the Word of life:

2. (For the life was manifested, and we have seen it, and bear witness, and shew unto you that eternal life, which was with the Father, and was manifested unto us.)

3. That which we have seen and heard declare we unto you, that ye also may have fellowship with us: and truly our fellowship is with the Father, and with his Son Jesus Christ.

4. And these things write we unto you, that your joy may be full.

5. This then is the message which we have heard of him, and declare unto you, that God is light, and in him is no darkness at all.

6. If we say that we have fellowship with him, and walk in darkness, we lie, and do not the truth;

7. But if we walk in the light, as he is in the light, we have fellowship one with another, and the blood of Jesus Christ his Son cleanseth us from all sin.

8. If we say that we have no sin, we deceive ourselves, and the truth is not in us.

9. If we confess our sins, he is faithful and just to forgive us our sins, and to cleanse us from all unrighteousness.

10. If we say that we have not sinned, we make him a liar, and his word is not in us.

Three tremendous fundamentals of the faith are brought out in the first epistle of John:
1. The manifestation of Life.
2. The manifoldness of God's love.
3. The marvel of Light.

We find Life, Love, and Light pointed out in concise, comprehensive phrases such as "the Word of Life . . . God is love . . . God is light." Life precedes light, and light makes it possible for us to see love.

Life eternal is revealed — *and operates* — in the Son of God. He is "THE LIFE" (John 14:6). Eternal life begins, continues, and climaxes in the Lord Jesus Christ who is *"the true God and eternal life"* (I John 5:20). He is the Author and finisher of faith; therefore faith in His shed blood and finished work brings life eternal. God does not *give forth* light — God IS Light. Love is not just a *part* of God, nor does God simply *demonstrate* love — God IS Love.

Life must precede light. Life was at the beginning — "in the beginning, GOD." When the beginning *began*, God was there; and God said, "Let there be light" (Gen. 1:3).

In the fulness of time God's love came down to man in a body (Gal. 4:4, 5); and when God's love was *revealed*, then all was completed as having to do with hell-deserving sinners receiving salvation by faith in the finished work of God's Son. By God's grace, Jesus the Son of God's love was permitted to taste death for every man (Heb. 2:9).

This first epistle of John is God's love letter to His "little children." Greek scholars tell us that John uses *two* words which are translated "children." The first (*teknon*) means "an offspring"; believers are not only *adopted*, we are *born* into the family of God (I John 3:1). The second word (*teknion*) is an endearing word, very tender, a word bursting with love such as a mother's love for her babe; and this word occurs seven times in the epistle:

"My little children . . . sin not" (ch. 2, v. 1).

"Little children . . . your sins are forgiven for His name's sake" (ch. 2, v. 12).

"Little children, abide in Him" (ch. 2, v. 28).

"Little children, let no man decieve you" (ch. 3, v. 7).

"My little children, let us love . . . in deed and in truth" (ch. 3, v. 18).

"Ye are of God, little children, and have overcome" (ch. 4, v. 4).

The epistle closes with these precious words: "Little children, keep yourselves from idols" (ch. 5, v. 21).

Surely there can be no doubt that this is God's love letter to His little children.

In this epistle we note *seven things* having to do with God:

1. The *Word* of God — which is the basis for all authority (ch. 2, v. 14).

2. The *love* of God — the secret and soul of all godliness and pure holiness (ch. 2, v. 5; ch. 4, v. 9; ch. 5, v. 3).

3. The *will* of God — which to know and to do is the bliss of all heaven's glory (ch. 2, v. 17).

4. The *children* of God. The believer is a born child of God, adopted into the family of God; and that relationship affords the believer all privilege that any son has in a family (ch. 3, vv. 1, 2; ch. 3, v. 10; ch. 5, v. 2).

5. The *Son* of God — Christ Jesus our Saviour, the center and soul of all revelation (ch. 3, v. 8; ch. 4, v. 15; ch. 5, vv. 5, 10, 12, 13, 20).

6. *Born* of God — which is the beginning of eternal life. One must be born of God, or die eternally (ch. 3. v. 9).

7. The *Spirit* of God — who draws the believer, "borns" the believer into the family of God, indwells, leads, and seals him. The Spirit of God is the power of all ability (ch. 4, v. 2).

These are words with a soul — bursting with meaning and filled with the energy of the Holy Spirit. The entrance of the Word brings light. To *hear and believe* the Word is to be born again (John 5:24; Rom. 10:17; I Pet. 1:23).

If these five glorious chapters of I John were the sky, we would see written there such words as "born," "know," "fellowship," "life," "love," "light," "truth"; for these words are spiritual stars — yea, planets and constellations! True *life* is the sum of all being; true *light* is the sum of all knowledge; pure *love* is the sum of all moral excellence. All three are found only in God and in those who possess Divine nature through faith in the Son of God's love. *God* is life, light, and love; *Jesus* is life, light, and love; and when we possess Divine nature imparted at the new birth (II Pet. 1:4), we possess the *life* of God, the *light* of God, and the *love* of God.

The Incarnation

Verses 1-3: "That which was from the beginning, which we have heard, which we have seen with our eyes, which we have looked upon, and our hands have handled, of the Word of life; (for the life was manifested, and we have seen it, and bear witness, and shew unto you that eternal life, which was with the Father, and was manifested unto us;) That which we have seen and heard declare we unto you, that ye also may have fellowship with us: and truly our fellowship is with the Father, and with His Son Jesus Christ."

"That which was from the beginning. . . ." There is no doubt

that the reference here is to the Lord Jesus Christ, "the Word" that was made flesh (John 1:1, 4). In the very beginning of this epistle, John offers evidence that Jesus was God incarnate, God manifested in the flesh. He declares that the proofs given had been subjected to trial of the senses — i.e., John was permitted to see whatsoever could be subjected to the test of the senses (sight, hearing, touch), as having to do with Christ's exalted nature, His character and His dignity.

"*That . . . which we have heard. . . .*" John the Beloved was with the Saviour throughout His earthly ministry, and he records more of the words of Jesus than do any of the other Gospel writers. He uses the words of Jesus as evidence that He WAS the Son of God — the Word incarnate, very God in flesh. This epistle was written that our joy might be full, and the first imperative for full joy is full assurance that Jesus was (and IS) everything He claimed to be.

"*That . . . which we have seen with our eyes. . . .*" John saw enough while he walked with Jesus to prove beyond any shadow of doubt that this was the Son of God. Here he is saying, "We saw His *Person,* we were eye-witnesses to His miracles. We saw Him as a *man* — yet we saw Him do things no *mortal* man could do! In His life and in His miracles we saw *proof* that He was very God in flesh." John wanted it understood that what he declared was not hearsay, it was not what *someone else* had heard or seen. He declared what he saw with his own eyes and heard with his own ears.

"*That . . . which we have looked upon. . . .*" The Greek word used here is more emphatic and intensive than that in the preceding phrase. It has a much *deeper* meaning than merely seeing (beholding) something. It suggests desire, or great pleasure, in that which is seen. John looked upon Jesus with great satisfaction, with deep affection and pleasure. What He saw in the Saviour's life, in His actions and in His miracles pleased him to such extent that he found great joy in looking upon Him. The Greek language also denotes *earnest gaze*; therefore, the evidences of the incarnation of the Son of God were subjected to an intense and earnest gaze by the beloved disciple.

"*That . . . which our hands have handled. . . .*" Here John declares evidence that Jesus was a man, subjected to the sense of touch by another man — even by John himself. If John and his brethren had only *seen* Jesus, it might have been declared that they had been the victims of an optical illusion; but the evidence went deeper than the eye. They had seen Him, they had heard Him — but they also put their hands upon Him. Therefore John declares that the Son of God was a man, *a real man of flesh, blood, and bone.*

(After His resurrection, when the disciples were hiding in the upper room because of their fear of the Jews, Jesus appeared to them; and when He observed that they were frightened, thinking they had seen a spirit, He said to them, "Behold my hands and my feet, that it is I myself: handle me and see; for a spirit hath not flesh and bones, as ye see me have" (Luke 24: 36-43). The same truth is declared in John 20:24-27.

". . . *of the Word of life*" — that is, the Word in which life resides; the Word which is the *source* of life. "The Word" here has reference to the Lord Jesus Christ. We are born of the "incorruptible seed," the Word of God (I Pet. 1:23). Inspired of God, John is saying here, "Whatever the *senses* could know pertaining to the Word of life that was manifested in the speech, actions, and miracles of Jesus, furnished evidence that He was the Word incarnate, very God in flesh. That is the message we declare unto you, that we may have fellowship with the Son in whom is life, love, and true fellowship."

"*For the life was manifested*" (made visible to us). "We saw the life, we *heard* the life, we put our hands on the living Christ." He who IS life and the *origin* of life was made known to men by the incarnation. He appeared as man that men might see Him, hear Him, touch Him; yet He was just as surely and truly God as He was man. He was in the beginning *with* God, in the *bosom* of God (John 1:1, 2, 18).

"*We have seen it, and bear witness.*" Here we find repetition, emphasizing the fact of the incarnation. The Holy Spirit is impressing upon us the fact that Jesus was the Word incarnate, very God; and that He was seen of men such as John the Beloved and the other disciples. John wants it known that he was a *personal* witness of what Christ Jesus the Saviour *was,* what He *did,* and what He *said.* The beloved disciple was thoroughly satisfied in his own heart that Jesus was God in flesh, that He was life, light, and love.

"*We . . . shew unto you that eternal life, which was with the Father.*" This statement declares the eternity of Christ Jesus, the Son of God. He was in the beginning with the Father, and as the Father had no beginning and will have no ending, so the *Son* is "from everlasting to everlasting" (Psalm 90:1, 2).

"In the beginning was the Word, and the Word was with God, and the Word was God. *The same was in the beginning WITH God*" (John 1:1, 2). Here is stated the Divine fact that the Son of God was (and IS) eternal. Before He was made manifest here on earth He was with the Father — the Word of life, the Eternal One. He is the Alpha and the Omega — the beginning and the ending, and all there is from eternity through eternity as having to do with salvation from sin.

"*. . . and was manifested unto us.*" Christ Jesus THE Life appeared unto men as a Man. There was never a time when the Son was not with the Father, but approximately two thousand years ago He was made known to men by the Incarnation. Before His Incarnation He was "the Word of Life," in the bosom of the Father (John 1:18) and that "Word of Life" was manifested on earth. He appeared among men in a body, He had a *real existence* on earth, not an "assumed appearance."

The *true characteristics* of Christ Jesus gave testimony that He was Man, and those who *saw* Him and were a long time with Him gave testimony that He was a real Man in a body of flesh; yet as Nicodemus declared, *no man* could do the miracles Christ did "*except God be with him.*" God *was* with Him, God was IN Him, *He WAS God:* ". . . God was in Christ, reconciling the world unto Himself, not imputing their trespasses unto them; and hath committed unto us the word of reconciliation" (II Cor. 5:19).

"*That which we have seen and heard declare we unto you.*" The errorists were already operating in the days of John the Beloved. There were those who denied that Jesus had come in the flesh, and John repudiates such doctrine by saying, "We are declaring that which we saw, that which we heard, and that which our hands handled: *even the Word of life in a body of flesh.*"

". . . *that ye also may have fellowship with us*" — that is, fellowship with the apostles of Christ Jesus the Saviour, those who actually saw Him, talked with Him, put their hands upon Him. John wants *all* believers to have the same faith in Jesus that the disciples had. He wants us to have the same hope, the same joy, and the same assurance that the Son of God, the Word Incarnate, *had* appeared among men in a body of flesh.

"*Truly our fellowship is with (God) the Father. . . .*" It was a source of joy to John that he was able to fellowship with God the Father. He and God, by media of the Word and prayer, partook together in aim, in joy, in feeling, in affection, desire, and plan. John was attached to the same things, he loved the same truths, he wanted the same fellowship, he was engaged in the same work. To be conscious of this divine relationship with the Father gave him joy this world cannot know and fellowship the world can never experience.

But ALL born again believers have fellowship with God. We are attached to Him through the miracle of the new birth, we are partakers of Divine nature. God's happiness is found in mery, justice, purity, truth, holiness — and the Christians' happiness lies in the same things. We should be humble — yet joyful — to know that "we are labourers together with God" (I Cor. 3:9). In II Corinthians 6:1 Paul says that we are "workers together with Him," III John 8 mentions "fellow helpers to the truth," and in Mark 16:20 we read that the disciples went forth, "and preached every where, *the Lord working with them,* and confirming the Word with signs following." The believer also has fellowship and direct communion with God in prayer and meditation, through the Lord's Supper and through the reading of His Word.

"*That ye also may have fellowship . . . with His Son Jesus Christ.*" In like manner as with God the Father, believers also have much in common with Christ Jesus the Saviour — in character, in desire, in plan, in spirit, in feeling. We are in definite union with Him; we are possessors of Divine nature and of the Holy Spirit — "Christ in you, the hope of glory" (Col. 1:27). The assurance of such tremendous truths gives the believer peace and joy.

Verse 4: "And these things write we unto you, that your joy may be full."

This is the *key verse* to the first epistle of John. *"These things"* have to do with Jesus in the flesh — seen by the apostles, heard and handled by them. They knew by personal experience that He was real, not mystic; and the knowledge of "these things" should bring US salvation and *full joy* — the birthright of every believer. If the devil cannot damn a soul, he does his utmost to rob the believer of the *joy* of salvation and keep us from being good stewards and soul-winners; and no one can have *full* joy unless he shares with others that which he has received by grace through faith in the finished work of the Lord Jesus Christ.

This verse contains almost the same words spoken by Jesus to His disciples just before He departed from them to return to the heavenly Father: "These things have I spoken unto you, that my joy might remain in you, and that your joy might be full" (John 15:11). It is impossible for a believer to experience full joy until he has unshakeable assurance that Jesus is the Son of God, that He was God incarnate, very God, and very man. Until the believer has complete assurance that Jesus is all He claimed to be, he cannot enjoy his spiritual birthright. Doubt destroys joy. Full joy is impossible if there is the slightest doubt concerning Jesus the Son of God, Saviour of sinners.

The Message

Verse 5: "This then is the message which we have heard of Him, and declare unto you, that God is light, and in Him is no darkness at all."

Notice it is not just *"a* message," but *"THE* message." There is only one true message, one pure Gospel. This is the substance of the announcement made by Jesus and received by the apostles.

"The message" here refers to the revelation given to the disciples through the words of Jesus — not necessarily "OF (about) Him," but the message they received *directly FROM Him* — words spoken by Him in their presence. This is the message John is giving to us, that our joy may be full.

"GOD IS LIGHT." Christ Jesus came to *declare* Him who is light —He came to declare God: "No man hath seen God at

any time; the only begotten Son, which is in the bosom of the Father, He hath declared Him" (John 1:18).

Light in the Word of God is an emblem of purity, holiness, truth, knowledge. Darkness is just the opposite. God is light; Satan is darkness. God is not "*the* light," He is not "*a* light" — He is simply *LIGHT itself*, and apart from Him there IS no light:

"Every good gift and every perfect gift is from above, and cometh down from the Father of lights, with whom is no variableness, neither shadow of turning" (James 1:17).

"In the beginning was the Word, and Word was with God, and the Word was God. The same was in the beginning with God. All things were made by Him; and without Him was not any thing made that was made. In Him was life; and the life was the light of men. And the light shineth in darkness; and the darkness comprehended it not. There was a man sent from God, whose name was John. The same came for a witness, to bear witness of the Light, that all men through Him might believe. He was not that Light, but was sent to bear witness of that light. That was the true Light, which lighteth every man that cometh into the world" (John 1:1-9).

"*In Him is no darkness at all.*" Here the Holy Ghost definitely affirms that God is absolutely perfect, absolutely holy, absolutely true. There is no imperfection in Him, nothing that could dim light *which God IS*. No shadow can ever mar the pure splendor of God's character.

The doctrine declared here (that God is pure light) lays the foundation for all true doctrine having to do with Christianity. We must accept *by faith* the truth that when the beginning began, God was already present. He has always been, He always will *be*. He has always been LIGHT, He always WILL BE light. No shadow has ever come over or upon Him, He cannot be tempted with evil, He cannot do wrong. We must believe IN such a God if we hope to receive the salvation provided in His only begotten Son.

Jesus was God in flesh, reconciling the world unto Himself. What God demanded, only God could provide. Neither mortal nor angel could provide *pure grace* to save a man who should burn in hell, and still let God remain just. Through the finished work of Jesus, God can now justify the ungodly and yet Himself remain *just*, and *pure*, and *holy*:

"But now the righteousness of God without the law is manifested, being witnessed by the law and the prophets; even the righteousness of God which is by faith of Jesus Christ unto all and upon all them that believe: for there is no difference: For all have sinned, and come short of the glory of God; being justified freely by His grace through the redemption that is in Christ Jesus: Whom God hath set forth to be a propitiation through faith in His blood, to declare His righteousness for the remission of sins that are past, through the forbearance of God; to declare, I say, at this time His righteousness: that He might be just, and the justifier of Him which believeth in Jesus. Where is boasting then? It is excluded. By what law? of works? Nay: but by the law of faith. Therefore we conclude that a man is justified by faith without the deeds of the law" (Rom. 3:21-28).

Since God is light and in Him is no darkness at all, those who fellowship with God must be compatible with Him: *"Can two walk together, except they be agreed?"* (Amos 3:3).

The Psalmist proclaimed, "Blessed is the people that know the joyful sound: they shall walk, O Lord, in the light of thy countenance" (Psalm 89:15).

Verse 6: "If we say that we have fellowship with Him, and walk in darkness, we lie, and do not the truth."

When a person testifies that he is saved, thereby declaring that he is a follower of Jesus, and then *lives* in the world, *walks* with the world, and *fellowships* with the world, the Word of God clearly declares that person a liar! Plain language — very blunt, but quite understandable. According to this verse of Scripture, they are not believers who — in their daily walk, manner of life, and company they keep — fellowship with the world. They may *profess* to be Christians, but they are not: *they are liars, "and do not the truth."*

I wonder how many preachers would dare step into the pulpit on next Lord's day and dogmatically declare that all the members of their church who profess to be followers of Jesus Christ are liars if they had rather be in a theatre, a dancehall, a nightclub, or at home watching television, or simply sitting at home in an easy chair, than to be in the house of God on prayermeeting night, Sunday night, and revival nights? How many pastors would have enough grace — and backbone — to look such parishioners in the face and declare that they are living a lie?

Those who practice sin are not born again. If they profess to be Christians and yet follow the things of the world, they are living a counterfeit life; they are deceived. If we love the world, the love of God is not in us (I John 2:15). God is pure, holy, and righteous. If we are born again we are partakers of Divine nature and the grace of God that saves us sets up a classroom in our hearts, teaches us and leads us:

"For the grace of God that bringeth salvation hath appeared to all men, teaching us that, denying ungodliness and worldly lusts, we should live soberly, righteously, and godly, in this present world: Looking for that blessed hope, and the glorious appearing of the great God and our Saviour, Jesus Christ, who gave Himself for us, that He might redeem us from all iniquity, and purify unto Himself a peculiar people, zealous of good works" (Tit. 2:11-14).

Paul clearly declares that born again persons are possessors of the Holy Spirit: "Ye are not in the flesh, but in the Spirit, if so be that the Spirit of God dwell in you. *Now if any man have not the Spirit of Christ, he is none of His*" (Rom. 8:9).

The Holy Spirit who indwells our hearts leads us into paths of righteousness: "For as many as are led by the Spirit of God, they are the sons of God" (Rom. 8:14).

The Spirit of God also assures our hearts: "The Spirit itself beareth witness with our spirit, that we are the children of God" (Rom. 8:16).

The Holy Spirit seals us: "Grieve not the Holy Spirit of God, whereby ye are sealed unto the day of redemption" (Eph. 4:30).

Certainly no honest person would accuse the Holy Spirit of leading him to places where many church members go, neither would the Holy Spirit lead us to *do* the things many church members do. Thus we know that those who profess to be followers of Jesus are living a lie if they follow the world and Satan. Not only are they living a lie, but the Scripture declares that they "*do not the truth*" — that is, they do not *act* according to truth; their profession is false. To DO the truth is to act and live *in accordance with truth.* Jesus said "I am truth" (John 14:6). He also prayed, "Father, sanctify them through thy truth. *Thy Word is truth*" (John 17:17). In John 8:32 He said, "Ye shall know the truth, and the truth shall make you free." If we know the truth, we know *Jesus;* if we know the truth we know *His Word;* and if we know Jesus and know His Word *we will walk in paths of righteousness* and whatsoever we do will be done to the glory of God.

Many churches today are filled with people who are strictly "religious," but a great majority of them have never been truly born again. Revelation 3:20 tells of Jesus standing at the door of the Laodicean church, knocking. He said, "Behold, I stand at the door, and knock: if any man hear my voice, and open the door, I will come in to him, and will sup with him, and he with me." But not even one member accepted His invitation. I am sure there are churches today where, like the Laodicean church, there is not one born again person, including the minister. According to the Apostle Paul, Satan has churches and ordained ministers; and "such are false apostles, deceitful workers, transforming themselves into the apostles of Christ. And no marvel; for Satan himself is transformed into an angel of light. Therefore it is no great thing if his ministers also be transformed as the ministers of righteousness; whose end shall be according to their works" (II Cor. 11:13-15).

There are tens of thousands who join a church, they are baptized, they conform to rituals and church ordinances; but they know nothing of the miracle of God's grace through the new birth. They have never personally trusted Jesus and asked Him to save them by His grace and cover their sins with His precious blood.

Christianity is a Person — *Christ.*

Christianity is light — Jesus said, "*I am the Light of the world.*"

Christianity brings "*peace that passeth all understanding.*" Jesus said, "Peace I leave with you, my peace I give unto you . . ." (John 14:27).

Christianity makes men pure: without holiness no man shall see God (Heb. 12:14).

Christianity brings "joy unspeakable and full of glory" (I Pet. 1:8).

Christianity causes men to live differently because they are new creations in Christ Jesus: "Therefore if any man be in Christ, he is a new creature: old things are passed away; behold, all things are become new" (II Cor. 5:17).

Verse 7: "But if we walk in the light, as He is in the light, we have fellowship one with another, and the blood of Jesus Christ His Son cleanseth us from all sin."

To walk in the light is to lead a life of purity and holiness, looking to Jesus, allowing Him to direct our steps, choose our changes, and lead us into paths of right living for His name's sake and for His glory. To walk in the light also means to walk in truth, to embrace truth in opposition to error. To walk in the light means to come out from liberalism, modernism, infidelity, and have no fellowship with the unfruitful works of darkness (Eph. 5:11; Cor. 6:17). Also study II Corinthians 4:6, I Corinthians 2:9-15, and Ephesians 1:18.

To walk in the light simply means to allow God to order our steps and direct us, by His Spirit and through His Word. Walking in the light means walking *in God's will* — not in our own will or way, not fulfilling the desires of our own heart and mind, but walking as He orders our steps in His will, to glorify His name in all that we say and do, and wherever we go."

"As He is the light" means that when we are truly born again, saved by God's grace, washed in the blood of Jesus, we are partakers of Divine nature (II Pet. 1:4), and therefore we possess the same kind of light that God IS. We do not of course possess that light in the *degree* that God is light, but we possess the same *kind* of light; we possess God's nature in the Person of the Holy Spirit (Rom. 8:9; John 3:5). Thus we have light *within* to direct us. We are not children of darkness, children of the night; *we are children of light,* and we have no excuse for walking in darkness — nor does the true believer have any *desire* to walk in darkness because he is created new in Christ Jesus, created to live and walk in good works and he longs to walk in light and lead a life that will please God and glorify the name of Jesus.

Christ promised the disciples that when the Holy Spirit did

come (He came at Pentecost) He would guide them into *ALL truth;* and when we walk in the truth we are free; we lead lives of liberty in light and love.

"We have fellowship one with another." All true believers belong to God's family and to the same Church – the Church of the living God. We become members of that Church when we are born again:

"For as the body is one, and hath many members, and all the members of that one body, being many, are one body: so also is Christ. For by one Spirit are we all baptized into one body, whether we be Jews or Gentiles, whether we be bond or free; and have been all made to drink into one Spirit. For the body is not one member, but many" (I Cor. 12:12-14).

Believers have much in common. All true believers possess the same Spirit (the Holy Spirit), the same nature (Divine nature), and if we cannot love our fellow believer whom we have seen, how can we love God whom we have NOT seen? When we are born again we walk in the light – the same light that God IS; and walking in the light we are all walking in the same path. We fellowship because we are blood kin in Jesus, we are covered by the same blood, possessors of the same Holy Spirit and the same Divine nature. We love the same God, we embrace the same truth of God's Word, we are living for the same Saviour, stewards for the same Lord. All truly born again people can fellowship. We may not see eye to eye on everything, but true believers can agree to disagree and still love each other and fellowship to the glory of God and for the sake of lost souls. An individual who cannot fellowship with other Christians is a Pharisee.

"The blood of Jesus Christ His Son cleanseth us from all sin." Please notice the word "CLEANSETH." This verse does not teach that the blood *has cleansed* (past tense), or that it *WILL CLEANSE* (future tense). But the blood of Jesus *cleanseth* us – day by day, moment by moment, as we trust in the finished work of Jesus.

The truth here is plain: For any and every sin of which we may be conscious, there is efficacy in the blood of the Lamb of God, slain for the remission of sins. There is efficacy in His

31

blood to remove *any* sin, *all* sin, and make the believer entirely pure and holy.

Our holiness is in His blood. The blood of Jesus is holy, and when God looks at the believer, covered by the blood, He sees the *blood*. No matter how ugly a sin may be, there is no stain so deep that the blood of Jesus cannot entirely take it away and cleanse the heart and soul, making it pure and holy.

John the beloved is giving the substance of the message which he had received (v. 5). He first declared, "God is light, and in Him is no darkness at all." He then declared that Christianity requires believers to resemble the Saviour and God the Father since they walk in the same light that He IS and possess Divine nature. They are created new in Christ, and therefore they should walk as He walked.

Also part of "THE message" — a very vital part — is that "the blood of Jesus Christ, God's Son, cleanseth us from all sin," making us holy and righteous — something no religious system on earth could do. Only the blood of the Lamb without spot or blemish could cleanse from sin, and in this day of bloodless religions the Word of God *still* thunders out, *"Without shedding of blood is no remission!"* (Heb. 9:22).

Paul instructed the Colossian believers to give thanks to God, "which hath made us meet to be partakers of the inheritance of the saints in light: who hath delivered us from the power of darkness, and hath translated us into the kingdom of His dear Son: *in whom we have redemption through His blood, EVEN THE FORGIVENESS OF SINS* . . . and, having made peace through the blood of His cross, by Him to reconcile all things unto Himself; by Him, I say, whether they be things in earth, or things in heaven" (Col. 1:12-14, 20).

In Mark 14:22-24 we read, "And as they did eat, Jesus took bread, and blessed, and brake it, and gave to them, and said, Take, eat: this is my body. And He took the cup and when He had given thanks, He gave it to them: and they all drank of it. And He said unto them, This is my blood of the new testament, which is shed for many."

Jesus is our Redeemer; we are redeemed through His blood: "Being justified freely by His grace through the redemption that is in Christ Jesus: whom God hath set forth to be a propititiou through faith in His blood, to declare His righteousness for the remission of sins that are past, through the forbearance of God" (Rom. 3:24, 25). But after we are redeemed we need a *Saviour* (Keeper), one who saves us from the power of sin, delivers and cleanses us from the pollution of sin day by day until we are in His presence in our glorified bodies. That is the meaning of the Greek word translated "cleanseth" in the last phrase of verse 7: the blood of Jesus cleanses — *and then goes ON cleansing.*

As long as we live in the flesh we are prone to sin — the spirit is willing, but the flesh is weak. God knows that we are dust, and in His great salvation He provided — not only redemption from the *penalty* of sin, but also the power to save us from the *power* of sin day by day — and glorious truth, in the sweet by-and-by He will save us from the very *presence* of sin!

Does this provision give the believer a license to sin? Certainly not! Romans 8:1 tells us, "There is therefore now no condemnation to them which are in Christ Jesus, *who walk not after the flesh, but after the Spirit.*" You will notice the Scripture does not say "*IF* we walk not after the flesh." It simply says that we "WALK NOT" after the flesh." We who are born again walk in paths of righteousness because we are led by the Holy Spirit and *HE leads us into paths of right living.*

We know that we are in Christ Jesus and in verse 5 of this chapter we learned that "in Him is no darkness at all." Christ is in US (Col. 1:27), therefore we possess the light, we are IN the light; and we walk in the light. Jesus said, "I am the light of the world: He that followeth me shall not walk in darkness, but shall have the light of life" (John 8:12).

Jesus said of Satan, "The prince of this world . . . hath nothing in me" (John 14:30). In other words, Satan is darkness, he is the originator of darkness, but in CHRIST is "*no darkness at all.*" The desire of the truly born again person is to have "*no part dark*" (Luke 11:36). A dark spot in the life of a believer will dim fellowship between him and the heavenly Father, and may also endanger the spiritual welfare of others.

In verses 3 and 5 we find the word "*declare.*" It is a solemn duty (as well as a glorious privilege) for the believer to declare to others what he has learned from the Word through the Spirit.

To know the truth, to experience the light and love of God, and yet fail to declare this glorious message to others is criminal negligence, spiritually speaking, and souls will burn in hell because some Christian failed to witness. All that we know, all that we learn, all that we possess concerning God — His love, mercy, and grace — we should declare to others. After His resurrection, Jesus commissioned the disciples to go and teach all nations, baptizing them and teaching them to observe "all things" — whatsoever He had commanded them. It is *our* duty to declare what we know concerning God, His great love and His saving grace. We are obligated to declare that "the wages of sin is death" — *and then make known the remedy to those who are living in sin!*

Are You Saved?

The threefold cord of salvation (salvation from the *penalty* of sin, from the *power* of sin, and eventually from the *presence* of sin) finds its fibre and strength in the cross of the Lord Jesus. Poor hell-deserving sinners are saved from condemnation only through faith in the finished work of Him who gave Himself for us. We are saved from wrath through Christ Jesus (Rom. 5:9). By and through the vitality of the risen, living Christ we are being saved daily from the *control* of sin as the vitality of the risen life of Christ pulsates within us; and because He abides within us, we overcome the law of sin and death (Rom. 5:10). We live because HE lives. He sits now at the right hand of the Father, in the holy of holies, to make intercession for us (I Tim. 2:5).

In the by-and-by (we believe it will be soon) we will be saved from this body of sin and death. This will occur when Christ comes back again. In I Thessalonians 5:9, 10 we read, "For God hath not appointed us to wrath, but to obtain salvation by our Lord Jesus Christ, who died for us, that, whether we wake or sleep, we should live together with Him."

Words could never express what was accomplished in the death of the Lamb of God on the cross. Had Christ stopped one step short of Calvary His mission to this earth would have been a total failure. The Holy Spirit of God declares that the climax and the *nature* of His ministry was that "HE APPEARED

TO PUT AWAY SIN BY THE SACRIFICE OF HIMSELF (Heb. 9:26).

The Need for Cleansing

Verse 8: "If we say that we have no sin, we deceive ourselves, and the truth is not in us."

Remember, this epistle was written to *believers*, and this verse *applies* to believers. Regardless of how consecrated we may be, regardless of how completely we are separated from the world, no matter how far advanced in holiness we may become, never in this tabernacle of flesh will we pass beyond the need for cleansing! Paul warned of this in I Corinthians 10:12: *"Wherefore let him that thinketh he standeth take heed lest he fall."*

Sin has roots; sin also bears fruits; and we must distinguish between the two. In this verse we are discussing sin as a *root*. ALL are born in sin and shapen in iniquity. There is none righteous — no, not one. Through the disobedience of Adam all men are sinners. Even if it were possible for a person to live above sin from the time he reaches the age of accountability until he dies, if his character were absolutely unmarked by sin, he still could not say "I have no sin." We are BORN sinners. In Ecclesiastes 7:20 we read, *"There is not a just man upon earth, that doeth good, and sinneth not."*

These tabernacles of flesh in which we live are fashioned after sin. There are those who teach that it is possible to completely eradicate this ugly root of sin; but this is not true. A little later in this epistle we will see what the word of God teaches concerning this matter. We will study the two natures of a believer — the flesh and the spirit; and we will search the Scriptures to learn all we can about the Christian and sin. The most consecrated believer — he who lives the holiest life — is but a poor sinner saved by grace.

The flesh, the old nature, the root that produces fruit, is always there. As long as we live we will be plagued with our own flesh; but thank God, the Holy Spirit is victor over the flesh, and He is the Divine Agent who gives US victory. Paul said to the Galatians, *"Walk in the Spirit, and ye shall not fulfil the lust of the flesh"* (Gal. 5:16).

By way of illustrating this point, consider a mold: whether it be a brick mold, a jelly mold, or a bread mold, *whatever* its design, it gives its identical pattern to its offspring. Whatever is molded in a certain mold *resembles* that mold; therefore, if the mold is chipped, all the products of that mold will bear the mark made by the chip. If a mold is scarred, everything molded in it will bear the imprint of the scar. Thus it is that we, being descended from Adam, bear the stigma (the mark or scar) of Adam's fall.

In the first Adam, all die; but in the last Adam (Jesus) all who *believe* are saved from sin and from the curse of the fall. It is JESUS the Righteous One who presents us faultless to the Father; it is not we ourselves. HE is the propitiation for our sins, He is our Redeemer, Sanctifier, Leader, Protector, Saviour — and He has promised never to leave us nor forsake us. He has declared that if we confess Him before men He will confess US before the heavenly Father.

Never entertain the thought that you are above sin. A magnet does not attract pieces of wood — it attracts only metal. If you move a magnet close to shavings from *wood*, nothing happens; but move the magnet close to *steel* shavings and the two are instantly attracted to each other. There is an element in the metal which finds in the magnet that which is desirable, and therefore the steel responds to the pull of the magnet. The same is true concerning the flesh (the old nature) and sin. We live in bodies that are attracted by sin. Study the seventh chapter of Romans, read it, re-read it, and then read the first three verses of Romans 8. It is only in the resurrection that we will be rid of this body and will have a glorious body that will be free from all sin, a body that *cannot* sin. But as long as we live in the flesh we must pray, "O God, order my steps. Set a guard at my lips. Deliver me from temptation, and guide me around the pitfalls Satan has set for me!" Satan will dig pitfalls and lay all the snares possible in an attempt to trap us and cause us to lose the joy of salvation and become a reproach instead of a blessing to the cause of Christ and the New Testament Church.

"*If we say we have no sin, we deceive ourselves.*" He who claims to be absolutely holy and sinless and claims that he cannot sin, knows little of his own heart. He knows nothing of the

36

weakness of the flesh and the wiles of the devil. Such a person is deceiving no one but himself. Certainly he is not deceiving God, nor is he deceiving his fellowman. *He* himself is the one deceived, *"and the truth is not in (him)."*

If the *truth* is not in a person, then Jesus is not in that person, for Jesus said, "I am the truth." If the *truth* is not in a person, then God's Word is not in that person, because Jesus said "Thy Word is truth." We are born again through the Word (I Pet. 1:23), and there can be no new birth apart from the Word. Therefore, if Christ is not in us and God's Word is not in us, then we are lost. Thus a person who claims to have no sin is not only deceived — he is also lost.

Sins Confessed Are Sins Forgiven

Verse 9: "If we confess our sins, He is faithful and just to forgive us our sins, and to cleanse us from all unrighteousness.

Notice the verse says, "If WE confess OUR sins." The personal pronouns included John the Beloved. He did not say "If YOU confess your sins," or "If THEY confess their sins." He said "WE" — meaning the little children, the born ones, we who are created anew in Christ Jesus. Even the most consecrated believer sins, and we need to *confess* our sins. When we DO confess, God is faithful and just to forgive.

If we are willing to face the Bible with open heart and open mind, not attempting to prove some church doctrine, we can see how sadly we come short of the glory of God and how sinful we really *are*. Those of us who have exercised faith in the finished work of Jesus and are covered by His precious blood are saved by grace — but we still live in the same *body* we occupied when God saved us by His grace; and we will carry this tabernacle of flesh until Jesus calls us to higher ground.

We sin because we are sinners, even though we are *sinners saved by grace*; we still have the old nature tagging along. A sheep is not a sheep because it bleats and produces wool: it bleats and produces wool because it is a *sheep*. A rooster is not a rooster because he crows; he crows because he is a *rooster*. A peachtree is not a peachtree because it bears peaches; it bears peaches because it is a peachtree. Sin was our nature when we were born into this world. When we are born *again* God puts within us a new heart but He does not give us new *flesh.* We will not receive new flesh until the resurrection — glorious day that will be!

Thank God, the Lord Jesus Christ was not only concerned with sin's characteristics, but also with sin's *character.* He did not come just to take away the fruits of sin — He came to put within us another *root*; and greater is He (the Holy Spirit) that is in you than he (the tempter) that is in the world. Through the miracle of the new birth, God puts Divine nature within us in the Person of the Holy Ghost, and then we become a *dual* person: the old nature (the flesh) is still with us, but Divine nature is on the throne within the heart: "A little leaven leaveneth the whole lump" (Gal. 5:9).

"Verily, verily, I say unto thee, Except a man be born of water and of the Spirit, he cannot enter into the kingdom of God" (John 3:5).

"But ye are not in the flesh, but in the Spirit, if so be that the Spirit of God dwell in you. Now if any man have not the Spirit of Christ, he is none of His" (Rom. 8:9).

"As many as are led by the Spirit of God, they are the sons of God" (Rom. 8:14).

"The Spirit (Himself) beareth witness with our spirit, that we are the children of God" (Rom. 8:16).

"This I say then, Walk in the Spirit, and ye shall not fulfil the lust of the flesh. For the flesh lusteth against the Spirit, and the Spirit against the flesh: and these are contrary the one to the other: so that ye cannot do the things that ye would" (Gal. 5: 16, 17).

"Grieve not the Holy Spirit of God, whereby ye are sealed unto the day of redemption" (Eph. 4:30).

Jesus the great Physician has dealt with the character of sin as well as with its characteristics. He has put within us another root, the Holy Ghost; and the *fruit* of the Spirit is "love, joy, peace, longsuffering, gentleness, goodness, faith, meekness, temperance: against such there is no law." (Gal. 5:22, 23).

Becoming a Christian Is No Minor Transaction

The beginning of the Christian life is no ordinary thing. For an unbeliever to become a Christian is God's greatest miracle —

Jesus called it a *birth*. Only a mother who has *given* birth knows the pain, anxiety, travail, many times *anguish*, and then the *joy* of a new life coming into the world. Only GOD knows what it cost the Father, Son, Holy Spirit — and all of heaven — to make possible the birth from above — the new birth, the spiritual birth, the Divine imperative of salvation (John 3:3, 5). When one becomes a Christian he is not just "a better man," he does not just reform and change his ways; he is a *new man* (II Cor. 5:17).

I doubt that many of us have ever really understood the full meaning of the words in Mark 10:15: *"Verily I say unto you, Whosoever shall not receive the kingdom of God as a little child, he shall not enter therein."* It is true that one must become humble and have the faith of a little child before he will truly repent and receive Jesus; but I believe the deeper meaning of these words to be this:

Except big men are willing to become as little children all over again, actually being born babes in Christ, they cannot enter heaven. If one hopes to enter the kingdom of heaven there must be a new beginning, and this is described as being *"born of God"* (John 1:12, 13). When one is born of God he is a babe in Christ (I Pet. 2:1, 2), but he is also a new creation. That is why Christians live differently — they ARE different. They live new lives because they are new creations. They follow the steps of Jesus because they are possessors of Divine nature. They walk in paths of righteousness because they are led by the Holy Ghost within them.

The reason many church members cannot live right and cannot stay straight is that they have never been created in Christ Jesus, they have never been born of the Spirit. Therefore, as the sow returns to her wallowing in the mire the unregenerate church member cannot but return to the beggarly elements of the world because he needs a new heart, a new nature. A hog loves the mire because it has a hog's heart. A dog chases rabbits because it has a dog's heart. A sheep does *not* chase rabbits because it has a sheep's heart and it is not the nature of a sheep to chase rabbits! Believers live differently because God puts a new heart within them (Ezek. 36:26).

Mark gives us the sad picture of an unregenerate heart: "For from within, out of the heart of men, proceed evil thoughts, adulteries, fornications, murders, thefts, covetousness, wickedness, deceit, lasciviousness, an evil eye, blasphemy, pride, foolishness: all these evil things come from within, and defile the man" (Mark 7:21-23).

"*If we confess our sins*" — yes, if believers will just confess to God — both sins of omission and of commission — God will forgive and abundantly pardon. Forgiveness comes as a result of true confession on the part of the one seeking forgiveness: "Wash me thoroughly from mine iniquity, and cleanse me from my sin. For I acknowledge my transgressions: and my sin is ever before me . . . Restore unto me the joy of thy salvation; and uphold me with thy free spirit" (Psalm 51:2, 3, 12).

"I will arise and go to my father, and will say unto him, Father I have sinned against heaven, and before thee" (Luke 15:18).

"*He is faithful and just to forgive us our sins.*" God is faithful to all of His children. He will do exactly what He has promised, He will do *ALL* that He has promised, and He will forgive us when we sin if we will *confess* our sin. God *must* be faithful because He is God. If He were unfaithful He would cease to BE God. But "through the redemption that is in Christ Jesus" God can be just and yet justify the ungodly:

"For all have sinned, and come short of the glory of God; being justified freely by His grace through the redemption that is in Christ Jesus: Whom God hath set forth to be a propitiation through faith in His blood, to declare His righteousness for the remission of sins that are past, through the forbearance of God; To declare, I say, at this time His righteousness: that He might be just, and the justifier of him which believeth in Jesus. Where is boasting then? It is excluded. By what law? of works? Nay: but by the law of faith. Therefore we conclude that a man is justified by faith without the deeds of the law" (Rom. 3:23-28).

God is not only faithful and just to forgive our sins, but He is also faithful "*to cleanse us from all unrighteousness.*" Righteousness is *imputed*; therefore when God imputes righteousness, all *unrighteousness* must be removed. Righteousness and unrighteousness cannot abide in the same heart. Ultimately God will remove all stains of guilt from soul, spirit, and body, and we will stand perfect before Him, holy, cleansed, without spot or wrinkle. Such can be ours only through the shed blood of Jesus and the unsearchable riches of His grace.

Verse 10: "If we say that we have not sinned, we make Him a liar, and His Word is not in us."

Here sin is regarded as an *act*. Believers DO commit deeds of unrightousness; we do things that we know are not pleasing to God, and we omit things that we know would please Him — deeds of godliness that we could do. We have all sinned — and even when we have done our very best we must admit that we are "unprofitable servants" (Luke 17:10). At our very best we still come short of God's glory.

We *can* have victory. Paul declares that we should be sanctified wholly, soul, spirit, and body, "preserved blameless unto the coming of our Lord Jesus Christ." That is, we should be blameless in that we live above reproach, lives that men may look upon and see Jesus in our daily walk, talk, and habits. Jesus said "Be ye therefore perfect, even as your Father which is in heaven is perfect" (Matt. 5:48). Does this mean that we can be as holy, sinless, pure, and righteous as God, the heavenly Father? No. Jesus meant that we are to be perfect in OUR sphere as God is perfect in HIS sphere. To whom much is given, of him the more is required; of him to whom little is given, not nearly so much is required. In our sphere as believers we should live blameless lives that cannot be criticized by the enemies of Jesus.

There is victory for those who desire it: "There hath no temptation taken you but such as is common to man: *but God is faithful, who will not suffer you to be tempted above that ye are able; but will with the temptation also make a way to escape, that ye may be able to bear it*" (I Cor. 10:13).

"*If we say that we have not sinned, we make God a liar.*" That is pretty definite language! I have met some wicked sinners, I have met some vile blasphemers; but I have yet to meet a man who would dare call God a liar. Yet this verse plainly declares that the person who boasts that he does not sin is making God a liar. *God's Word* says that ALL have sinned. God's Word says that "there is not a just man upon the earth that doeth good and sinneth not." And listen to James 4:17: "*To him*

41

that knoweth to do good, and doeth it not, TO HIM IT IS SIN!"
It is sin to fall short of doing all the good and living all the god-
liness we possibly can. So — if we say we *have* no sin, we make
God a liar.

Romans 3:22, 23 tells us that "there is no difference, *for ALL
have sinned, and come short of the glory of God."* Oh yes,
there may be a difference in the *degree* of sin. Some are vile,
wretched, outrageous sinners, and others are mild, nice, "religious" sinners who belong to a big church. There IS a difference in degrees of sin committed, but there is no difference in the
disease of sin: all have it. The fact of sin is there although the
degree of sin may differ. The symptoms and the results of sin
appear more evident in some than in others, but the fact of sin
abides in all, for all have sinned.

The Word of God is not in us if we *deny* this fact. If we
claim to be exempt from sin, not having sinned, not sinning
now, we deny the truth; and to deny the truth means that the
Word of God is not in us; and if the Word of God is not in us,
then we are lost, because we can only be born again *through*
the Word. We are begotten of the Word (I Pet. 1:23, James
1:18). If we are born again we are begotten with the Word of
truth; and if the Word of truth is not in us, we certainly are lost.

Glorious Truth

The sinner is saved and cleansed by the precious blood of
Jesus (I John 1:7).

Redemption is God's gift to hell-deserving sinners through the
finished work of the Son of God. We are redeemed by His
blood. After we are born again we are not called upon to make
painful sacrifices, we do no pennances or voluntary scourgings,
we make no pilgrimages. All God requires of us is that we
confess to Him when we have sinned, and He forgives us for
Christ's sake (Eph. 4:32).

Faith in His Finished Work

"Behold, his soul which is lifted up is not upright in him:
but the just shall live by faith" (Hab. 2:4).

"For therein is the righteousness of God revealed from faith to faith: as it is written, *The just shall live by faith*" (Rom. 1:17).

"But that no man is justified by the law in the sight of God, it is evident: for, *The just shall live by faith*" (Gal. 3:11).

"*Now the just shall live by faith*: but if any man draw back, my soul shall have no pleasure in him" (Heb. 10:38).

I JOHN — Chapter II

1. My little children, these things write I unto you, that ye sin not. And if any man sin, we have an advocate with the Father, Jesus Christ the righteous:

2. And he is the propitiation for our sins: and not for our's only, but also for the sins of the whole world.

3. And hereby we do know that we know him, if we keep his commandments.

4. He that saith I know him, and keepeth not his commandments, is a liar, and the truth is not in him.

5. But whoso keepeth his word, in him verily is the love of God perfected: hereby know we that we are in him.

6. He that saith he abideth in him ought himself also so to walk, even as he walked.

7. Brethren, I write no new commandment unto you, but an old commandment which we had from the beginning. The old commandment is the word which ye have heard from the beginning.

8. Again, a new commandment write I unto you, which thing is true in him and in you: because the darkness is past, and the true light now shineth.

9. He that saith he is in the light, and hateth his brother, is in darkness even until now.

10. He that loveth his brother abideth in the light, and there is none occasion of stumbling in him.

11. But he that hateth his brother is in darkness, and walketh in darkness, and knoweth not whither he goeth, because that darkness hath blinded his eyes.

12. I write unto you, little children, because your sins are forgiven you for his name's sake.

13. I write unto you, fathers, because ye have known him that is from the beginning. I write unto you, young men, because ye have overcome the wicked one. I write unto you, little children, because ye have known the Father.

14. I have written unto you, fathers, because ye have known him that is from the beginning. I have written unto you, young men, because ye are strong, and the word of God abideth in you, and ye have overcome the wicked one.

15. Love not the world, neither the things that are in the world. If any man love the world, the love of the Father is not in him.

16. For all that is in the world, the lust of the flesh, and the lust of the eyes, and the pride of life, is not of the Father, but is of the world.

17. And the world passeth away, and the lust thereof: but he that doeth the will of God abideth forever.

18. Little children, it is the last time: and as ye have heard that anti-christ shall come, even now are there many anti-christs; whereby we know that it is the last time.

19. They went out from us, but they were not of us; for if they had been of us, they would no doubt have continued with us; but they went out, that they might be made manifest that they were not all of us.

20. But ye have an unction from the Holy One, and ye know all things.

21. I have not written unto you because ye know not the truth, but because ye know it, and that no lie is of the truth.

22. Who is a liar but he that denieth that Jesus is the Christ? He is anti-christ, that denieth the Father and the Son.

23. Whosoever denieth the Son, the same hath not the Father: [but] he that acknowledgeth the Son hath the Father also.

24. Let that therefore abide in you, which ye have heard from the beginning. If that which ye have heard from the beginning shall remain in you, ye also shall continue in the Son, and in the Father.

25. And this is the promise that he hath promised us, even eternal life.

26. These things have I written unto you concerning them that seduce you.

27. But the anointing which ye have received of him abideth in you, and ye need not that any man teach you; but as the same anointing teacheth you of all things, and is truth, and is no lie, and even as it hath taught you, ye shall abide in him.

28. And now, little children, abide in him; that, when he shall appear, we may have confidence, and not be ashamed before him at his coming.

29. If ye know that he is righteous, ye know that every one that doeth righteousness is born of him.

In the opening of this chapter John the Beloved makes known his primary objective in writing to believers — namely, *that we should not SIN*. Yet he makes it plain that if we DO sin, we should not despair when we realize our guilt before a holy God, because we have an Advocate with the Father — One who has already made propitiation for the sins of the whole world (vv. 1 and 2). Also see I Timothy 2:5. This is actually a continuation of what John was saying in the closing of chapter 1.

In verses 3 through 6 we find the evidence whereby we know that we know God and that we are true believers. This assurance is ours because we keep His commandments — and "the commandments" referred to here are *not* the Ten Commandments of the Mosaic Law. Romans 10:4 tells us that "Christ is the *end* of the law for righteousness to every one that believeth."

In verses 7 through 11 John declares that the truth he had set forth was no *new* commandment, but *the same truth* they had always heard concerning the nature of the pure Gospel. Even though in *this* respect the law of love was no new commandment, from another aspect it WAS new because it was, in its singularity and peculiarity, originated by Christ Jesus our Saviour. It was a commandment which Christ meant to make the the characteristic of pure religion (*Christianity*). A good part of this entire epistle is given over to explaining and emphasizing the importance of this commandment which requires Christians to love each other.

In verses 12 through 14 John points out several reasons why he was writing to "the little children," reasons derived from the peculiar character of different classes in the family of God — the "little children," the "fathers," and the "young men." To each of these John gives a solemn command — not a *suggestion* — that they "love not the world, neither the things that are IN the world," because things which make up this world are not of the Father. The world will soon pass away, but those who do the will of God shall abide forever (vv. 15-17).

In verses 18 through 20 the Holy Spirit calls attention to the fact that these are the closing days of this dispensation, as evidenced by the presence of antichrists even in John's day.

In verses 21 through 26 our attention is directed to the *characteristics* of Antichrists: they would deny that Jesus was the Christ of God, very God in flesh — and to deny Christ the Son is to deny God the Father. John lived in the first century of Christianity, yet antichrists were already operating. There were teachers who had already begun to teach the doctrine of Antichrist.

In the closing verses of chapter 2 John assures us that we have "the anointing from above," (the Holy Spirit within us), and that the Holy Spirit teaches and *leads* the believer, thus assuring us that we will not be led astray. Antichrist cannot deceive a true believer: "Wherefore also it is contained in the Scripture, Behold, I lay in Sion a chief corner stone, elect, precious: and he that believeth on him shall not be confounded" (I Pet. 2:6).

The Holy Spirit earnestly pleads that the "little children" will abide in God the Saviour, that when Jesus appears in the blessed hope they might have confidence, and not be ashamed (because of unfaithfulness) at His coming. When we stand before God to give an account of our labors and stewardship, there will be some believers who will be *ashamed* of their life here on earth.

Christ Our Advocate

Verse 1: "My little children, these things write I unto you, that ye sin not. And if any man sin, we have an Advocate with the Father, Jesus Christ the righteous."

"*My little children. . . .*" Greek authorities tell us that the words used here for "little children" actually mean "*little born ones.*" We need not *guess* as to whom these words are directed. The Holy Spirit is speaking here to born again believers, children of God, *not sinners.*

"*These things write I unto you, that ye sin not.*" ("These things" are the things just studied in chapter 1.) God does not want His little children to sin. *Natural* parents (if they are what parents *should* be) do not want their children to do wrong; they want them to live honest, clean, upright lives and refrain from doing things that would bring shame and disgrace upon the family name. Much more, then, God desires that HIS children sin not.

All that the Holy Spirit has given us through the pen of John has been in order that believers may see the sin problem stated — *and solved.* Believers should not sin, they *need not* sin; but "*if any man sin, we have an Advocate with the Father, Jesus Christ the righteous.*" This does not imply that it is right, or proper, or natural for a believer to sin; but any and all believers are *liable* to sin because we live in a tabernacle of flesh, and the flesh is capable of committing any sin in Satan's catalog if we are caught off guard or in a weak moment when we are not fully trusting and leaning heavily on the strong arm of Christ Jesus, our Saviour and Lord. We live in a corrupt world (though we are not OF the world); and we are subject to temptation. So long as we abide in this tabernacle of flesh even the very best of us is liable to sin.

Even though we are saved by grace through faith plus nothing, God does not give His little "born ones" a license to sin. Even though the grace of God that saves us also teaches and keeps us, the Holy Spirit instructs us that regardless of how dedicated we may be, we are still subject to temptation; and when we realize that we have sinned we should not just throw up our hands and say, "What's the use? I cannot overcome." We should not let failure cause us to despair. We should immediately cry out to God for forgiveness — and *"He is faithful and just to forgive."*

Thank God, Christ Jesus who died to *redeem* us also lives to save and keep us *daily*. He is our Intercessor:

"For when we were yet without strength, in due time Christ died for the ungodly. For scarcely for a righteous man will one die: yet peradventure for a good man some would even dare to die. But God commendeth His love toward us, in that, while we were yet sinners, Christ died for us. MUCH MORE THEN, BEING NOW JUSTIFIED BY HIS BLOOD, WE SHALL BE SAVED FROM WRATH THROUGH HIM. For if, when we were enemies, we were reconciled to God by the death of His Son, MUCH MORE, BEING RECONCILED, WE SHALL BE SAVED BY HIS LIFE" (Rom. 5:6-10).

We are justified by His blood NOW, we *shall be* saved from wrath day by day, moment by moment, until we reach Paradise — but notice that we are saved from wrath *through HIM*. We were reconciled to God by Christ's *death*, we shall be saved by His *life*. Because HE lives, WE live — *Christ IS our life* — and when He who is our life shall appear, we shall also appear with Him in glory. He died to redeem us, and as our Advocate He lives to deliver us from sin day by day.

Only GOD can forgive sin. Luke 5:17-26 records the account of the healing of the paralytic. When Jesus told the man to rise, take up his bed, and *walk*, the Pharisees began to reason among themselves, saying, "Who is this which speaketh blasphemies? Who can forgive sins, but God alone?" The Pharisees were correct in that statement — *no one but God CAN forgive sins.* As individuals we cannot approach God because we have sinned and come short of His glory; but there is One upon whom we can depend to take care of our interests with the Father. Our Redeemer and Saviour, Christ Jesus, can approach God, because through suffering He learned obedience and became the Heir of eternal salvation. He was made like unto His brethren in all things (sin apart), that He might be a faithful and compassionate High Priest unto God pertaining to things that have to do with believers and the heavenly Father. He can plead our cause and present our need to God: "For there is one God, and one Mediator between God and men, the Man Christ Jesus" (I Tim. 2:5).

The word here translated "Advocate" in other places is translated "paraclete." *"Advocate"* as used here points out that Jesus is eligible to stand in our stead before God and is capable of pleading our case before Him. In Greek language — as well as in Greek life — the same word was used with reference to a lawyer or counsellor.

As our Advocate before the Father, the Man Christ Jesus admits the guilt of those for whom He advocates. He admits that the law of God has been broken, He makes no apology for the sin having been committed. He does not deny the *fact* of sin, nor does he attempt to show that the individual has a *right* to sin. But as our Advocate, He is our surety; and while He does not excuse us, He does present to the Father what He has done on our behalf. Through His sufferings and death, through His shed blood and His resurrection, He is now seated at the right hand of God the Father; the fact of His being there is Divine proof that in all things He pleased the Father, and therefore He has the right to *remind* the Father that He willingly took our sin (and our *sins*) and nailed them to His cross.

"For even hereunto were ye called: because Christ also suffered for us, leaving us an example, that ye should follow His steps: Who did no sin, neither was guile found in His mouth: Who, when He was reviled, reviled not again; when He suffered, He threatened not; but committed Himself to Him that judgeth righteously: WHO HIS OWN SELF BARE OUR SINS IN HIS OWN BODY ON THE TREE, THAT WE, BEING DEAD TO

SINS, SHOULD LIVE UNTO RIGHTEOUSNESS: BY WHOSE STRIPES YE WERE HEALED. For ye were as sheep going astray; but are now returned unto the Shepherd and Bishop of your souls" (I Pet. 2:21-25).

Christ Jesus our Advocate is also surety for us. He gives God a pledge that He will guide and direct us in paths of righteousness, obedience, and truth. Such a pledge of surety cannot be given in *human* courts of justice. Our courts can *pardon* a thief, but no court, judge, or lawyer can give surety that he will never steal again; but in the Court of Heaven the Man Christ Jesus *does* become just such surety or pledge for every Christian in his standing before God.

"For the law made nothing perfect, but the bringing in of a better hope did; by the which we draw nigh unto God. And inasmuch as not without an oath He was made priest: (For those priests were made without an oath; but this with an oath by Him that said unto Him, The Lord sware and will not repent, Thou art a priest for ever after the order of Melchisedec:) *BY SO MUCH WAS JESUS MADE A SURETY OF A BETTER TESTAMENT.* And they truly were many priests, because they were not suffered to continue by reason of death: But this Man, because He continueth ever, hath an unchangeable priesthood. WHEREFORE HE IS ABLE ALSO TO SAVE THEM TO THE UTTERMOST THAT COME UNTO GOD BY HIM, SEEING HE EVER LIVETH TO MAKE INTERCESSION FOR THEM. For such an high priest became us, who is holy, harmless, undefiled, separate from sinners, and made higher than the heavens; who needeth not daily, as those high priests, to offer up sacrifice, first for his own sins, and then for the people's: for this He did when He offered up Himself. For the law maketh men high priests which have infirmity; but the word of the oath, which was since the law, maketh the Son, who is consecrated for evermore" (Heb. 7:19-28).

"*Jesus Christ the Righteous.*" Jesus was God incarnate. What God demanded, only God could provide. Therefore, God Himself came down to man in a body. God was in Christ, He is the Righteous One, and being altogether righteous in Himself He possesses the means of rendering others righteous.

Righteousness is not attained; it is *imputed*: "But to him that worketh is the reward not reckoned of grace, but of debt. *But to him that worketh not, but believeth on Him that justifieth the ungodly, his faith is counted for righteousness"* (Rom. 4: 4, 5).

"But of Him are ye in Christ Jesus, who of God is made unto us wisdom, and righteousness, and sanctification, and redemption: That, according as it is written, He that glorieth, let him glory in the Lord" (I Cor. 1:30, 31).

We are saved (justified) on account of *Christ's* righteousness. God will receive us because of His righteousness which is imputed to us. Christ Jesus our Saviour (and now our Advocate) is the only Person who ever lived on this earth who did not sin. He was altogether righteous, there was no guile, no trace of sin, in Him. He satisfied God in every minute detail, and He is therefore eligible to sit at the right hand of the Majesty and plead our case.

Verse 2: "And He is the propitiation for our sins: and not for our's only, but also for the sins of the whole world."

The Greek word here translated "propitiation" occurs again in chapter 4, verse 10, and these are the only times that we find this particular word so translated in the entire New Testament, though words of the same derivation and having the same essential meaning often occur. A similar word occurs in Romans 3:25 and is rendered "propitiation," and another similar word occurs in Hebrews 9:5 where it is rendered *"mercy seat."* The verb of the same word is found in Luke 18:13 where the publican prayed, "God, be merciful to me a sinner." We find a similar word in Hebrews 2:17, rendered "reconciliation."

The proper meaning of this word is "turning away anger, making reconciliation between God and man." It means to "render favorable," and here signifies that Christ Himself, through the expiatory sacrifice of His death, is the personal means by whom God shows mercy to those who believe on Christ. The only way we can stand in God's favor is for Jesus to plead for us.

God is angry with sin, and the truth set forth here is that the wrath of God must be poured out upon sin. God has been offended and it is needful that His anger be turned away and His wrath against sin satisfied *by a suitable sacrifice.* Jesus offered such a sacrifice — once, for all, forever, never to be repeated. He offered His own blood. (Study the entire tenth chapter of Hebrews.)

When we confess our sins in the name of Jesus we are reconciled to God. His anger is turned away and He forgives us for Christ's sake: "Be ye kind one to another, tenderhearted, forgiving one another, even as God for Christ's sake hath forgiven you" (Eph. 4:32). Jesus is the propitiation for our sins. He has done whatever is necessary to maintain the honor of God's law, God's justice and truth, making it consistent for a holy God to offer pardon and forgiveness.

Propitiation (to make atonement) does not change God nor His attitude toward sin. It does not mean that God overlooks sin as a fact. It simply means that Jesus paid the sin-debt in full, and since He offered His own blood for the remission of sin, God can now be just and yet justify the ungodly when the ungodly confess their sins and believe on Jesus. I would emphasize the fact that *God forgives us and saves us for Christ's sake.*

If the believer sins *after* redemption, God can still be just and forgive the sins of the believer for Christ's sake, on the merit of His finished work. God does not want us to sin, but if we DO sin, we have assurance that propitiation has been provided and pardon will be freely extended to us. If we confess our sins He is faithful and just to forgive us, and to cleanse us from all unrighteousness.

"*And not for our (sins) only, but also for the sins of the whole world.*" Thank God for the last part of this verse! Jesus paid the penalty for all sins of all sinners of all times. There are those who teach limited atonement, hyper-Calvinism. They teach that the "elect" can be saved, and all others must be *damned* — but such a doctrine is not found in the Word of God. The Scripture tells us that "*God so loved THE WORLD.*" Therefore Christ is the propitiation for the *sins* of the whole world: "*The Lord is . . . not willing that ANY should perish, but that ALL should come to repentance*" (II Pet. 3:9). To His own people Jesus said, "Ye *will NOT* come to me that ye might have life!"

Certainly the blood of Jesus is *sufficient* for our sins, and for the sins of all the world. Any sinner can be saved if he will hear the Gospel and believe on the name of Jesus Christ. He did not die for one race, one nationality, nor for an elect, select group: He died for the whole world, and His invitation is to *all* :" . . . Let him that is athirst come. And *whosoever will*, let him take the water of life freely" (Rev. 22:17).

The atonement was planned and provided for all, it is truly fitted to all, and the propitiation is sufficient in merit for all. Jesus paid the sin-debt and satisfied the heart of God concerning sin for *all* peoples, and *whosoever will* can be saved. Christ Jesus our Saviour and Lord so completely fulfilled the law (Matt. 5:17), so gloriously magnified the law and honored God the Father in every detail of His life and service, so fully expressed the Divine sense of the evil and ugliness of sin, that through His finished work the offer of the great salvation is made as freely to one as to the other. Any and all who will believe can be saved. "For the love of Christ constraineth us; because we thus judge, that if One died for *all*, then were all dead" (II Cor. 5:14).

"But we see Jesus, who was made a little lower than the angels for the suffering of death, crowned with glory and honour; that He by the grace of God should taste death for *every* man" (Heb. 2:9).

"For I reckon that the sufferings of this present time are not worthy to be compared with the glory which shall be revealed in us. For the earnest expectation of the creature waiteth for the manifestation of the sons of God. For the creature was made subject to vanity, not willingly, but by reason of Him who hath subjected the same in hope. Because the creature itself also shall be delivered from the bondage of corruption into the glorious liberty of the children of God. For we know that the whole creation groaneth and travaileth in pain together until now. And not only they, but ourselves also, which have the firstfruits of the Spirit, even we ourselves groan within ourselves, waiting for the adoption, to wit, the redemption of our body" (Rom. 8:18-23).

It is the plan and program of God to save the entire creation from the curse of sin; and eventually, in the by-and-by, the whole creation that now groans and travails *will be* delivered, the curse will be completely removed. There will be peace on earth and good will toward men. In Isaiah II we read that the curse will be lifted from the animal kingdom also, and "they shall not hurt nor destroy in all (God's) holy mountain: for the earth will be full of the knowledge of the Lord, as the waters cover the sea" (Isa. 11:9).

True Believers Have Assurance

Verse 3: "And hereby we do know that we know Him, if we keep His commandments."

Remember the key verse of this epistle: *"These things write we unto you that your joy may be full."* Certainly there cannot be full joy in our salvation apart from absolute assurance. In the beginning of the epistle John assured us that he knew what he was talking about; he declared that he was giving the message "which was from the beginning, which we have heard, which we have seen with our eyes, which we have looked upon, and our hands have handled, of the Word of life."

Now in this verse he declares that *"we do know that we know Him."* There is no such thing as salvation apart from assurance. Any person who does not KNOW that he is saved as surely as he knows that he is breathing, has a counterfeit experience. Paul said, "I KNOW WHOM I HAVE BELIEVED, and am persuaded that He is able to keep that which I have committed unto Him against that day" (II Tim. 1:12).

The blind boy in John 9 declared, "Whether He be a sinner or not, I know not: *ONE THING I KNOW, that, whereas I was blind, now I see"* (John 9:25).

Romans 8:16 tells us, "The Spirit (Himself) *beareth witness with our spirit,* that we are the children of God."

Later in our present study John declares, "WE KNOW that we have passed from death unto life, because we love the brethren. He that loveth not his brother abideth in death . . . And hereby WE KNOW that we are of the truth, and shall assure our hearts before Him. For if our heart condemn us, God is greater than our heart, and knoweth all things. Beloved, if our heart condemn us not, then have we confidence toward God" (I John 3:14, 19-21).

If you are a believer, you KNOW it. If you are genuinely saved, you KNOW it. And if you do not KNOW that you are saved, then my advice to you is to slip away to some quiet place, open your Bible, and read John 5:24, Ephesians 2:8, 9, Romans 10:9, 10, 13, and I John 1:9. Then get down on your knees and ask the Lord to forgive your sin, cover you with His precious blood, and write your name in the Lamb's book of life. I assure you on the authority of God's Word that if you will *hear* His Word and believe in the finished work and shed blood of Jesus, God will save you — AND YOU WILL KNOW IT!!

We know that we know Him *"if we keep His commandments."* Is John speaking here of the Ten Commandments — the law of Moses? According to Romans 10:4, "Christ is the END of the law for righteousness to every one that believeth," and in Matthew 5:17 Jesus said, "Think not that I am come to destroy the law, or the prophets: *I am not come to destroy, but to FULFIL."*

We know, then, that John is not speaking of the Ten Commandments, for Christ is the end of the Mosaic system; He fulfilled every jot and tittle. John is speaking of a *new* commandment. In Galatians 6:2 we read, "Bear ye one another's burdens, *and so fulfil the LAW OF CHRIST."* II John 5 says, "And now I beseech thee, lady, not as though I wrote a *new* commandment unto thee, *but that which we had from the beginning, THAT WE LOVE ONE ANOTHER."*

The "new commandment," the Law of Christ, is the Divine love that He puts within the heart of every believer. When we are born of the Spirit, the *fruit* of the Spirit is LOVE:

"Hope maketh not ashamed; because *the love of God is shed abroad in our hearts* by the Holy Ghost which is given unto us" (Rom. 5:5).

"Whereof the Holy Ghost also is a witness to us: for after that He had said before, This is the covenant that I will make with them after those days, saith the Lord, *I will put my laws into their hearts, and in their minds will I write them"* (Heb. 10:15, 16).

The new commandment is *law written in the heart,* not on tables of stone or in a book. The new Law of Christ is the New Covenant of Hebrews 8:8; it is the law of liberty:

"But whoso looketh into *the perfect law of liberty,* and continueth therein, he being not a forgetful hearer, but a doer of the work, this man shall be blessed in his deed . . . So speak

ye, and so do, as they that shall be judged *by the law of liberty*"
(James 1:25; 2:12).

The law of Moses *demanded* love (Lev. 19:18; Deut. 6:5;
Luke 10:27), but Christ's law IS love. God is love (I John
4:8), therefore CHRIST is love.

Verse 4: "He that saith, I know Him, and keepeth not His
commandments, is a liar, and the truth is not in him."

The person who professes to be a believer, one who testifies
that Jesus is his Saviour, *"and keepeth not His commandments, is
a liar."* Those who profess Christ should practice the habits of a
Christian — first and foremost, *love for the Lord*; and then love
for the brethren. If love is not demonstrated in the life of one
who professes to be a Christian, that person is living a lie, he
is counterfeit, and he professes what he does not possess —
namely, *the Holy Spirit and Divine nature*. There can be no
genuine repentance, no true conversion, where one does not
obey the Word of God. Jesus said, "By this shall all men know
that ye are my disciples, if ye have love one to another" (John
13:35).

The person who professes without possessing is not only a
liar, but *"the truth is not in him."* The incorruptible seed, the
Word of God, is not in such a person; and since the Word is
the incorruptible seed that brings eternal life, any person who
testifies that he knows Jesus and yet "keepeth not His commandments" is living a lie and is hopelessly lost.

This is the second time in fourteen verses that the Holy Spirit
has declared certain persons to be *liars*. We do not hear such
plain preaching from pulpits today; yet the most scathing,
scorching words ever to fall from the lips of man fell from the
lips of the Son of God. (Read Matthew 23; study it carefully.)

Verse 5: "But whoso keepeth His Word, in him verily is the
love of God perfected: hereby know we that we are in Him."

Obedience is the test that determines whether or not we are
really born again. Obedience always follows true conversion.
Obedience is also the measure of our love for God. We obey
His Word and follow His commands, seeking to know and to do
His perfect will, in measure corresponding to the depth, the
purity, and the fulness of our love for Him. The disobedient
child — one who does not do the things that bring joy and satis-

faction to the hearts of the parents — may profess love for them over and over again; but the words are meaningless when the child persistently disobeys and ignores the parents' wishes. Just so, there are those who *with their lips* profess to love God — but they do not obey His Word, they do not follow His commands. Our attitude toward Christ in obeying His Word will determine what degree of love we have for the heavenly Father — He who loved US so much that He gave His only begotten Son to die for us in payment of our sin-debt.

In John 14:15 Jesus said, "If ye love me, keep my commandments." (Greek scholars tell us that the pure Greek reads, "If ye love me, YE WILL KEEP my commandments.") Believers who truly love the Lord Jesus as they should will take great joy in obeying His Word. His commands are not grievous or burdensome, and obedience brings deep and satisfying joy to the heart of the believer.

The Greek word translated *"keepeth"* is in the present tense, implying not just a single act, but *continuous activity* — day by day obedience, in *material* things as well as in the spiritual realm; obedience not only when people are watching us, but when we are in secret. "Whatsoever He saith unto you, *do it*" (John 2:5) were the words spoken by the mother of Jesus to the servants at the wedding in Cana where Jesus performed His first miracle. What He asked them to do seemed very insignificant — He simply asked them to fill the wine jars with water; but there are no "little" things in what Jesus commands or invites us to do.

> Trust and obey, for there's no other way
> To be happy in Jesus, but to trust and obey."

In the Great Commission Jesus said, "All power is given unto me in heaven and in earth. Go ye therefore, and teach all nations, baptizing them in the name of the Father, and of the Son, and of the Holy Ghost: teaching them to observe all things whatsoever I have commanded you: and, lo, I am with you alway, even unto the end of the world. Amen" (Matt. 28:18-20).

Here is the Saviour's prerogative. He has all power, and His program reads thus: "Go into all the world, and teach all nations." In other words, *make disciples*; and He has promised that if we go, and teach, and preach, He will be with us all of our days, even to the consummation of the age. What He has spoken, that He will do!

What a tremendous set-up under which to work! Divinely planned, all the world before us, and our invitation is to preach to all nations. We are backed up by the promise of all power given to us from Him who HAS all power. Christ is the all-powerful One, He is able to keep His promise.

It is worthy of note, however, that in the teaching of our Saviour's program we many times forget to emphasize His instructions to teach people "to observe ALL things whatsoever I have commanded you." Not only do we forget to emphasize "ALL things" He has commanded us, but we neglect His instructions to teach them "*to OBSERVE* all things" whatsoever He has commanded us. From Matthew through Revelation the Word of God emphasizes *doing, observing, keeping, obeying* the commandments of Jesus. We teach, we preach, we emphasize them, but we do not command the people to *observe* them. Today it has become customary for the Word to be hidden in the *head*, not in the heart; we have head-knowledge, but not heart-obedience. It is the Word hidden in the heart that keeps believers from sinning. It is the Word hidden in the heart that leads the Christian to obey, to observe, to do and to keep His commandments. It is possible to have a head full of Scripture and a heart full of sin. It is possible for one to speak great swelling words from the pulpit, and yet the Word of God not abide in the heart of the speaker.

True love is always accompanied by obedience. If true love exists in the heart it will be manifested in the life — i.e., if we love we obey, and if we obey it is because we love. In the spiritual realm it is Jesus whom we love and obey. The apostles said, "We ought to obey God rather than men" (Acts 5:29).

"Whoso keepeth His Word, *in him verily is the love of God perfected.*" Without love and obedience to God it is impossible for an individual to develop, grow in grace, and know perfect love. I John 4:18 tells us that "there is no fear in love; but *perfect love casteth out fear*: because fear hath torment. He that feareth is not made perfect in love."

"*Hereby know we that we are in Him.*" Love that produces

obedience to God assures the heart that we are genuinely born again and that the love of God abides in our hearts, because *apart* from the love of God we could not be obedient to Him. The natural man does not obey God, he does not follow the leadership of the Spirit, because he has no love for God in his heart. Paul said "the natural man receiveth not the things of the Spirit of God: for they are foolishness unto him: neither can he know them, because they are spiritually discerned" (I Cor. 2:14). God is love, and when our hearts are permeated by the love of God we will obey Him because we love Him.

Verse 6: "He that saith he abideth in Him ought himself also so to walk, even as He walked."

In John 15:1-14 Jesus gives an illustration concerning the believer's abiding in Him:

"I am the true vine, and my Father is the husbandman. Every branch in me that beareth not fruit He taketh away: and every branch that beareth fruit, He purgeth it, that it may bring forth more fruit. Now ye are clean through the Word which I have spoken unto you. Abide in me, and I in you. As the branch cannot bear fruit of itself, except it abide in the vine; no more can ye, except ye abide in me. I am the vine, ye are the branches: He that abideth in me, and I in him, the same bringeth forth much fruit: for without me ye can do nothing.

"If a man abide not in me, he is cast forth as a branch, and is withered; and men gather them, and cast them into the fire, and they are burned. If ye abide in me, and my words abide in you, ye shall ask what ye will, and it shall be done unto you. Herein is my Father glorified, that ye bear much fruit; so shall ye be my disciples. As the Father hath loved me, so have I loved you: continue ye in my love. If ye keep my commandments, ye shall abide in my love; even as I have kept my Father's commandments, and abide in His love.

"These things have I spoken unto you, that my joy might remain in you, and that your joy might be full. This is my commandment, That ye love one another, as I have loved you. Greater love hath no man than this, that a man lay down his life for his friends. Ye are my friends if ye do whatsoever I command you."

So important is this passage that I have given it here in its entirety, so there will be no excuse for not reading and studying these tremendous verses. Jesus is the true Vine, the heavenly Father is the husbandman, WE are the branches; and the branch cannot hope to bear fruit except it abide in the Vine. You will notice Jesus mentioned "fruit," "more fruit," and "*much* fruit." We glorify God when we bear MUCH fruit.

Just before Jesus was crucified He said to His heavenly Father, "I have glorified thee on the earth: I have finished the work which thou gavest me to do" (John 17:4). I wonder, if the Lord should call me home today, if I could say "I have glorified Jesus upon the earth." What about YOU? Are you obedient? Are you abiding? Are you bearing fruit? more fruit? *much* fruit? Think it over — and remember, Jesus is glorified when we bear *much fruit*.

We ourselves ought "*so to walk, even as HE walked.*" This is the Bible rule concerning the walk of a Christian. Every step Jesus walked upon the earth, everything He said and everything He did, was to glorify God the Father. He never performed one miracle for His own comfort or satisfaction. His ministry was always to glorify God first, and to benefit mankind second; and when we walk as HE walked we are displaying an outward sign that Jesus lives within us. "The steps of a good man are ordered by the Lord: and he delighteth in His way" (Psalm 37:23).

The words of our present verse were written to believers, not sinners. In Ephesians 2:1 we are told that unbelievers are "dead in trespasses and sins." They walk according to the course of this world, and before they can walk as believers should walk, they must be *raised* from the dead, they must be born again, new creatures in Christ Jesus. We need not invite the sinner to walk as the Master walked; he needs to be born again first. We are not converted by *walking*, but by believing in the shed blood and finished work of the Lamb of God.

As we read and study the life of Christ as recorded in the Gospels, on every page we see His example in His daily walk set before us — an example that reached from His boyhood to Calvary; and as He walked, so should WE walk who bear His name. This is the rule of dedicated spiritual living. We must not follow the examples set by *people*, we dare not even get our eyes on preachers, teachers, evangelists, or missionaries. We must have a single eye, looking to Jesus, and always, in all things, we are to follow HIM — not man, not tradition, not "religion," not dogma — *but the Man, Christ Jesus.*

It is true that times have changed, customs and habits of life have changed since Jesus walked upon this earth; but the basic things today are the same as when Jesus lived and ministered among men. Sin has not changed, Satan has not changed, temptation has not changed. So regardless of what we face today we can follow in the steps of Jesus and know that we will come out right every time: "There hath no temptation taken you but such as is common to man: but God is faithful, who will not suffer you to be tempted above that ye are able; but will with the temptation also make a way to escape, that ye may be able to bear it" (I Cor. 10:13).

He who saves us gives us strength to walk as we *should* walk: "If thou shalt do this thing, and God command thee so, then thou shalt be able to endure, and all this people shall also go to their place in peace" (Ex. 18:23).

"Be ye therefore followers of God, as dear children" (Eph. 5:1). We are God's "little born ones" and if we have faith in God as we should (Mark 11:22) we need not doubt that we can *do* all that we should. Those of us who abide in Jesus and walk in His steps will *grow* day by day as we follow Him and feed upon the milk, the bread, and the meat of His Word and obey the leadership of the Holy Spirit.

The born again believer possesses Divine nature (II Pet. 1:4).
The believer possesses the Holy Spirit (Rom. 8:9).
We are led by the Spirit (Rom. 8:14).
We are assured by the Spirit (Rom. 8:16).
Christ dwells in the believer (Col. 1:27).
The believer is hid with Christ in God (Col. 3:3).
The believer is united to Jesus (I Cor. 12:12-14).
We are members of His body, of His flesh, and of His bones (Eph. 5:30).

Since these things are true, we certainly ought to imitate Him in all things.

Verse 7: "Brethren, I write no new commandment unto you, but an old commandment which ye had from the beginning.

The old commandment is the Word which ye have heard from the beginning."

The Holy Spirit would have us understand that what is being declared here is not new; it is the same pure, Divine doctrine that was preached in the beginning. What John wrote here under inspiration was not a doctrine or commandment which he originated; the message He is giving is the message that was from the beginning — pure doctrine given to Him by the Holy Spirit and penned down for us *that our joy might be full.*

Even in the days of John the Beloved there were false teachers who were preaching man-made doctrines, some of which were so attractive and inviting that they were leading astray some of the people who had listened to John preach the pure Gospel. These false teachers came along offering something new, and some of those who were not truly born again were attracted because of the novelty of it. John assures those to whom he is writing that these are not HIS words, but the pure Word of God, the pure Gospel which they had heard from the very beginning. He is laying down the familiar truths of the faith once delivered unto the saints — the same truths Jesus had taught and preached, and which believers had received.

It was no *new* commandment which he wrote unto them, *"but an OLD commandment"* — that is, it is old in the sense that it has *always been*; it is not something John made up himself. It is that *"which ye had from the beginning."* These people had heard the Gospel of the grace of God, and true believers certainly should not be led astray by every wind of doctrine. What John had penned down were fundamentals of the faith preached when the Gospel was first proclaimed, and those same truths had been preached all along the way.

"The old commandment is the Word which ye have heard from the beginning." That settles it! John was teaching, preaching, and writing as the Holy Ghost dictated the Word of God that was "in the beginning" (John 1:1), the Word that is forever settled in heaven (Psalm 119:89), the Word that is the power of God unto salvation to everyone who will believe (Rom. 1:16), the Word that makes men clean (John 15:3). In reality, John is saying, "All that I have written, all that I have

said, all that I have preached to you is a commandment as old as the beginning — the same commandment, the same Word, that you have always heard and obeyed. Nothing new has been added, nothing has been taken away or *replaced* with something new."

Verse 8: "Again, a new comandment I write unto you, which thing is true in Him and in you: because the darkness is past, and the true Light now shineth."

This may sound like a contradiction in Scripture, but not so. John is speaking here of the commandment of Jesus that we "love one another." He speaks of it as a "new commandment" — not in the sense that JOHN declared it, but new in that Jesus the Saviour gave it to His disciples as a token whereby the world might recognize the true Christian: *"By this shall all men know that ye are my disciples, if ye have love one to another"* (John 13:35).

In the Sermon on the Mount Jesus said, "Ye have heard that it hath been said, Thou shalt love thy neighbour, and hate thine enemy. BUT I SAY UNTO YOU, Love your enemies, bless them that curse you, do good to them that hate you, and pray for them which despitefully use you, and persecute you; that ye may be the children of your Father which is in heaven: for He maketh His sun to rise on the evil and on the good, and sendeth rain on the just and on the unjust. For if ye love them which love you, what reward have ye? Do not even the publicans the same? And if ye salute your brethren only, what do ye more than others? Do not even the publicans so? Be ye therefore perfect, even as your Father which is in heaven is perfect" (Matt. 5:43-48).

"A new commandment . . . *which thing is true in Him*" (that is, in the Lord Jesus). The law of love was *perfected* in Christ Jesus, illustrated in Him, and manifested by Him as He ministered here upon this earth. He loved His disciples, and "having loved His own which were in the world, He loved them unto the end" (John 13:1).

The law of love was true in Jesus, *"and in you."* Here John speaks of the believers to whom he addressed this epistle, as well as to you and to me. His meaning is that among Christians, brotherly love is displayed. We manifest love one for another as we fellowship together in the community and in the church.

"*The darkness is past, and the true Light now shineth.*" Here we are reminded that we are not children of darkness, we are not children of the night. He who is the Light of the world has come for the believer, darkness no longer exists — not even twilight. "God is light, and in Him is no darkness at all." His Word is a lamp unto our feet and a light unto our pathway. We walk in the light, and because GOD is love, *Christianity* is love. We love Him because He first love US. If we do not love each other, if we do not love our Christian brother whom we have *seen*, how can we love God whom we have NOT seen? And according to Jesus' teaching in the passage just quoted from Matthew, if we love only those who do good to us and speak well of us, we are doing no more than the hypocrites and Pharisees!

"In Him was life; and the life was the light of men. And the light shineth in darkness; and the darkness comprehended it not . . . That was the true Light, which lighteth every man that cometh into the world" (John 1:4, 5, 9).

The Apostle Paul said, "But ye, brethren, are not in darkness, that that day should overtake you as a thief. Ye are all the children of light, and the children of the day: we are not of the night, nor of darkness. Therefore let us not sleep, as do others; but let us watch and be sober" (I Thess. 5:4-6).

In Colossians 1:12-14 we read, "Giving thanks unto the Father, which hath made us meet to be partakers of the inheritance of the saints *in light*: Who hath delivered us from the power of *darkness*, and hath translated us into *the kingdom of His dear Son*: In whom we have redemption through His blood, even the forgiveness of sins." Jesus is the Light of the world, and therefore His kingdom is a kingdom of light; and He will be the light of the Pearly White City (Rev. 21:23).

Believers are children of light, we walk in the light, we *possess* the Light, we have been translated into the *kingdom* of light. Therefore "*the darkness is past, and the true Light now shineth.*" There is no excuse for spiritual ignorance concerning the commandments of Jesus as related to the believer.

Light vs. Darkness — Love vs. Hate

Verses 9-11: "He that saith he is in the light, and hateth his brother, is in darkness even until now. He that loveth his brother abideth in the light, and there is none occasion of stumbling in him. But he that hateth his brother is in darkness, and walketh in darkness, and knoweth not whither he goeth, because that darkness hath blinded his eyes."

Hatred is of the devil, it is of the kingdom of darkness and it proceeds from a dark heart. These verses give us a terrible picture of a man who hates another: he abides in darkness. By way of illustration, suppose we take a beautiful plant, put it in the basement and close out the light. The plant would grow for a few days, and then its beautiful color would fade, it would become drab and would soon begin to droop, and finally it would die. That is what the spirit of hatred does to the soul. There are few things a man can do that are as ugly as hate; for an unloving, unforgiving spirit, the spirit of hatred, will actually cause its victim to become sick. Darkness! Few people really *like* darkness. Jesus said, *"men loved darkness rather than light, because their deeds were EVIL"* (John 3:19).

The man who hates his brother not only *lives* in darkness, He *"walketh in darkness and knoweth not whither he goeth."* The man who harbors hatred in his heart does not know where he is going, he has no idea where that hatred will lead him. The vicious thoughts that control his mind may — and many times do — lead to bloodshed and murder. In chapter 3, verse 15 of this epistle John tells us that *"whosoever hateth his brother is a murderer: and ye know that no murderer hath eternal life abiding in him."* According to God's Word, hatred is murder, and many times hatred brings forth the actual killing of one's fellowman!

Moreover, from the spiritual standpoint hatred is a deadly poison; it dulls the mind, warps the soul removes the smile from a face and, unless uprooted by the grace of God, will actually *poison* body, mind, and soul. When a person lives in the spirit of hatred, the seeds of hate may grow into deeds that are unthinkable. Many times, words cannot describe what hatred will cause one to do, because *"darkness hath blinded his eyes."*

One who hates also gropes in darkness; he is in far more piti-
ful condition than if he were *physically* blind. The physically
blind can find their way by use of a cane, they can be led by
a friend, or they can follow a "seeing-eye dog"; but the person
whose eyes are blinded by hatred cannot be led by *anyone*
until God works a miracle in the heart and the *love* of God
comes into the soul! The Holy Spirit can then take over and
hatred will depart.

Hate blinds the mind. He who lives in the spirit of hatred cannot see reason, he cannot recognize truth: "But if our Gospel be
hid, it is hid to them that are lost: *in whom the god of this
world hath blinded the minds* of them which believe not, lest
the light of the glorious Gospel of Christ, who is the image of
God, should shine unto them" (II Cor. 4:3, 4). When hatred
permeates the soul the mind cannot think in the right direction. Such a person needs to pray, *"Lord, that I may receive
my sight!"* (Luke 18:41).

Jesus said "I am the Light of the world," and if we believe
on Him He abides within us and we abide in Him. Therefore
we have the Light of life and according to Matthew 5:14 we
are lights in a dark world. It is true that many believers need
to trim their lamps and clean their reflectors. Some need to remove their lamps from beneath a bushel. But we have received
light from the *true Light* and we should shine in this dark world
to point unbelievers to the Lamb of God who taketh away the
sin that damns the soul.

Notice the life of a man who lives in love, who is filled and
controlled by the love of God. The law of love is "an old commandment" — as old as God Himself, because God IS love. God
was in the beginning, God is a God of grace, and *because* of His
grace God's love was brought down to man. While we were yet
unlovely He loved us. The law of love was in the beginning
with God, love is OF God, and we who belong to the same
body, walk in the same light, possess the same Spirit, should
love *each other.* He who loves his brother *"abideth in the light,
and there is none occasion of stumbling in him."*

Let me use a very crude — but true — illustration: A man
who works in the sunlight shows *on his face* that he is a man
who works in the sun; his face is tanned. The man who works

indoors and is seldom exposed to the sunlight also shows it; his face is untanned, much whiter than the face of the man who lives and works in the outdoors. The light of the sun will change the appearance of the skin — and the same is true, figuratively, in the spiritual realm: If we walk in the light of God and His love, it will change our appearance and our habits of life as well. Walking in the light of God changes us *throughout*.

The original Hebrew language of Psalm 34:5 reads, "They looked unto Him *and were RADIANT.*" God's love puts radiance in the face of the believer, just like the sun puts color in the face of the person who is exposed to its light.

The man who walks in the light has *"none occasion of stumbling in him."* When we walk in the light we are walking in JESUS, and when we walk with Him in the light of His countenance and love, we can rest assured that we will not stumble. He who walks in the light can see the pitfalls of Satan in his path, he can see the stumbling blocks Satan has placed in the way, and — if he so wills — he can *avoid* those pitfalls and stumblingblocks. Sad to say, not all believers *desire* to live a separated, consecrated, spirit-filled life that will glorify God and point others to salvation; but the Christian who *wants* victory can certainly have it:

"What shall we then say to these things? If God be for us, who can be against us? . . . Nay, in all these things we are more than conquerors through Him that loved us" (Rom. 8:31, 37).

"Ye are a chosen generation, a royal preisthood, an holy nation, a peculiar people; that ye should shew forth the praises of Him who hath called you out of darkness into His marvellous light" (I Pet. 2:9).

The Message to Little Children, Young Men, and Fathers

Verses 12-14: "I write unto you, little children, because your sins are forgiven you for His name's sake. I write unto you, fathers, because ye have known Him that is from the beginning. I write unto you, young men, because ye have overcome the wicked one. I write unto you, little children, because ye have known the Father. I have written unto you, young men, because ye are strong, and the Word of God abideth in you, and ye have overcome the wicked one."

In the family of God there are "little born ones" (those who are babes in Christ); there are "young men" (those who have grown in grace); and there are "fathers" (those who are spiritually mature, having fed many years on the milk, bread, meat, and living water of the Word). Throughout the New Testament we are taught that in the spiritual life, as in the physical, we should go forward. There should be progress in the life of the believer. Paul admonishes us to leave "the principles of the doctrine of Christ," and go on to perfection (Heb. 6:1) — not that we should *throw away* the first things, for even the mature Christian needs the milk of the Word; but we need to feed on the deeper things of God as we grow: "As ye have therefore received Christ Jesus the Lord, so walk ye in Him: Rooted and built up in Him, and stablished in the faith, as ye have been taught, abounding therein with thanksgiving" (Col. 2:6, 7).

"*I write unto you, little children.* . . ." In the fuller sense, John is speaking here to *all* believers, because all believers are children of God; but he specifies "little" children — and in the spiritual realm we need to always have and exercise the faith of a little child.

"Little children . . . *your sins are forgiven you for His name's sake.*" I pray that every believer who reads these lines will see this truth as clearly as the Holy Spirit has shown it to me. I have often asked, "Why did God save a poor, miserable, wretched sinner such as I?" In the words of the familiar song,

> Why should He love me so?
> Why should He love me so?
> Why should my Saviour to Calvary go?
> Why should He love me so?

And then one day I read these wonderful words: "Be ye kind one to another, tenderhearted, forgiving one another, even as God FOR CHRIST'S SAKE hath forgiven you" (Eph. 4:32).

God the Father saves us for Christ's sake — but WHY does He save us for Christ's sake? Ephesians 2:6, 7 answers: God "hath raised us up together, and made us sit together in heavenly places in Christ Jesus: THAT IN THE AGES TO COME HE MIGHT SHEW THE EXCEEDING RICHES OF HIS GRACE

IN HIS KINDNESS TOWARD US THROUGH CHRIST JESUS."

God does not save sinners simply to give us a more comfortable life. He does not save us just for the purpose of our inhabiting the Pearly White City. He saves us in order to complete the Church which will *occupy* the Pearly White City suspended between heaven and earth; and as we dwell there *God will display the EXCEEDING RICHES OF HIS GRACE in His kindness toward us.*

"*I write unto you, fathers, because ye have known Him that is from the beginning.*" This then is the supreme mark of spiritual parenthood — one who has grown spiritually to a place of maturity. He is no longer a "little born one," he is no longer a "young man"; he is a seasoned, instructed, spiritual father. He knows the Gospel intimately and is assured that what God's Word teaches about Jesus, God, heaven, hell and judgment is true — that which was "from the beginning." Spiritual "fathers" know the Gospel in their hearts as well as in their minds. They are mature servants of God, with a deep love for souls and a deep concern for fellow Christians.

Believers today can look into the "perfect law of liberty" which is able to make us wise. We are commanded to study to show ourselves approved unto God, workmen who need not be ashamed, rightly dividing the Word of truth (II Tim. 2:15). Paul's testimony was, "I count all things but loss for the excellency of the knowledge of Christ Jesus my Lord: for whom I have suffered the loss of all things, and do count them but dung, that I may win Christ, and be found in Him, not having mine own righteousness, which is of the law, but that which is through the faith of Christ, the righteousness which is of God by faith: *THAT I MAY KNOW HIM, AND THE POWER OF HIS RESURRECTION, AND THE FELLOWSHIP OF HIS SUFFERINGS, being made comformable unto His death*" (Phil. 3:7-10). The number one desire of Paul's life was "that I may know HIM," and to Timothy, his son in the ministry, he testified, "I KNOW WHOM I have believed, and am persuaded that He is able to keep that which I have committed unto Him against that day" (II Tim. 1:12).

To know God and to trust Him completely is to have the desire to move forward with a will of steel. In Daniel 11:32 we read, " . . . THE PEOPLE THAT DO KNOW THEIR GOD SHALL BE STRONG, AND DO EXPLOITS." The world has its "dare-devils"; we need more "dare-*saints*" today, Christians who dare to attempt great things for God.

The most joyous experience that could come to a believer (apart from his own salvation) is that of becoming a spiritual father, leading souls to Christ. The Apostle Paul rejoiced in Timothy, to whom he referred as "my own son in the faith" (I Tim. 1:2) and "my dearly beloved son" (II Tim. 1:2). To Philemon he wrote of "my son Onesimus, whom I have begotten in my bonds" (Phm. 10). John the Beloved wrote, "I have no greater joy than to hear that my children walk in truth" (III John 4). It should be the determined desire of every born again believer to grow in grace and in the knowledge of our Lord and Saviour Jesus Christ until we have truly become spiritual "fathers."

"*I write unto you, young men, because ye have overcome the wicked one.*" "*Young men*" speaks of those who are *growing*, but are not yet spiritually mature. This does not mean that they are not fully saved. When a baby is born in the flesh, that baby is an individual, as truly a person as it will ever be. If it is a normal child it will *grow*, but at the age of threescore and ten it will be no more a *person* than when it was an hour old. The same is true of the spiritual babe. When we are born again we are children of God just as surely and as fully as we will EVER be; but we should not remain children in the faith. We should not be content to feed only on the milk of the Word and remain babes in Christ; we should grow to become young men and, eventually, spiritual fathers.

These young men to whom John writes had "*overcome the wicked one*" — Satan; but HOW did they overcome? The answer is in the Word of God: "Wherewithal shall a young man cleanse his way? by taking heed thereto according to thy Word. With my whole heart have I sought thee: O let me not wander from thy commandments. Thy Word have I hid in mine heart, that I might not sin against thee. Blessed art thou, O Lord: teach me thy statutes. With my lips have I declared all the judgments of thy mouth. I have rejoiced in the way of thy testimonies, as much as in all riches. I will meditate in thy precepts, and have respect unto thy ways. I will delight myself in thy statutes: I will not forget thy Word" (Psalm 119:9-16).

You will notice that these "young men" overcame — not temptation, but the *Tempter*, a personal devil. Paul said "we wrestle not against flesh and blood, but against principalities, against powers, against the rulers of the darkness of this world, against spiritual wickedness in high places" (Eph. 6:12). There are those who deny that Satan is a person; they declare that he is just an influence. But JESUS met and was tempted by *a personal devil*. Just after His baptism He was led of the Holy Spirit into the wilderness to meet Satan. *Notice*:

"And when the TEMPTER came to Him . . ." — not when "temptation" came to Him. The devil is very real, but there is victory for the believer. There is no excuse for Christians' living defeated lives and allowing sin to have dominion over them: "Likewise reckon ye also yourselves to be dead indeed unto sin, but alive unto God through Jesus Christ our Lord. Let not sin therefore reign in your mortal body, that ye should obey it in the lusts thereof. Neither yield ye your members as instruments of unrighteousness unto sin: but YIELD YOURSELVES UNTO GOD, as those that are alive from the dead, and your members as instruments of righteousness unto God. FOR SIN SHALL NOT HAVE DOMINION OVER YOU: FOR YE ARE NOT UNDER THE LAW, BUT UNDER GRACE!" (Rom. 6:11-14).

"Who shall separate us from the love of Christ? shall tribulation, or distress, or persecution, or famine, or nakedness, or peril, or sword? As it is written, For thy sake we are killed all the day long; we are accounted as sheep for the slaughter. *Nay, in all these things we are MORE than conquerors through Him that loved us. For I am persuaded, that neither death, nor life, nor angels, nor principalities, nor powers, nor things present, nor things to come, nor height, nor depth, nor any other creature, shall be able to separate us from the love of God, which is in Christ Jesus our Lord*" (Rom. 8:35-39).

"For (whosoever) is born of God overcometh the world: and this is the victory that overcometh the world, EVEN OUR FAITH" (I John 5:4).

We know there are those who are weak and who fall victims to temptation; but Paul speaks of those who receive ABUNDANCE OF GRACE and who shall reign in life by Jesus Christ (Rom. 6:17). *These* will reign over fears, feelings, habits, circumstances, temptations, sin, the world, the flesh, and the devil — and that is much greater than reigning as king over a great country.

"*Ye are strong.*" A weak Christian is not a normal Christian. We are commanded to "be strong in the Lord, and in the power of His might" (Eph. 6:10). Certainly one who does not feed on the Word of God, one who has no appetite for the Word, will be a delicate, weak, "invalid" Christian — and it is sad that there are *so many of them*; but feeding upon the Word and spending much time in prayer will make one strong.

Also, we need to *exercise* our spiritual life in service to God. A natural child who does not get proper exercise will not develop as it should, and the same is true in the spiritual life. We need the right exercise, we need to be working for Jesus, sowing seed, winning souls. It is by the exercise of our spiritual faculties that we grow and develop. When Jesus said "Be ye therefore perfect, even as your Father which is in heaven is perfect" (Matt. 5:48), He was speaking of maturity, full growth in the Lord. Study Joshua 1:9-18 and Haggai 2:4. Romans 15:1 admonishes, "We then that are strong ought to bear the infirmities of the weak, and not to please ourselves."

"*The Word of God abideth in you.*" Herein is the secret of spiritual development. All mature Christains, "fathers" in the spiritual realm, are Bible believing, Bible studying Christians, "*mighty in the Scriptures*" (Acts 18:24); but this does not happen overnight. First we must feed on the *milk* of the Word, then on the living bread, then on the meat. We become mighty in the Scriptures when we show ourselves "approved unto God."

Most Christians *read* the Bible, but not too many read it consistently and *few* of them really *study* it. We need to heed Paul's admonition given in Colossians 3:16: "*Let the word of Christ dwell in you richly in all wisdom;* teaching and admonishing one another in psalms and hymns and spiritual songs, singing with grace in your hearts to the Lord."

"Little children . . . ye have known the Father" (v. 13). The same is said of the "fathers" in the first part of this verse. In Galatians 4:6 we read, "And *because ye are sons,* God hath sent forth the Spirit of His Son into your hearts, crying, Abba, Father." The Holy Spirit teaches even the *babe* in Christ to say "Abba" (Father). The spiritual babe *just born* into the family of God knows the Father, because the Holy Spirit takes up His abode in the heart the very moment one believes unto salvation; but the newborn babe in Christ does not know the Father in the same way that the spiritual "fathers" know Him, nor even as the "young men" know Him. The newborn Christian knows the Father as the One to whom he must look for food, for strength, and for guidance; but he also has the Holy Spirit, the Teacher of the Holy Scriptures, in his heart to teach and lead him into all truth concerning spiritual matters. Every believer — whether a babe in Christ, a strong "young man," or a mature "father" — has within his heart this Divine, inexhaustible power, this source of information and inspiration, and through the indwelling Holy Spirit he can know, understand, and be led according to God's direction, regardless of the circumstances or conditions in which he may find himself. Even the *youngest* of believers can know all that is *needful* to know in order to be what he *should* be to the glory of the God who saved him for Christ's sake. The admonition to the newborn babe in Christ is, *"As newborn babes, desire the sincere milk of the Word, that ye may grow thereby"* (I Pet. 2:2).

Paul said to young Timothy, "From a child thou hast known the holy Scriptures, which are able to make thee wise unto salvation through faith which is in Christ Jesus. All Scripture is given by inspiration of God, and is profitable for doctrine, for reproof, for correction, for instruction in righteousness: *that the man of God may be perfect* (mature), *thoroughly furnished unto all good works"* (II Tim. 3:15-17).

Each of us should search our hearts and ask ourselves just what we *are,* spiritually speaking. Are we "little children" — babes? Are we strong "young men"? Or are we "fathers" — full grown, mature Christians? There are many church members who are "old" from the standpoint of years, but they are carnally minded, they do not understand spiritual things, and truly spiritual believers cannot fellowship with them. There are very few spiritual "fathers."

The Apostle Paul is a good example of one who had reached the *fullest* Christian maturity, and such is reached only through feeding upon the Word of God and fellowshipping with God in prayer. Such practice must begin at the beginning of the Christian experience and continue throughout life.

Forbidden Love

Verse 15: "Love not the world, neither the things that are IN the world. If any man love the world, the love of the Father is not in him."

I believe in a positive Gospel, but at the same time we cannot ignore the *negative* part of the Gospel. There are many spiritual negatives. In this verse we find forbidden love: Jesus commanded, "*Love not the world.*"

We do not become Christian by hating sin and ungodliness; we become Christian by receiving Jesus into our hearts by faith. But *when we receive Him* and the love of God comes into our hearts, there are spiritual negatives that will automatically follow. Some people think that the Christian life is easy — smooth sailing. They seem to think that to believe on Jesus will take care of all difficulties, and that the Christian then "takes it easy" until he reaches Paradise; but this not true in Bible doctrine. *Jesus said*, "In the world ye shall have tribulation: but be of good cheer; I have overcome the world" (John 16:33). He also said, "No man, having put his hand to the plough, and looking back, is fit for the kingdom of God" (Luke 9:62). In Matthew 10:38 He said, "He that taketh not his cross, and followeth after me, is not worthy of me."

Three "Can Not's"

"And there went great multitudes with Him: and He turned, and said unto them, If any man come to me, and hate not his father, and mother, and wife, and children, and brethren, and sisters, yea, and his own life also, *he CAN NOT be my disciple*. And whosoever doth not bear his cross, and come after me, *CAN NOT be my disciple* . . . So likewise, whosoever he be of you that forsaketh not all that he hath, *he CAN NOT be my disciple*" (Luke 14:25-27, 33).

This passage is clear and to the point: If Christ does not mean more to us than family, friends, business — even our own lives; if we are not willing to bear the cross and walk with Him; if we are not willing to forsake all that we have to follow Him and give Him first place in our hearts and lives, we CAN NOT be His disciples.

Notice, dearly beloved: The Scriptures do not say that we will be *weak* disciples, *poor* disciples, or *backslidden* disciples, but that we cannot be His disciples *at all*. It makes no difference how much ministers try to tone it down, smooth it over, and sugarcoat it, the Scripture still says we CAN NOT be His disciples unless we are willing to let all else take second place in our lives. Many preachers today are interested in counting heads and reporting numbers. They major in "catch-all" invitations — and they CATCH all! They bring in a "mixed multitude" (Ex. 12:38), but when that mixed multitude is put to the test of the three "can not's," there are not many true disciples.

Certainly any evangelist would be flattered by a following of such multitudes as followed Jesus; but when He delivered messages such as that just quoted from Luke, the crowd dwindled away, declaring that He preached doctrine that was "hard to hear." We are living in a day of statistics and numbers. The order of the day is to make an outstanding record and have a good report to give at the annual convention. But *God* keeps a record, and all that will matter when we stand before Him will be what we have done in Jesus' name to glorify God and bring honor to Him. Too many ministers today are trying to make a name for themselves instead of glorifying the Name that is already made — the precious name of *Jesus*.

"*Love Not the World*"

There are three deadly, powerful evils that are determined to damn your soul and send you to hell; but if you believe on the Lord Jesus Christ and are saved, your sins covered by the blood and your name written in the Lamb's book of life, the same three deadly evils will then attempt to discourage and discredit you as a good steward for the Lord.

1. *The world in which you live* is determined to damn you, and if you become a believer the world will do everything possible to hinder your Christian life. The *systems* of this world are controlled by the *god* of this world — *Satan,* "the prince of the power of the air" (Eph. 2:2); and those systems, under his influence, operate to destroy and damn souls.

2. *The flesh* is against you, the very body you live in will damn you unless you believe on Jesus and allow Him to give you a new heart: "For from within, out of the heart of men, proceed evil thoughts, adulteries, fornications, murders, thefts, covetousness, wickedness, deceit, lasciviousness, an evil eye, blasphemy, pride, foolishness: all these evil things come from within, and defile the man" (Mark 7:21-23).

"The heart is deceitful above all things, and desperately wicked: who can know it?" (Jer. 17:9).

"A new heart also will I give you, and a new spirit will I put within you: and I will take away the stony heart out of your flesh . . ." (Ezek. 36:26).

3. *The devil* "as a roaring lion walketh about seeking whom he may devour." If he cannot devour your soul, he will do his best to devour your testimony and your stewardship. He will never leave you alone until you are safe in Paradise with Jesus. As long as you live on this earth Satan will be on your trail — as a serpent, as a roaring lion, or as an angel of light.

Man has three strikes aginst him — but praise God, *JESUS conquered* all three — the world, the flesh, and the devil — *and we are more than conquerors through Him!*

What is meant here by "love not *the world?*" It does not mean the world of matter, nor does it refer to the world of nature even though, in spite of the curse, nature provides beauty that words cannot describe. We know that the "world" spoken of here is not the world of *people,* as such, because in John 3:16 we are told that God *so loved* the world that He gave His only begotten Son to die for the *sins* of the world — and certainly He does not want us to hate people. We are to hate sin and hate the ways of the sinner, but God loves all men and He commands US to love all men, "especially they of the household of faith."

What then IS "the world" we are to "love not"? The meaning here is simply that we are not to love anything IN this world that is alienated from God, whether it be "things," or people, or influences. *Satan* is "the prince of this world" (John 14:30), he is "the god of this world" (II Cor. 4:4), and "the whole world lieth in wickedness" — or, "lieth in the wicked one" (I John 5:19).

The systems of this world are in the hands of Satan — and sad but so, the vast majority of *people* are in his hands; but even though spiritually minded people are in the minority, with JESUS we are always the *majority,* and we will win in the end because we are with Him who IS the victory!

The more lightly we cling to things of this world, the tighter grip we have on God and things eternal. The Scripture here makes it crystal-clear that the world can draw the love of the believer away from the Father. When a Christian begins participating in worldly amusements, attending questionable places, and keeping company with unbelievers, he will soon discover that his love for God, his interest in God's Word and in fellowship with other believers, has begun to slip away. Prayer meeting, revival night, Sunday school and worship will become of secondary concern, and one sad day, all too late, that person will wake up to the fact that his joy and peace have gone. Exactly when it happened he may not know; it may have happened so gradually that he was not aware of its going until it was too late.

The most miserable person on earth is the Christian who is out of fellowship with God and out of God's will, as Peter was the night He cursed, blasphemed, and denied his Lord. But when Jesus looked at him so tenderly, Peter went out and wept bitterly in repentance. In my experience in meetings down through the years, the most bitter tears I have seen shed were not tears of sinners, but tears of *backsliders.* The Christian who has known God and served Him in full surrender, and then allowed the cares of the world to dampen his fervor and zeal for God and the things of God, is of all people most miserable.

When Paul was in prison he said, "Demas hath forsaken me, having loved this present world" (II Tim. 4:10). There is no neutral ground here: the believer cannot love God completely and love the world any at all. One bit of love for the world, and the spiritual fulness of complete surrender begins to slowly ebb away.

The world and its attractions are all about us, always bidding for the testimony of fine young Christians. The devil takes great joy in causing a strong Christian to become weak. There are *some* believers whom Satan seldom bothers because they do not cause him too much worry, they do not threaten his program; but strong Christians are always his targets and he puts countless snares and pitfalls in their way. Therefore the admonition to those who have "overcome the wicked one" is to *"love not the world, neither the things that are IN the world."*

I would emphasize again that this does not refer to the *earth* as such. This globe which God created has nothing to hurt souls. It is not a sin to love nature (so long as we do not *worship* nature). Surely the Lord Jesus loved the beauty of the out-of-doors; in His Sermon on the Mount He said, ". . . Consider the lilies of the field, how they grow; they toil not, neither do they spin: And yet I say unto you, That *even Solomon in all his glory was not arrayed like one of these!"* (Matt. 6:28).

The *world systems* to which this Scripture refers began back in Genesis 4:16, when "Cain went out from the presence of the Lord." He built a city, and from that day forward the systems of this world began to attract the souls of men, offering pleasures and many things that promised satisfaction without God. Satan has made it more attractive and more convenient to go to hell today than ever before! There are more species of attractions to lure people away from God and crowd God out of their lives. The devil and his cohorts take no time off, they work overtime, scheming, planning, "programming," devising new things to keep man away from God.

God's Word tells us that just before the flood "the wickedness of man was great in the earth, and . . . every imagination of the thoughts of his heart was only evil continually. And it repented the Lord that He had made man on the earth, and it grieved Him at His heart. And the Lord said, I will destroy man whom I have created from the face of the earth; both man, and beast, and the creeping thing, and the fowls of the air; for it repenteth me that I have made them" (Gen. 6:5-7).

Noah found grace in the eyes of the Lord, and he and his family were saved from the flood; but when they came out of the ark they brought with them *the same flesh* that had led man into such vileness as to make the flood necessary, and wickedness quickly started multiplying again.

Some people think of "the world" as the old-fashioned saloon, gambling halls, and the street of forgotten men and women; but Satan does not operate in these places alone. Many times he appears as "an angel of light" (II Cor. 11:14). He operates in the world of arts and culture, appealing to the flesh through these things, and even dedicated believers often find themselves attracted to and spending entirely too much time in things which the average Christian would call "harmless." It is not uncommon for the *business* world to become a stumbling block and a snare to the believer. We must be on guard at all times against the evils of this world. In John 17:15 Jesus said, "I pray not that thou shouldest take them out of the world, but that thou shouldest keep them from the evil."

Three Avenues of Temptation

Verse 16: "For all that is in the world, the lust of the flesh, and the lust of the eyes, and the pride of life, is not of the Father, but is of the world."

Regardless of what our temptation may be, it comes through one of these three avenues: (1) the lust of the flesh, (2) the lust of the eyes, or (3) the pride of life. These things are not of God, and in verse 15 we were told that "if any man love the world, the love of the Father is not in him." It is possible for a person to be *attracted* to some of the things this world has to offer and still be a believer, but one who is *in love* with the world cannot be in love with God at the same time. Jesus made this clear in Matthew 6:24: "No man can serve two masters: for either he will hate the one, and love the other; or else he will hold to the one, and despise the other. *Ye cannot serve God and mammon!*"

Whatever temptations come to us, they will come through the three avenues given in our present verse. This was evidenced in the temptation of Jesus:

1. *The lust of the flesh*:

Just after the baptism of Jesus, He was "led up *of the Spirit* into the wilderness to be tempted of the devil." Notice that *the Holy Spirit,* not Satan, led Him. James gives us the truth concerning this matter: "Let no man say when he is tempted, I am tempted of God: for God cannot be tempted with evil, neither tempteth He any man" (Jas. 1:13). Jesus was God, and God cannot be tempted with evil. From the heart, Jesus did not yield to temptation. A sinful heart did not lead Him into the wilderness; the Spirit of God led Him there to meet — *and defeat* — a personal devil.

"And when He had fasted forty days and forty nights, He was afterward an hungred" (Matt. 4:2). The devil then approached Him with these words: "*IF thou be the Son of God,* command that these stones be made bread." Jesus had flesh exactly like ours, sin apart; and after forty days of fasting, certainly He was hungry — and Satan knew it. He therefore made his first attack at what he considered the Saviour's weakest point — *hunger*; and he put an "IF" in his challenge. "*If*" does not belong to God's vocabulary; "if" is not the language of faith; and without faith we cannot please God. Satan was at enmity with God, and the "if" suggested that he was not interested in knowing Jesus as *the SON of God*. He was only interested in causing him to *fall* so that He could not save sinners and, in the end, could not bruise Satan's head (Gen. 3:15).

Jesus answered thus: "IT IS WRITTEN, Man shall not live by bread alone, but by every word that proceedeth out of the mouth of God" (Matt. 4:4). Please notice: *Jesus quoted Scripture* (from Deuteronomy 8:3). He could have *spoken* Scripture — anything He said would have been the Word of God. He did not need to quote Scripture that had already been written, He could have spoken *new* words; but in this we see how much Jesus respected the written Word.

2. *The pride of life*:

Jesus conquered the lust of the flesh — in this instance, *hunger*; but Satan did not give up — he never *does!* He simply approaches from another angle:

"Then the devil taketh (Jesus) up into the holy city, and setteth Him on a pinnacle of the temple, and saith unto Him, If thou be the Son of God, cast thyself down: for it is written, He shall give His angels charge concerning thee: and in their hands they shall bear thee up, lest at any time thou dash thy foot against a stone" (Matt. 4:5, 6).

Here Satan quoted from Psalm 91:11, but if you will read that verse you will notice that he *misquoted* it. He is proficient at warping and twisting the Scriptures, adding a bit, taking out a little, but giving enough truth to lead astray those who do not know the Word of God as thoroughly as they should. But Jesus KNEW what the Old Testament Scriptures said, and He answered, "IT IS WRITTEN AGAIN, Thou shalt not tempt the Lord thy God."

Certainly Jesus *could* have hurled Himself from the pinnacle of the temple in spectacular display of His power, and He would not have been injured; but He did not come into this world to be spectacular, He did not come to earth to make a name for Himself: He came to declare God (John 1:18), and He *declared* God — not by leaping from the pinnacle of the temple, but by doing God's will, by doing the works God sent Him to do, and by giving forth words that are spirit and life.

3. *The lust of the eyes*:

Satan then came to Jesus from the third avenue of temptation: "Again, the devil taketh Him up into an exceeding high mountain, and sheweth Him all the kingdoms of the world, and the glory of them; and saith unto Him, *All these things will I give thee, if thou wilt fall down and worship me.*" Jesus replied, "Get thee hence, Satan: FOR IT IS WRITTEN, Thou shalt worship the Lord thy God, and Him only shalt thou serve" (Matt. 4:8-10).

Jesus is the only one who ever commanded Satan to depart. He is the only one who is more than a match for him. Even

Michael the archangel feared to rebuke Satan when he dis-
puted with him about the body of Moses. Michael said,
"The LORD rebuke thee" (Jude 9). For the third time the
Lord employed Old Testament Scriptures, the written Word of
God, to defeat the devil. How important God's Word is! What
victory it brings. The devil then departed from Jesus, and
angels came and ministered unto Him. Study the entire passage
of Matthew 4:1-11.

We are born in a body that is determined to damn us. God
gave up the flesh in the Garden of Eden; He made no provision
to repair or redeem the flesh, but many "church members" are
still attempting to repair what God gave up. To Adam He
said, "Dust thou art, and unto dust shalt thou return." In Psalm
103:14 the Spirit reminds us that God "knoweth our frame;
He remembereth that we are dust." We must recognize that
in the flesh "dwelleth no good thing," it is wicked, totally
depraved. Man's heart is desperately wicked; and no one can
know its degree of wickedness. The unregenerate heart is capable of manufacturing and producing any sin or wickedness
that has ever been committed by any man from Adam to this
present moment (Mark 7:21-23).

Christians need to hear Paul's instruction to the Corinthians:
"For though we walk in the flesh, we do not war after the
flesh: (For the weapons of our warfare are not carnal, but
mighty through God to the pulling down of strong holds;)
casting down imaginations, and every high thing that exalteth
itself against the knowledge of God, and bringing into captivity every thought to the obedience of Christ" (II Cor. 10:3-5).

Even the most spiritual of born again believers must be
constantly on guard concerning the flesh, because when we are
born again the flesh *remains* flesh and there is continual warfare between the flesh and the Spirit. But thank God, greater
is He who is *within* than he who is without (I John 4:4).
Jesus conquered the world, the flesh, and the devil — and *we*
can be *more* than conquerors if we will look to Him. We
cannot conquer in our own strength, and Paul warns, "Let him
that thinketh he standeth take heed lest he fall" (I Cor. 10:12)
God sent His own Son in the likeness of sinful flesh and,
through HIM, did what none other could have accomplished:

"There is therefore now no condemnation to them which are in Christ Jesus, who walk not after the flesh, but after the Spirit. For the law of the Spirit of life in Christ Jesus hath made me free from the law of sin and death. *For what the law could not do, in that it was weak through the flesh, God sending His own Son in the likeness of sinful flesh, and for sin, condemned sin in the flesh, that the righteousness of the law might be fulfilled in us,* who walk not after the flesh, but after the Spirit" (Rom. 8:1-4).

Concerning *the lust of the eyes,* Jesus said, "If thine eye offend thee, pluck it out: it is better for thee to enter into the kingdom of God with one eye, than having two eyes to be cast into hell fire: where their worm dieth not, and the fire is not quenched" (Mark 9:47, 48).

Evil desires enter through the eye-gate. Our first parents sold the human race into wholesale slavery and death because of sin — and it all happened when Eve *looked*: "And when the woman *saw* that the tree was good for food, and that it was *pleasant to the eyes,* and a tree to be desired to make one wise, she took of the fruit thereof, and did eat, and gave also unto her husband with her; and he did eat" (Gen. 3:6).

Another tragedy as a result of the lust of the eye is recorded in Joshua chapters 6 and 7. Please read both chapters for the complete account. God had given specific instructions to Joshua and his army concerning the things of Babylon; but Achan saw among the spoils "a goodly Babylonish garment, and two hundred shekels of silver and a wedge of gold of fifty shekels weight." He saw, he coveted, and he *took* the forbidden spoil. His disobedience brought tragedy upon Israel and upon Achan and his family.

I Kings 19 records the account of the mighty Elijah losing his spiritual stamina because of an ungodly woman. God had blessed Elijah in a most unusual way, he was fresh from his overwhelming victory at Carmel where he had slain Jezebel's prophets with the sword. He should have been filled with courage and thanksgiving. But when Jezebel heard that Elijah had slain her prophets, she sent him a message, saying, *"So let the gods do to me, and more also, if I make not THY life as the life of one of them by to morrow about this time!"*

In spite of the great victory God had given the prophet, when an ungodly queen threatened him he panicked and ran for his life! The Scripture tells us, *"when he SAW that,* he arose, and went for his life, and came to Beer-sheba, which belongeth to Judah, and left his servant there. *But he himself went a day's journey into the wilderness, and came and sat down under a juniper tree: and he requested for himself that he might die*; and said, It is enough; now, O Lord, take away my life; for I am not better than my fathers" (I Kings 19:3, 4).

What a sad, sad story! What a shame that Elijah did not see the GOD who had given him outstanding victory, instead of seeing the poor, weak, wicked Jezebel! The eye can be most destructive if it is not singled on Jesus.

In the *New* Testament, Matthew 14:22-31 gives an account of the eyes bringing defeat when victory could have been assured. These verses tell of Christ's walking on the water — certainly a very extraordinary thing: "And when the disciples saw Him walking on the sea, they were troubled, saying, It is a spirit; and they cried out for fear. But straightway Jesus spake unto them, saying, Be of good cheer; it is I; be not afraid. And Peter answered Him and said, Lord, if it be thou, bid me come unto thee on the water. And (Jesus) said, Come. And when Peter was come down out of the ship, he walked on the water, to go to Jesus. *BUT WHEN HE SAW the wind boisterous,* he was afraid; and beginning to sink, he cried, saying, Lord, save me. And immediately Jesus stretched forth His hand, and caught him, and said unto him, O thou of little faith, wherefore didst thou doubt?" (Matt. 14:26-31).

"The pride of life" is vainglory — evil desires born in a heart that longs for position, power, wealth and comfort. Many a man has been brought down to the sides of the pit because of pride. James 4:6 tells us, ". . . God resisteth the proud, but giveth grace unto the humble." I Timothy 6:10 says, "The *love of money* is the root of all evil: which while some coveted after, they have erred from the faith, and pierced themselves through with many sorrows. The pride of life takes in many things. It is surprising what *some* people will do in order to be noticed, to get their names in the paper, or to be popular.

The right *kind* of pride is honorable, but fleshly pride is of the devil. Proverbs 16:18 says, "Pride goeth before destruction, and an haughty spirit before a fall. Better it is to be of an humble spirit with the lowly, than to divide the spoil with the proud." *Jesus* was in the world made by Him — yet not once did He demonstrate pride in any way.

The way UP with God is DOWN. We must be humble if we would be blessed of Him. I say this with fear and trembling, but it is true: *God cannot save the proud.* We must come to Him with a broken and a contrite heart, we must humble ourselves before Him; *then* He will hear our prayer, forgive our sin, and save us for Jesus' sake:

"The Lord is nigh unto them that are of a broken heart: and saveth such as be of a contrite spirit" (Psalm 34:18).

"The sacrifices of God are a broken spirit: a broken and a contrite heart, O God, thou wilt not despise" (Psalm 51:17).

The lust of the flesh, the lust of the eyes, the pride of life — all these are of the world.

Verse 17: "And the world passeth away, and the lust thereof: but he that doeth the will of God abideth for ever."

Fellow believer, let us "look not at the things which are seen, but at the things which are not seen: for the things which are seen are temporal; but the things which are not seen are eternal" (II Cor. 4:18).

One day "the elements shall melt with fervent heat, the earth also and the works that are therein shall be burned up" (II Pet. 3:10). One day the stars of heaven will fall to the earth, "even as a fig tree casteth her untimely figs, when she is shaken of a mighty wind" (Rev. 6:13). This world will pass away, but the born again ones, the Church of the living God, *"abideth forever!"* We will abide forever, and we will occupy the Pearly White City which Jesus is now preparing for His bride.

When we are born again, God puts a new nature within us — Divine nature (II Pet. 1:4). Thus the Christian has *two* natures — the flesh which we received from Adam, and the Spirit which we receive from God when we are born again. This brings about a warfare in the life of the believer — the flesh against the Spirit, the Spirit against the flesh: "For the flesh lusteth against the Spirit, and the Spirit against the flesh: and these are contrary the one to the other: so that ye cannot do the things that ye would" (Gal. 5:17).

But the Christian has much about which to rejoice, because we are assured of victory: "Ye are of God, little children, and have overcome them: because *greater is He that is in you, than he that is in the world*" (I John 4:4). Paul puts it this way: "I am crucified with Christ: nevertheless I live; *yet not I, but Christ liveth in me: and the life which I now live in the flesh I live by the faith of the Son of God, who loved me, and gave Himself for me*" (Gal. 2:20).

Believers Warned against Apostates

Verse 18: "Little children, it is the last time: and as ye have heard that antichrist shall come, even now are there many antichrists; whereby we know that it is the last time."

Apostates will come *in the last days,* denying the Deity of Christ — and most of us never realize that we have been *living* in "the last days" ever since Jesus was born in Bethlehem of Judaea.

The *first coming* of Jesus was in "the last days": "God, who at sundry times and in divers manners spake in time past unto the fathers by the prophets, hath *in these last days* spoken unto us *by His Son,* whom He hath appointed heir of all things, by whom also He made the worlds" (Heb. 1:1, 2).

The *crucifixion* of Jesus was in "the last days" — the end of the age: "For then must He often have suffered since the foundation of the world: but now once *in the end of the world* hath He appeared to put away sin by the sacrifice of Himself" (Heb. 9:26).

In our King James version, "world" in the Greek means "age" — this Age (dispensation) of Grace. The Holy Spirit came at Pentecost "in the last days": "And it shall come to pass *in the last days,* saith God, I will pour out of my Spirit upon all flesh: and your sons and your daughters shall prophesy, and your young men shall see visions, and your old men shall dream dreams" (Acts 2:17).

The Church Age runs its course in "the last days": "Now all these things happened unto them for ensamples: and they are written for our admonition, upon whom *the ends of the world* are come" (I Cor. 10:11). Paul directed these words to the believers in the church at Corinth, and if *they* were living in the end of the age, surely today WE are living in the end of the age. These are the *last days* of the "last days."

The Word of God tells us that in the last days scoffers will come. They were in the days of Jesus, they were in the days of the apostles, they were in the days of Luther and Wesley, and we have them today:

"Knowing this first, that there shall come in the last days scoffers, walking after their own lusts, and saying, Where is the promise of His coming? for since the fathers fell alseep, all things continue as they were from the beginning of creation" (II Pet. 3:3, 4).

Several years after Peter penned these words, Jude said, "These are murmurers, complainers, walking after their own lusts; and their mouth speaketh great swelling words, having men's persons in admiration because of advantage. But, beloved, remember ye the words which were spoken before of the apostles of our Lord Jesus Christ; how that they told you there should be mockers in the last time, who should walk after their own ungodly lusts" (Jude 16-18).

John the beloved disciple, to whom God dictated the words of this epistle, did not hesitate to proclaim that it was "the last time" when he penned this verse 1900 years ago.

Last but not least, we are assured in the Word of God that the mediatorial kingdom (the kingdom of heaven on earth, known as the Millennium) will be established in the earth *in the last days*: "And it shall come to pass in the last days, that the mountain of the Lord's house shall be established in the top of the mountains, and shall be exalted above the hills; and all nations shall flow unto it" (Isa. 2:2).

In the language of God, "the last days" covers the entire sweep of God's dealings with a lost world from the birth of Christ Jesus the Saviour to the ushering in of the new heavens and the new earth. This will occur just before the eternity of eternities begins. We have been living in "the last days" for more than 1900 years, and we do not know how much longer they will continue: but remember, beloved, GOD has plenty of time and His ways are not our ways, His thoughts are not our thoughts. "But, beloved, be not ignorant of this one thing, that one day is with the Lord as a thousand years, and a thousand years as one day" (II Pet. 3:8). So you see it has not been quite two days yet. It has been almost 2,000 years since Jesus was born, so we know God's program is running on schedule. Fret not, little one; Jesus is coming again, and it may be this very day!

"Nevertheless we, according to His promise, look for new heavens and a new earth, wherein dwelleth righteousness" (II Pet. 3:13).

"But every man in his own order: Christ the firstfruits; afterward they that are Christ's at His coming. *Then cometh the end,* when He shall have delivered up the kingdom to God, even the Father; when He shall have put down all rule and all authority and power" (I Cor. 15:23, 24).

John tells us that *"even now there are many antichrists."* What is the meaning of "antichrist"? "Anti" means opposite (or against); and in the last days many will be anti-*Christ.* There will be many deceivers, many false prophets. Study Matthew 24 — the entire chapter.

These antichrists (plural) are NOT the Man of Sin, Antichrist (singular); they are his *forerunners.* After the rapture of the Church, the Man of Sin will be unveiled:

"For the mystery of iniquity doth already work: only He (the Holy Spirit)who now letteth will let, until He be taken out of the way. *And then shall that Wicked* be revealed, whom the Lord shall consume with the spirit of His mouth, and shall destroy with the brightness of His coming: Even him, whose coming is after the working of Satan with all power and signs and lying wonders" (II Thess. 2:7-9).

These antichrists who deny the Deity of our Lord are forerunners of the Antichrist who will be *the devil incarnate.* He will sit in the temple and announce that he is God, he will blaspheme the God of heaven. He will be the one world ruler known in the Bible as "the King of Fierce Countenance . . . the Man of Sin . . . the Antichrist . . . Son of Perdition" and many other names.

Even in the days of John there were *many* antichrists, and because there were many at that time *"we know that it is the last time.*" In Matthew 24 Jesus warned the disciples that "many deceivers" would come, and would announce that they were Christ. Today we have men who claim to be Christ, they claim everything Jesus claimed. These are some of the antichrists of whom John speaks. There are many things today which assure us that the second coming of Jesus is at hand; but one of the most *outstanding* indications is the fact that there are so many false teachers, so many who deny the fundamentals of the faith — the Deity of Christ, the verbal inspiration of the Scriptures, the bodily resurrection, the second coming All these are antichrists. We call them modernists and liberals, but they are antichrists as well. The number one fundamental of the faith is that Jesus was God in flesh; antichrists deny this Bible truth.

Verse 19: "They went out from us, but they were not of us; for if they had been of us, they would no doubt have continued with us: but they went out, that they might be made manifest that they were not all of us."

The antichrists mentioned here were members of a local church — a *local* church, not the body of Christ. They were operating inside the assembly, but notice that John tells us *"they were not OF us."* To become a member of the Church of the living God, the body of Christ, one must believe that Jesus is the Son of God, and these antichrists denied that truth. They had united with the local assembly, but they "went out from it" because they were not really part OF it. They joined in name, but they were never born into the family of God.

Today, some would refer to these people as "backsliders," but they were NOT backsliders: *they were never born again,* In heart and experience they were never members of the true Church.

Using denominational terms causes a lot of confusion and division among believers. If ministers (including myself) would use *Bible terms only,* and not employ terms coined by denominations, there would be less friction and less misunderstanding in the Church.

There are those who believe and teach that all church members are Christians, and therefore when a church member turns his back on the church and goes back to the world they call him a backslider; but most of the time that person has never been truly born again. There ARE true backsliders, it is *possible* for a born again person to backslide; but most of the people today who claim to be backsliders have never experienced the new birth. Peter describes them thus: "But it is happened unto them according to the true proverb, The *dog* is turned to his own vomit again; and the *sow* that was washed to her wallowing in the mire" (II Pet. 2:22). These people were "dogs" and "pigs" all the time; they were never "*sheep.*" The born again person follows righteousness, and thus, before men, proves the new birth. Those who wallow in unrighteousness have never been made new creatures in Christ (John 2:29; II Cor. 5:17).

Greek scholars tell us that the word here translated *antichrist* means "instead of" — that is, there were those who professed to be followers of Christ, they united with the local church, but all the time in their hearts they were *opposed* to Christ. Today in the pulpits of America there are men who profess to be ministers of the Gospel, and yet they use the pulpit to deny the Deity and the miracles of Jesus, they deny His virgin birth, His atoning death, His shed blood, His bodily resurrection, and His personal return. They deny God's Word even while professing to be ministers of Jesus Christ. They ARE ministers, it is true; but they are ministers of the devil. Paul describes them in II Corinthians 11:13-15:

"For such are false apostles, deceitful workers, transforming themselves into the apostles of Christ. And no marvel; for Satan himself is transformed into an angel of light. Therefore it is no great thing if his ministers also be transformed as the ministers of righteousness; whose end shall be according to their works."

John says that if these persons had been true believers, "*they would no doubt have continued with us.*" A tremendous truth is declared here: Born again, blood washed, true believers *continue* in the faith. They may at times grow weak, they may even backslide; but they never completely turn their backs on God, His Church, and His Word. There is no "maybe-so" about this. John says, "If they had been OF us *they would NO DOUBT* have continued with us."

They went out, left the church and turned their backs on

believers, *"that they might be made manifest that they were not all of us."* God exposes error, and all who walk in the light can *recognize* error. It is possible for an antichrist to remain in the local assembly without being detected for a season, but he cannot continue long without true believers recognizing him as counterfeit. God will not long allow a liberal or a modernist to live under the guise of a true minister; He will expose that person in one way or another. Sooner or later he will say or do something (or *teach* something) that will brand him anti-Christ, anti-Bible, anti-Christian.

True Believers Are Not Deceived by Antichrists

Verses 20 — 26: "But ye have an unction from the Holy One, and ye know all things. I have not written unto you because ye know not the truth, but because ye know it, and that no lie is of the truth. Who is a liar but he that denieth that Jesus is the Christ? He is antichrist, that denieth the Father and the Son. Whosoever denieth the Son, the same hath not the Father: but he that acknowledgeth the Son hath the Father also. Let that therefore abide in you which ye have heard from the beginning. If that which ye have heard from the beginning shall remain in you, ye also shall continue in the Son, and in the Father. And this is the promise that He hath promised us, even eternal life. These things have I written unto you concerning them that seduce you."

"Ye have an unction from the Holy One." It is a glorious truth and a comforting fact that every born again believer has the unction (the anointing) from the Holy Ghost, the great Teacher — He who leads us into paths of right living and guides us around the pitfalls and snares of the devil. In II Corinthians 1:21, 22 Paul tells us, "Now He which stablisheth us with you in Christ, and hath anointed us, is God; who hath also sealed us, and given the earnest of the Spirit in our hearts."

Thank God for the tremendous truth of I Peter 2:6: "Wherefore also it is contained in the Scripture, *Behold, I lay in Sion a chief corner stone, elect, precious: and he that believeth on Him shall not be confounded."*

John 7:17 assures us, "IF ANY MAN WILL DO HIS WILL, he shall KNOW the doctrine, whether it be of God. . . ." The believer who wills to do GOD'S will shall know the teaching of truth. He will not be led around by "every wind of doctrine," nor will he be led astray by the doctrine of antichrists.

Any person who does not recognize error, one who does not know truth from false doctrine, needs only one thing: *he needs to be born again.* The Holy Spirit guides the believer into all truth and we can know *"all things"* because He who dictated this Bible to holy men of old abides in our bosom as our Teacher and Guide.

In verse 21 John makes it clear that he is writing to people who know the truth — and truth and error will not mix. God is light, not twilight; He is Shekinah glory — *pure righteousness.* Believers — whether "little born ones," strong "young men," or spiritual "fathers," know the truth; we become members of the body of Christ through the truth: "Ye shall know the truth, and the truth shall make you free . . . If the Son therefore shall make you free, ye shall be free indeed" (John 8:32, 26). "Jesus saith unto (Thomas), I am the Way, the Truth, and the Life: no man cometh unto the Father, but by me" (John 14:8).

"Who is a liar but he that denieth that Jesus is the Christ?" Jesus is The Truth. Antichrist, the Man of Sin, will be exactly opposite Jesus — he will be The Lie. Jesus said to His own people, "I am come in my Father's name, and ye receive me not: *if another* (Antichrist) *shall come in his own name, HIM YE WILL RECEIVE"* (John 5:43). Any person who denies the incarnation and the virgin birth of the Son of God is a liar — and this is the fourth time we have found this blunt statement in this epistle: Chapter 1, verse 8, "If we say that we have no sin . . . *the truth is not in us."* Chapter 1, verse 10, "If we say that we have not sinned, we make Him a liar. . . ." Chapter 2, verse 4, "He that saith, I know Him, and keepeth not His commandments, is a liar. . . ." And in our present verse, he is a liar who denies that Jesus is the Christ.

A very solemn warning is voiced in II John 7-11 concerning those who deny the virgin birth, the Deity, the incarnation of Jesus Christ: "For many deceivers are entered into the world, who confess not that Jesus Christ is come in the flesh. This

is a deceiver and an antichrist. Look to yourselves, that we
lose not those things which we have wrought, but that we
receive a full reward. Whosoever transgresseth, and abideth
not in the doctrine of Christ, *hath not GOD*. He that abideth
in the doctrine of Christ, *he hath both the Father and the
Son. If there come any unto you, and bring not this doctrine,
receive him not into your house, neither bid him God speed*:
*FOR HE THAT BIDDETH HIM GOD SPEED IS PARTAKER
OF HIS EVIL DEEDS."*

These tremendous verses make it very plain that we are not
to support anyone who denies the virgin birth, the Deity, the
incarnation of Christ; and if we DO support them, we thereby
become partaker of their evil deeds.

"Let that therefore abide in you" — (that is, adhere stedfastly
to the truth) *"which ye have heard from the beginning"* — the
beginning of their Christian experience, not the beginning as
in Genesis 1:1, but in the beginning of the declaration of the
Gospel of the grace of God. Believers are admonished to hold
stedfastly to these cardinal doctrines.

"Ye also shall continue in the Son, and in the Father" — united
to the Son, united to the Father, born of the Spirit and hidden
with Christ in God.

"Verily, verily, I say unto thee, Except a man be born of
water and of the Spirit, he cannot enter into the kingdom of
God" (John 3:5).

"For ye are dead, and your life is hid with Christ in God"
(Col. 3:3).

*"And this is the promise that He hath promised us, even
eternal life."* John thus encourages believers to hold fast the
truths which they had accepted concerning the Incarnation and
virgin birth of the Son of God. In essence he is saying that
true believers will hold to these truths and therefore have the
promise of eternal life; but perdition will be the portion of
those who deny the truth (as some in the book of Hebrews
did in departing *from* the truth). Eternal life is promised to
those who believe on the Lord Jesus Christ, repent of their
sins, and receive Him by faith.

"And this is the record, that God hath given to us eternal
life, and this life is in His Son. He that hath the Son hath

life; and he that hath not the Son of God hath not life" (I John 5:11, 12). We will of course study these verses later, but because it is altogether possible that some dear soul who reads these lines may never *complete* this commentary, I would point out here that *today* is the day of salvation, *now* is the accepted time. *"Boast not thyself of tomorrow; for thou knowest not what a day may bring forth"* (Prov. 27:1). "Seek ye the Lord while He may be found, call ye upon Him while He is near" (Isa. 55:6).

"He that believeth on Him is not condemned: but he that believeth not is condemned already, because he hath not believed in the name of the only begotten Son of God" (John 3:18).

"He that believeth on the Son hath everlasting life: and he that believeth not the Son shall not see life; but the wrath of God abideth on him" (John 3:36).

And now hear the words of Paul and Silas to the jailer at Philippi: When he asked, "What must I do to be saved?" they replied, "Believe on the Lord Jesus Christ, and thou shalt be saved, and thy house" (Acts 16:31).

"These things have I written unto you, concerning them that seduce you." Here John speaks again of the false prophets, the antichrists. *"Seduce"* means to lead astray. Thus believers are warned concerning teachers who would lead them astray and turn them aside from the cardinal truths of the Gospel. We should remember that the early Christians did not have Bibles in the home, they did not have portions of Scripture to carry in their pockets as we carry the New Testament today. Therefore they needed to be warned and instructed concerning antichrists and false teachers who would lead them into dangerous error. There is no excuse for Christians' being led astray today. We have the written Word of God, and that Word is final. "Let God be true, but every man a liar" (Rom. 3:4). We can use the Word of God as the scales upon which to weigh a man's message; and if the message deviates from the pure Gospel we know that he is anti-Gospel. He is anti-Christ, a minister of the devil.

John was not saying here that the believers had *already been* seduced; he was warning them in case false teachers should

94

attempt to lead them astray, and in the very next verse he makes
it plain that believers are kept from error because of the
Teacher within. Truly blood washed, born again believers will
not follow after error because we have within our bosom the
Holy Ghost, He who detects ALL error. He is our instructor,
our guide, our protector, and our seal.

Verse 27: "But the anointing which ye have received of Him
abideth in you, and ye need not that any man teach you: but
as the same anointing teacheth you of all things, and is truth,
and is no lie, and even as it hath taught you, ye shall abide in
Him."

The "anointing" here is the same as the "unction" in verse 20.
Before Jesus was crucified, He promised the coming of the
Spirit: "And I will pray the Father, and He shall give you
another Comforter, that He may abide with you for ever; even
the Spirit of truth; whom the world cannot receive, because it
seeth Him not, neither knoweth Him: but ye know Him, for He
dwelleth with you, and shall be in you. I will not leave you
comfortless: I will come to you. Yet a little while, and the
world seeth me no more; but ye see me: because I live, ye shall
live also. At that day ye shall know that I am in my Father, and
ye in me, and I in you" (John 14:16-20).

The Holy Spirit convicts us of sin and draws us to God (John
6:44; 16:7-11).

The Holy Spirit "borns" us into the family of God (John
1:12, 13; 3:5).

The Holy Spirit baptizes us into the body of Christ (I Cor.
12:12, 13).

The Holy Spirit indwells us, leads us, and assures us (Rom.
8:9, 14, 16).

The Holy Spirit seals us until the day of redemption (Eph.
4:30).

From the moment we are saved until we depart this life to be
with the Lord, the Holy Spirit teaches us all things. He brings
to our memory the things we need to know about spiritual
matters, He is the Teacher of the Scriptures. *"All Scripture is
given by inspiration of God,* and is profitable for doctrine, for
reproof, for correction, for instruction in righteousness: that the

man of God may be perfect, thoroughly furnished unto all good works" (II Tim. 3:16).

"We have also a more sure word of prophecy; whereunto ye do well that ye take heed, as unto a light that shineth in a dark place, until the day dawn, and the day star arise in your hearts: Knowing this first, that no prophecy of the Scripture is of any private interpretation. *For the prophecy came not in old time by the will of man: but holy men of God spake as they were moved by the Holy Ghost*" (II Pet. 1:19-21).

The Holy Spirit does not come upon us and then leave us as was true in Old Testament days. He abides permanently within us, He is always present to guide us into all truth and to guide us away from all error. "This I say then, Walk in the Spirit, and ye shall not fulfil the lust of the flesh" (Gal. 5:16). Here is a Divine guarantee that those who are born of the Spirit and who walk as He leads will not fulfill nor follow after the lust of the flesh; and according to I Peter 2:6, those who are trusting in Jesus will not be confused by error nor led astray by false doctrine. We know from God's Word that those who go after every "ism," schism, and religion that comes to town have never been born of the Spirit nor washed in the blood.

"*And ye need not that any man teach you.*" This "teaching" refers to things pertaining to Christianity. The deep things of God are revealed by the Spirit, not through human wisdom or ability. The only possible way for any man to *understand* the things of God is for him to be taught by the Spirit. I thank God for Christian schools and for great Bible teachers who are themselves taught of the Spirit; but all of their teaching would be as sounding brass and tinkling cymbals to us were it not for the Holy Spirit within us and His application of the message to our hearts. Teachers can help us to know how to study, they can help us to train our minds to think; but the deeper things of the Spirit are *revealed* to us BY the Spirit.

"*But as the same anointing teacheth you of all things*" (all things pertaining to Christianity and spiritual living) "*and is truth and is no lie. . . .*" The Holy Spirit leads us TO truth and then guides us IN the truth. No one has ever yet been led into false doctrine or error by the Holy Spirit. He guides around and away from these things, not *into* them.

96

"*And even as (He) hath taught you, ye shall abide in Him.*"
As the Holy Spirit teaches us, we are to obey His teaching.
We are to walk in the light and abide in Him; and to abide
in Him is to abide in Christ.

Verse 28: "And now, little children, abide in Him; that, when
He shall appear, we may have confidence, and not be ashamed
before Him at His coming."

Abiding in Christ is the secret of power: "If ye abide in me,
and my words abide in you, *ye shall ask what ye will, and it
shall be done unto you*" (John 15:7).

Abiding in Christ brings freedom from the *power* of sin and
freedom from the *love* of sin: "Whosoever abideth in Him sinneth not: whosoever sinneth hath not seen Him, neither known
Him" (I John 1:6).

Abiding in Christ means keeping the Lord's commandments —
not the Mosaic law, for Christ is the end of the law to all
who believe (Rom. 10:4) — but the keeping of the commandments of Jesus: "And he that keepeth His commandments
dwelleth in Him, and He in him. And hereby we know
that He abideth in us, by the Spirit which He hath given us"
(I John 3:24). A heart indwelt by the Holy Spirit and filled
with the love of God shows itself in ready response to the
directions that the Holy Spirit gives us. In the spiritual life,
obedience is the key to every door, the solution to every
difficulty, the killer of every worry and doubt. Obedience brings
every blessing and every good gift. Obedience is the measure
of the power we have with God in prayer. Obedience is divine
proof that we are abiding in Christ Jesus the Lord.

Abiding in Christ shows itself in fruit-bearing: "I am the
vine, ye are the branches: He that abideth in me, and I in
him, the same bringeth forth much fruit: for without me ye
can do nothing" (John 15:5) "The fruit of the Spirit is love,
joy, peace, longsuffering, gentleness, goodness, faith, meekness
temperance: against such there is no law" (Gal. 5:22, 23).

Abiding in Christ displays itself in pure love: "No man hath
seen God at any time. If we love one another, God dwelleth
in us, and His love is perfected in us. Hereby know we that
we dwell in Him, and He in us, because He hath given us
of His Spirit . . . And we have known and believed the love

that God hath to us. God is love; and he that dwelleth in love dwelleth in God, and God in him" (I John 4:12, 13, 16).

Abiding in Christ means walking in His footsteps: "He that saith he abideth in Him ought himself also so to walk, even as HE walked" (I John 2:6). To walk in the footsteps of Jesus means to be submissive to His Word, dependent upon the Holy Spirit, humble in heart. It means to lead a prayerful life, loving and doing God's will and work.

Abiding in Christ means that the believer continues in His Word: "Then said Jesus to those Jews which believed on Him, If ye continue in my Word, then are ye my disciples indeed" (John 8:31). How does a believer continue in the Word? First he *hears* the Word, then he continues by believing it fully, with no doubt whatsoever *concerning* the Word. He obeys it unhesitatingly. When the Word of God speaks, the abiding Christian moves swiftly. To abide in Him is to love His Word supremely.

Abiding in Christ means that the believer is faithful to God's Word: "Let that therefore abide in you which ye have heard from the beginning. If that which ye have heard from the beginning shall remain in you, ye also shall continue in the Son, and in the Father" (I John 2:24).

Someone has said, *"Truth is the mold in which character is formed, the magnet by which people are attracted from the haunts of sin to the heart of God."*

To abide in Him is to be spiritually minded, dedicated soul, spirit, and body (I Thess. 5:23).

". . . *That, when He shall appear*" (in the Rapture, when the dead saints will be raised incorruptible and the living saints will be changed — I Cor. 15:51-55) *"we may have confidence.* . . ." The Greek word means "boldness," and is used in several places in the New Testament with reference to boldness in *speaking* (Mark 8:32; John 7:4; Acts 2:29; II Cor. 3:12); but here it means the boldness of unshakeable assurance that becomes ours because we are abiding believers — spiritually minded Christians.

". . . *and not be ashamed at His coming.*" Those who will be ashamed at His coming are Christians who have buried their talent instead of using it to gain other talents (Matt. 25:14-30).

It is possible for the soul to be saved while testimony and stewardship are lost. There are believers who do not live an abiding life controlled by the Holy Spirit. They have *buried* their influence, testimony, and service because of other attractions.

Paul warns that there is but one foundation — Jesus Christ; and "if any man build upon this foundation gold, silver, precious stones, wood, hay, stubble; every man's work shall be made manifest: for the day shall declare it, because it shall be revealed by fire; and the fire shall try every man's work of what sort it is. If any man's work abide which he hath built thereupon, he shall receive a reward. *If any man's work shall be burned, he shall suffer loss: but he himself shall be saved; yet so as by fire"* (I Cor. 3:12-15).

The "fire" is the Word of God (Jer. 23:29). His Word will try every man's works of what "sort" they are. If the works abide, that man will receive a reward; but if the works are *burned* he will suffer loss. Thus he will be *ashamed,* because he will stand before God empty handed, with no crowns to cast at the feet of Jesus when we crown Him King of kings and Lord of lords!

I have pointed out several times that salvation is free, but rewards are earned by faithful stewardship and works that glorify God. II Corinthians 5:10 tells us, "We must all appear before the judgment seat of Christ; that every one may receive the things done in his body, according to that he hath done, whether it be good or bad." When Jesus comes in the Rapture, rewards will be given to all who have been faithful; and those who have NOT been faithfully abiding will lose their rewards: "BEHOLD, I COME QUICKLY; AND MY REWARD IS WITH ME, TO GIVE EVERY MAN ACCORDING AS HIS WORK SHALL BE" (Rev. 22:12).

Redemption and stewardship are two distinctly different things. *Redemption* is by grace through faith, the gift of God. *Stewardship* is our good works. We are *created UNTO good works* in Christ Jesus, and faith without works is dead. We are rewarded for our works, we glorify God when we bring forth "much fruit."

If Jesus should come today, would *we* be ashamed to stand

before Him — ashamed of what we have done for Him and of what we have given Him? He gave *His life* for us; what have we given to *Him?* May we sincerely ask ourselves this question, and then hear the plea of the Apostle Paul in Romans 12:1:

"I beseech you therefore, brethren, by the mercies of God, that ye present your bodies a living sacrifice, holy, acceptable unto God, which is your reasonable service."

How We May Know the Children of God

Verse 29: "If ye know that He is righteous, ye know that every one that doeth righteousness is born of Him."

There are certain marks of identification which every believer possesses as evidence that he belongs to Christ:

1. *Heart marks*: The believer's heart is surrendered to Jesus, resting on Him, cleansed and indwelt by Him: "For with the heart man believeth unto righteousness; and with the mouth confession is made unto salvation" (Rom. 10:10).

"Blessed are the pure in heart; for they shall see God" (Matt. 5:8).

Paul speaks of being "strengthened with might by His Spirit in the inner man; that Christ may dwell in your hearts by faith" (Eph. 3:16, 17).

2. *Ear marks*: The ear of the believer is tuned to the Word of God. We listen to His Word and learn of Him: "My sheep hear my voice, and I know them, and they follow me" (John 10:27).

3. *Tongue marks*: The believer *confesses* Christ and speaks *for* Christ. God has no tongue but our tongue to give forth verbal testimony to His saving grace, His keeping power, and His ability to supply our every need. Paul said to the Corinthian church, "Ye seek a proof of Christ speaking in me, which to youward is not weak, but is mighty in you" (II Cor. 13:3). Also read Acts 1:1-8, Philippians 4:6, and John 14:14.

4. *Eye marks*: The believer looks to Jesus, author and finisher of our faith, author of eternal salvation: "But we all, with open face beholding as in a glass the glory of the Lord, are changed into the same image from glory to glory, even as by

The Spirit of the Lord" (II Cor. 3:18). Also read Hebrews 12:2; 5:9.

5. *Face marks*: Because of his communion with Christ, the *glory* of Christ is reflected in the face of the believer. When Moses came down from Mount Sinai where God gave him the Ten Commandments, his face shone so brightly that Aaron and the children of Israel were afraid to come near him (Ex. 34:28-30). In Acts 4:13, the people "saw the boldness of Peter and John, and perceived that they were unlearned and ignorant men, (and) they marvelled; *and they took knowledge of them, that they had been with Jesus.*"

6. *Hand marks*: The hands of Christ were marked that we might be saved, and the hands of true believers bear the marks of service. We work for Jesus — not to BE saved, but because we ARE saved. Every believer brings forth fruit — some bring forth thirty, some sixty, some a hundredfold; but nowhere in God's Word do we read that a Christian produces NO fruit at all. We labor *for* Christ and *with* Him, ministering to Him in supplying the need of others: "We then as workers together with Him, beseech you also that ye receive not the grace of God in vain" (II Cor. 6:1). "And the King shall answer and say unto them, Verily, I say unto you, Inasmuch as ye have done it unto one of the least of these my brethren, ye have done it unto me" (Matt. 25:40).

7. *Feet marks*: The precious feet of Jesus were marked with the nails at Calvary that we might be saved and walk with Him, following in His footsteps in suffering and in service. If we suffer with Him we will reign with Him; if we deny Him He will deny us. "And (Jesus) said to them all, If any man will come after me, let him deny himself, and take up his cross daily, and follow me" (Luke 9:23). "If any man serve me, let him follow me; and where I am, there shall also my servant be: if any man serve me, him will my Father honour" (John 12:26).

8. *Head marks*: Along with a new heart, God gives the believer a new spirit, a new "thinking apparatus": "Casting down imaginations, and every high thing that exalteth itself against the knowledge of God, *and bringing into captivity every thought to the obedience of Christ*" (II Cor. 10:5).

Paul said, "From henceforth let no man trouble me: for I bear in my body the marks of the Lord Jesus" (Gal. 6:17). In other words, "I bear *branded on my body* the marks of the Lord Jesus." These words were given under inspiration by one of the most faithful, fearless followers of Jesus the world has ever known.

When we exercise faith in the shed blood and finished work of Jesus, this satisfies the Father; but while we satisfy God *by faith,* it is by works and by the marks of Christ that we bear that we prove to men that we are saved. The rough hand of the laborer testifies that he is the servant of unceasing toil. The sailor's weather-beaten face, tanned by the salt air, testifies that he is a man of the sea. Medals worn on the breast of a soldier's uniform give evidence that he has fought in many battles. Feeble steps, a furrowed brow, and hair that is white are marks of old age. In like manner, the marks upon the body of the beloved Apostle Paul gave testimony of his sufferings for and with Christ as he lived for Him and preached His Word. Paul gloried in tribulation, he wore his scars with confidence. They reminded him of the day he met Jesus, the day his life was completely changed.

How many scars do *I* bear as testimony before the world that I have lived a righteous, godly, separated, Christ-centered life, faithful in stewardship to Him who was marred, scarred, bruised, and crucified that I might have life and have it abundantly?

Believers are signboards for Jesus in this world. We are living epistles read of men (II Cor. 3:2) and therefore we should live clean, dedicated, blameless lives. Righteous living testifies that the righteous Saviour has saved us and abides within us. Such living by believers will influence others to come to Jesus and be saved.

Paul said, ". . . forgetting those things which are behind, and reaching forth unto those things which are before, *I press toward the mark for the prize of the high calling of God in Christ Jesus*" (Phil. 3:13, 14 in part). There IS a prize for the faithful, abiding child of God. There is much in the New Testament concerning a *full reward.*

We may suffer persecution, we may be laughed at and

criticized, even by those near and dear to us; but if we are consistently abiding in Christ, we can say with Paul, "None of these things move me, neither count I my life dear unto myself, so that I might finish my course with joy, and the ministry, which I have received of the Lord Jesus, to testify the Gospel of the grace of God" (Acts 20:24).

Romans 8:16-19 tells us, "The Spirit itself beareth witness with our spirit, that we are the children of God: and if children, then heirs; heirs of God, and joint-heirs with Christ; if so be that we suffer with him, that we may be also glorified together. *For I reckon that the sufferings of this present time are not worthy to be compared with the glory which shall be revealed in us!*"

II Timothy 3:12 tells us plainly that "all that will live godly in Christ Jesus shall suffer persecution." Jesus told His disciples, "If the world hate you, ye know that it hated me before it hated you. If ye were of the world, the world would love his own: but because ye are not of the world, but I have chosen you out of the world, therefore the world hateth you" (John 15:18, 19).

God help us, that our daily prayer may be, "Lord, help ME to live right, do right, walk right, that others may see Jesus in me. May I glorify God this day by living righteously, looking only to Jesus, doing all to the glory of God, not standing in the way of sinners nor sitting in the seat of the scornful; but delighting in thy Word, walking in the steps of Jesus, doing righteousness that my life may testify that Christ abides in me and I in Him!"

I JOHN — Chapter 3

1. Behold, what manner of love the Father hath bestowed upon us, that we should be called the sons of God: therefore the world knoweth us not, because it knew him not.
2. Beloved, now are we the sons of God, and it doth not yet appear what we shall be: but we know that, when he shall appear, we shall be like him; for we shall see him as he is.
3. And every man that hath this hope in him purifieth himself, even as he is pure.
4. Whosoever committeth sin transgresseth also the law: for sin is the transgression of the law.
5. And ye know that he was manifested to take away our sins; and in him is no sin.
6 Whosoever abideth in him sinneth not: whosoever sinneth hath not seen him, neither known him.
7. Little children, let no man deceive you: he that doeth righteousness is righteous, even as he is righteous.
8. He that committeth sin is of the devil; for the devil sinneth from the beginning. For this purpose the Son of God was manifested, that he might destroy the works of the devil.
9. Whosoever is born of God doth not commit sin; for his seed remaineth in him: and he cannot sin, because he is born of God.
10. In this the children of God are manifest, and the children of the devil: whosoever doeth not righteousness is not of God, neither he that loveth not his brother.
11. For this is the message that ye have heard from the beginning, that we should love one another.
12. Not as Cain, who was of that wicked one, and slew his brother. And wherefore slew he him? Because his own works were evil, and his brother's righteous.
13. Marvel not, my brethren, if the world hate you.
14. We know that we have passed from death unto life, because we love the brethren. He that loveth not his brother abideth in death.
15. Whosoever hateth his brother is a murderer: and ye know that no murderer hath eternal life abiding in him.
16. Hereby perceive we the love of God, because he laid down his life for us: and we ought to lay down our lives for the brethren.
17. But whoso hath this world's good, and seeth his brother have need, and shutteth up his bowels of compassion from him, how dwelleth the love of God in him?
18. My little children, let us not love in word, neither in tongue; but in deed and in truth.

19. And hereby we know that we are of the truth, and shall assure our hearts before him.

20. For if our heart condemn us, God is greater than our heart, and knoweth all things.

21. Beloved, if our heart condemn us not, then have we confidence toward God.

22. And whatsoever we ask, we receive of him, because we keep his commandments, and do those things that are pleasing in his sight.

23. And this is his commandment, That ye should believe on the name of his Son Jesus Christ, and love one another, as he gave us commandment.

24. And he that keepeth his commandments dwelleth in him, and he in him. And hereby we know that he abideth in us, by the Spirit which he hath given us.

In this chapter we will see that Christians are sons of God NOW, and the world does not know us because it did not know Jesus; as *He* was, so are *we* in this world. We will learn that when Jesus appears, we will be *like Him,* and having the hope of the second coming of Christ, we purify ourselves; we live holy lives (vv. 1-3).

We will see that that which is born of God does not commit sin (vv. 4-10). We will learn the *definition* of sin (v. 4) and that Christ Jesus our Saviour and Lord was manifested to *take away* our sins, and he who commits sin is of the devil.

We will see clearly that Christianity is manifested by love: a Christian loves God and loves his fellowman. If he cannot love his brother whom he has *seen,* he cannot love God whom he has *not* seen (vv. 10-18). One of the commandments of Jesus is that Christians love one another. Love for the brethren is proof that we have passed from death unto life (v. 14). A man who hates his brother is a murderer, and certainly a murderer is not a child of God (v. 15). We should love the brethren because *Jesus loved US* while we were yet sinners; and "having loved His own which were in the world, He loved them unto the end" (John 13:1).

Jesus proved His love by laying down His life for us (v. 16). If we who claim to be Christians see a brother in need and refuse to help him, we dare not say that God dwells in us

(v. 17). We prove our love for God and for the brethren by "doing" — by works as well as by words (v. 18).

In verses 19-21 believers have evidence that the love of God is in us. We have assurance of our love for God because of the testimony of our heart.

In verses 22 and 23 we see that if we keep His commandments our prayers will be answered. If we keep His commandments we may also have assurance through the Holy Spirit that God abides in us and we in Him.

Chapter 3 is largely given over to declaration of the evidences of true faith, true Christianity. There is perhaps no place in the Bible where we might study to greater advantage than this chapter concerning how we may know that we are truly saved, genuinely Christian. It is one of the *great* chapters in the Word of God.

It is easy to discover the two main sections of I John:

1. *God is light* — declared in chapter 1, verse 5, expounded in chapters 1 and 2.
2. *God is love* — declared in chapter 1 verse 8, used as the theme of chapters 3, 4, and 5. There are sixty-six verses in these three chapters, and in those verses the word *"love"* is used forty-six times. It occurs sixteen times as a noun, five times as an adjective, and twenty-five times as a verb.

The Manner of the Father's Love

Verse 1: "Behold, what manner of love the Father hath bestowed upon us, that we should be called the sons of God: therefore the world knoweth us not, because it knew Him not."

God does not call every man "son." There is a doctrine abroad in the land that teaches "the fatherhood of God and the brotherhood of man," but it is a doctrine of men, not of God. From the *natural* aspect we are all descendants of Adam and Eve — brothers in the flesh; but from the *spiritual* standpoint there is no such thing as the fatherhood of God and the brotherhood of man. Born again, blood washed believers are sons of God, but Jesus said of those who are *not* born again, *"Ye are of your father, the devil"* (John 8:44). There are two groups of children upon this earth: children of God, and children of the devil.

Paul said to the Galatian believers, "Ye are all the children of God *by faith in Christ Jesus*" (Gal. 3:26). We *become* children of God by faith in Christ Jesus, and all who do not HAVE that faith are children of the devil. John 1:12, 13 declares, "*As many as received Him,* to them gave He power to *become* the sons of God, even to them that believe on His name: which were born . . . of God."

"*Behold, what MANNER of love the Father hath bestowed upon us. . . .*" We sing "Amazing grace! How sweet the sound that saved a wretch like me." It was the "amazing" grace of God the Father that made possible the love He bestowed upon us. Had it not been for *grace,* God could and would not have bestowed His *love* upon us:

"*But we see Jesus, who was made a little lower than the angels for the suffering of death, crowned with glory and honour; that He BY THE GRACE OF GOD should taste death for every man*" (Heb. 2:9).

It was *God's grace* — unmerited and unearned — that allowed Jesus to take a body, and in that body come to earth to declare God to man. Since God is love, Jesus *declared* that love: "For God SO loved the world, that He gave His only begotten Son, that whosoever believeth in Him should not perish, but have everlasting life" (John 3:16).

God did not love us because we were *worthy* of His love; we were everything BUT worthy. He did not love us because we were *lovely*; we were ugly and despicable. He did not love us because we were desirable; we were ungodly sinners, and sin is repulsive to the holy nature of God. In Romans 5:1-10 Paul describes God's great love:

"Therefore being justified by faith, we have peace with God through our Lord Jesus Christ: by whom also we have access by faith into this grace wherein we stand, and rejoice in hope of the glory of God. And not only so, but we glory in tribulation also: knowing that tribulation worketh patience; and patience, experience; and experience, hope: and hope maketh not ashamed; because the love of God is shed abroad in our hearts by the Holy Ghost which is given unto us.

"*For when we were yet without strength, in due time Christ died for the ungodly.* For scarcely for a righteous man will one die: yet peradventure for a good man some would even dare to die. *But God commendeth His love toward us, in that, while we were yet sinners, Christ died for us.* Much more then, being now justified by His blood, we shall be saved from wrath through Him. For if, when we were enemies, we were reconciled to God by the death of His Son, much more, being reconciled, we shall be saved by His life."

God commended His love toward us while we were strengthless, hopeless, ungodly sinners, enemies to Him. No wonder John opens this chapter with "BEHOLD!" We need to stop and literally *gaze* at the cross, because Jesus on the cross was God's love on display for ungodly, hopeless, wretched sinners, who were His enemies. On Calvary God put on display heaven's best — the only begotten Son, loving a sinful world, *dying* for that world. Yes, God gave heaven's Best to die for earth's worst — and He did it willingly.

Greek scholars tell us that the root of the word "manner" is used in many other places in the New Testament. For example, when the ship was about to sink beneath the stormy waves and Jesus was asleep in the ship, the disciples cried out, "Lord, save us: we perish!" Jesus rebuked the winds, they ceased to blow, and the sea became calm. The disciples then asked of each other, "What *manner* of Man is this, that even the winds and the sea obey Him?" (Matt. 8:27). Those fishermen had never before come in contact with such a Man as He who rebuked the winds and caused them to obey. They knew that He belonged to another world.

No other person ever loved like Jesus loved. His "manner" of love is singular: He not only *loved,* He IS love. But we need to remind ourselves often that the Scripture says, *"For GOD so loved the world. . . ."* It was the grace of God the Father that allowed Jesus the Son to leave the bosom of the Father and be born of the virgin, and at the end of His earthly ministry, die for sinners.

In Romans 5:11 we read, ". . . *but we also JOY IN GOD through our Lord Jesus Christ,* by whom we have now received the atonement." It was God the Father who by His grace set forth Jesus to be a propitiation for our sins. It was God the Father who literally turned His head while Jesus died on the cross and paid the sin-debt in full. In His dying hour He cried out, "My God! My God! Why hast thou forsaken me?" (Matt. 27:46). God *did* forsake Jesus while He paid the sin-debt, because God cannot look upon sin, and Jesus was made to be sin for us (II Cor. 5:21). He bore our sins in His own body (I Pet. 2:24).

"Christ hath redeemed us from the curse of the law, being made a curse for us: for it is written, Cursed is every one that hangeth on a tree" (Gal. 3:13). Jesus, the only begotten of God, was made a curse for us, God forsook *Jesus* that He might *receive US*, ". . . that we should be called the sons of God.*"* Think of it, beloved! We who were poor, lost, ungodly, hopeless sinners, enemies of God, through God's love and the shed blood of Jesus are *now* sons of God. What a privilege to be numbered with the children of God, to be members of the eternal family of the Most High, members of the body of Christ (Eph. 5:30; II Cor. 12:12, 13).

"*THEREFORE the world knoweth us not.*" Unbelievers cannot understand why Christians act as they do, walk as they do, and live as they do. People of the world look upon spiritually minded believers as foolish "fanatics and crackpots." To them, any person is considered "simple" who turns his back on pleasure and all that the world has to offer, and lives a "narrow" life such as Christians are thought to live. Unbelievers are blind, they cannot see nor understand. They cannot receive the things of the Spirit of God (I Cor. 2:14). They cannot understand that at His right hand are "pleasures forevermore" (Psalm 16:11), and that "no good thing will He withhold from them that walk uprightly" (Psalm 84:11).

The world does not know US "*because it knew HIM not.*" John 1:10 tells us, "He was in the world, and the world was made by Him, and the world knew Him not." The world will not know US if we are truly born again and walk in the Spirit. Paul tells us that by and through the cross the believer is crucified unto the world, and the world is crucified unto the believer (Gal. 6:14). Let me illustrate: Suppose we go into a mortuary, into a room where two dead men rest, each in his own casket. How much fellowship do those two men have? *None,* of course, because they are *dead* to each other. Just so,

the world is dead to a spiritually minded believer and *he* is
dead to the world; therefore there is no fellowship between
them. The believer and the unbeliever cannot fellowship together — two cannot walk together except they be agreed
(Amos 3:3). The Christian and the unbeliever do not see
alike, they do not walk alike, talk alike, or live alike because
they are sons of two different families — sons of God, and
sons of Satan. There IS no fellowship between light and darkness, between a believer and an atheist. If we are true believers, walking in the light, the world does not know us and
does not want us. If you go back into the world it will not be
because the world led you astray; it will be because you imposed
yourself upon the world until it took you in. You may rest
assured that you will never be invited to a poker game nor to
a nightclub with a Bible under your arm, witnessing to the
saving grace of God and His marvelous love that was displayed on Calvary when Jesus suffered, bled, and died to save
"whosoever will."

By His brethren in the flesh, Jesus was called an imposter,
an illegitimate, a blasphemer. They said "We will not have
Him to reign over us. Give us Barabbas!" If they said such
things about our Saviour, they will say the same about His
children. If you are a born again child of God you need not
be surprised at what the world says about you!

The world does not know us because there is a secret in-
gredient in the Christian that makes him completely different
from the unbeliever. When our enthusiasm is kindled by the
fires of the cross of Jesus and the love He displayed there,
that enthusiasm will find outlet in ministering to others as HE
ministered, walking in His footsteps and being conformed to
His image. Pure love is an *eradicator*. It is also an *indicator*.
Love for Jesus not only expels sin and evil, it also compels
to obedience. If we love Him as we should we will not find
it difficult to obey His Word and His will. True love is never
concerned about ease, but takes great joy in sacrifice for others.
Because Jesus laid down His life for us, we ought to lay down
our lives for the brethren (I John 3:16).

The love of God within us is power to move us, to direct
us; it is also a sphere to limit us and put brakes on us when

needful. His love is a fulness to enrich us. When we are filled with God's love, when all that we do is permeated by that love, we live a full life and others are blessed because of it.

To know Christ in the heart is the Divine secret of power.

To feed upon the Word of God is the secret of Christian growth.

To love Christ supremely is the secret of "joy unspeakable and full of glory."

To abide in Christ fully is the secret of victory.

To follow Christ and walk in His steps is the secret of faith.

To listen to Christ moment by moment is the secret of knowledge.

To walk in the yoke with Christ is the Divine secret of rest.

God loved us *so much* that He gave His only begotten Son, that we might be saved, and He hungers for love from His people. He visited Adam and Eve in the Garden every day. He not only wants to visit *us* daily, He also desires to abide *within us*. He wants all of our love; and when we behold the manner of love He bestowed upon US — love that transforms hell-deserving sinners into sons, heirs of God and joint-heirs with Christ — how *can* we love Him less than with our entire being?

Sons Now

Verse 2: "Beloved, now are we the sons of God, and it doth not yet appear what we shall be: but we know that, when He shall appear, we shall be like Him; for we shall see Him as He is."

We are redeemed NOW. We do not pray "Lord, *at last* save us in heaven" — we are sons of God NOW. We are members of the body of Christ NOW. Our citizenship is in heaven NOW. We sit together in heavenly places in Christ Jesus NOW. Beloved, NOW ARE WE THE SONS OF GOD!

There are those who say that it is presumptuous to speak so dogmatically and with such certainty about salvation; but I would say that the ugliest sin mortal man can commit against a holy God is to hear God's Word and refuse to believe it. We may not *understand* all of it, but if it is HIS WORD, *believe it because God said it.*

Every truly born again believer *knows* that he is a believer, that he is born again. If you do not know that you are a child of God as positively as you know that you are living physically, then God help you to get alone somewhere with the Word of God, go down upon your knees before the open Word, and stay there until you can say "Blessed assurance, Jesus is mine! O, what a foretaste of glory divine!"

Sons of God possess the Holy Spirit — He dwells within our hearts.

We are *born* of the Spirit (John 3:5).

We are baptized into the body of Christ by the Spirit (I Cor. 12:12, 13).

We are led by the Spirit (Rom. 8:14).

We are assured by the testimony of the Spirit (Rom. 8:16).

We are sealed by the Spirit (Eph. 4:30).

Therefore it is a divine impossibility to be born again, washed in the blood, indwelt by the Spirit, and not know it! NOW are we the sons of God.

"*And it doth not yet appear what we shall be.*" What we shall be hereafter is not fully revealed, but we know that we are *sons of God NOW* and that we are predestined to be conformed to the image of His dear Son (Rom. 8:29). "*We shall be like HIM.*" What is involved in this tremendous declaration we do not fully know now, and even if God had seen fit to explain it to us, we would not be able to understand it with our poor, limited, finite minds! Why do I say that? The Scriptures tell us that after His resurrection Jesus ascended to the Father and then returned to earth again — perhaps in a matter of seconds. He entered a room where all doors were closed and the windows were locked, and appeared in the midst of His disciples (John 20:19-28). He invited them, "Behold my hands and my feet, that it is I myself: handle me, and see; for a spirit hath not flesh and bones, as ye see me have . . . and they gave Him a piece of a broiled fish, and of an honeycomb. And He took it, and did eat before them" (Luke 24:36-43).

We cannot understand a body, a personality, like that, we cannot comprehend such tremendous truth with these finite minds. Therefore God did not explain in detail what it will mean to be like Jesus. We will just wait and let Him show us in that glorious resurrection morning.

"*We know that when He shall appear, we shall be like Him.*" In this God reveals to us the fact that our glorified bodies will be like the resurrection body of the glorified Christ. Also read Philippians 3:21 and II Corinthians 3:18. True believers are satisfied with this. To be like Christ is too wonderful for words. We could never explain such a marvelous blessing in the weak, inadequate words of man's language. It would require heaven's language to explain what Christ is like as He sits at the right hand of the Majesty on high; but we know from the assurance of God's Word that *we will be like Him.*

"*We shall see Him as He is.*" We shall SEE Him!! Beloved, weigh those words. What an indescribably glorious, magnificent moment that will be when we experience our first sight of Jesus our Saviour, He who said "I go to prepare a place for you . . . I will come again and will receive you unto myself, that where I am, there ye may be also." What a joyous, blessed, purifying hope to know that one day we shall SEE Him!

In brief review of the first two verses of this chapter, we noted first of all that God the Father wants us to behold His amazing love — the love He bestowed upon us, love that transforms us from sinners to sons, love that innoculates us against the world. We also have the assurance that we are sons of God *now,* we do not yet fully understand what we *shall be,* but we know that when He appears *we shall be like Him* and we shall see Him as He is. There are many things about the future that we will never know in this world, and if those things had been written down and given to us we could not have understood them; but we *do* understand the glorious fact that HE SHALL APPEAR, and "*we shall be like Him!*"

All truly born again believers expect the return of the Lord. Do I have Scripture to support that statement? Indeed I do:

"For the grace of God that bringeth salvation hath appeared to all men, teaching us that, denying ungodliness and worldly lusts, we should live soberly, righteously, and godly, in this present world; looking for that blessed hope, and the glorious appearing of the great God and our Saviour Jesus Christ; who gave Himself for us, that He might redeem us from all iniquity, and purify unto Himself a peculiar people, zealous of good works" (Tit. 2:11-14).

Grace brings salvation, apart from grace there IS no salvation, therefore *every saved person possesses grace*; and the same grace that saves us also teaches us to look for Jesus. His return is the hope of the Church, the hope of our departed loved ones (insofar as the body is concerned), and the hope of all creation:

"For we know that the whole creation groaneth and travaileth in pain together until now. And not only they, but ourselves also, which have the firstfruits of the Spirit, even we ourselves groan within ourselves, waiting for the adoption, to wit, the redemption of our body" (Rom. 8:22, 23).

The Purifying Hope

Verse 3: "And every man that hath this hope in him purifieth himself, even as He is pure."

What IS *"this hope"*? It is the hope of the return of Jesus — a blessed, happy, purifying hope, a comforting hope. In the Greek language, "hope" does not mean "I do not have it but I *hope* that I may get it." "Hope" means "I do *not* have it YET, but I am assured and know for certain that *I shall get it.*" Thus hope becomes certainty; there is no shadow of doubt about it. The *second* coming of Jesus is just as sure and positive as His *first* coming. If He came the first time born of a virgin, as a Lamb for the slaughter, as Saviour of mankind, He is coming the second time as King of kings, Lord of lords, the Lion of the Tribe of Judah. The same Bible that prophesied and promised His *first* coming has much *more* to say about His *second* coming. Jesus Himself said, "Be ye also ready; for in such an hour as ye think not the Son of man cometh" (Matt. 24:44).

The two messages the devil hates above all others are those which proclaim (1) that the blood of Jesus Christ, God's Son, cleanses from all sin; and (2) that the grace of God that brings salvation teaches us to look for the blessed hope of His return. Satan knows that if he can keep the *blood* out of the message from the pulpit he can damn every person who sits under such a ministry because "without shedding of blood is no remission." But if the minister preaches the blood, and souls are saved, the devil then does his diabolical best to keep that minister from preaching the second coming, because he knows that believers who are looking for Jesus will be working, serving, winning souls. A church that expects the immediate return of the Lord will be an evangelistic church, a soul-winning church, a pure church.

Every man who has this hope *"purifieth himself."* I am sure someone is asking, "What does *that* mean? You ministers preach that HE does the purifying — and yet in this verse we read that we are to *purify ourselves.*" The answer to this question is found in God's Word. In James 1:18-25 we read, "Of His own will begat He us with the Word of Truth, that we should be a kind of firstfruits of His creatures. Wherefore, my beloved, brethren, let every man be swift to hear, slow to speak, slow to wrath: For the wrath of man worketh not the righteousness of God. Wherefore lay apart all filthiness and superfluity of naughtiness, and receive with meekness the engrafted word, which is able to save your souls. But be ye doers of the Word and not hearers only, deceiving your own selves. For if any be a hearer of the Word, and not a doer, he is like unto a man beholding his natural face in a glass: for he beholdeth himself, and goeth his way, and straightway forgetteth what manner of man he was. But whoso looketh into the perfect law of liberty, and continueth therein, he being not a forgetful hearer, but a doer of the work, this man shall be blessed in his deed."

The Word of God is the incorruptible seed. We are *begotten* through the Word. Jesus said to His disciples, "Now ye are clean through the Word which I have spoken unto you" (John 15:3). Thus the Word of God is our spiritual bathtub, our spiritual washcloth, our spiritual bar of soap. BUT — *does the Word automatically cleanse and purify us as the Bible is placed on a table in the home?* Indeed it does not! We are commanded to *study* the Word, *eat* the Word, *receive* the Word with meekness. We are commanded to be doers of the Word, we are commanded to look into the perfect law of liberty — the looking glass, the mirror; and when we look into God's mirror we will see the dirty blotches and spots that need to be removed. We will find cleansing in the washing of water by the Word (Eph. 5:26). It is the WORD that does the purifying as we study, assimilate, and receive the Word.

In II Corinthians 3:18 we read, "But we ALL with an open face" (with nothing between us and Jesus) "beholding as in a glass" (looking into the mirror of God's Word) "the glory of the Lord, are changed into the same image" (as we look into the Word) "from glory to glory, even as by the Spirit of the Lord."

Primarily and fundamentally, *God does the purifying*; but He does it as we look into the mirror of the Word. As we get into the water of the Word, God does the cleansing *through* His precious, powerful Word. Moment by moment we are cleansed and purified through the Word as we exercise faith in the Lord Jesus Christ and His finished work.

Verse 4: "Whosoever committeth sin transgresseth also the law: for sin is the transgression of the law."

If we should ask a dozen ministers for a definition of sin, the chances are good that we would get a dozen different answers. If we should ask one minister if it is a sin to drink intoxicants, he would tell us that *he* occasionally takes a drink. If we should ask another minister if it is a sin to gamble, he would tell us that his congregation plays "Bingo" in the church basement. By contrast, other ministers would declare that drinking and gambling are *gross sins*. Preachers and religious leaders do not agree on what constitutes sin, so let us look at the *Bible* definition of sin as set forth so clearly in this verse:

"Sin is the transgression of the law." Since sin is the transgression of the law, then *whosoever* (that takes in everybody) *transgresses the law commits sin.* That settles it! To break God's law is to sin, and according to Romans 3:23 *"ALL have sinned,* and come short of the glory of God." Romans 3:10 tells us that "There is *none* righteous, no, not one." In Ecclesiastes 7:20 we read, "There is not a just man upon the earth, that doeth good, and sinneth not." Isaiah 53:6 tells us, "All we like sheep have gone astray; we have turned every one to his own way; *and the Lord hath laid on Him (Jesus) the iniquity of us all!"*

Are we then saved by keeping the commandments? Definitely not. In Romans 3:20 Paul tells us, "Therefore by the deeds of the law there shall no flesh be justified in His sight. . . ." The law was never given to save sinners; it was given that man might see the exceeding sinfulness of sin. Galatians 3:24, 25 tells us, "Wherefore the law was our schoolmaster to bring us unto Christ, that we might be justified by faith. But after that faith is come, we are no longer under a schoolmaster."

In Matthew 5:17 Jesus said, "Think not that I am come to destroy the law, or the prophets: I am not come to destroy, but to fulfil." And He did just that. He fulfilled the law, He fulfilled the prophets — *and He filled them full*. Therefore, *"Christ is the end of the law* for righteousness to every one that believeth" (Rom. 10:4). We are not justified by law, we are justified by faith *without* the deeds of the law.

Read what Jesus said about the law in Matthew 22:36-39: "Then one of them, which was a lawyer, asked Him a question, tempting Him, and saying, *Master, which is the great commandment in the law?* Jesus said unto him, Thou shalt love the Lord thy God with all thy heart, and with all thy soul, and with all thy mind. This is the first and great commandment. And the second is like unto it, Thou shalt love thy neighbour as thyself. *On these two commandments hang all the law and the prophets."*

In Romans 6:14, 15 Paul said, ". . . Ye are not under the law, but under grace. What then? *Shall we sin,* because we are not under the law, but under grace? *God forbid."*

We are not saved by keeping the law, but God's law reminds us that we have obligations, and God's marvelous *grace* — "grace that is greater than all our sin" — so fills the heart of the true believer that he wants to *meet* those obligations. *Law* is love's divine gift to man; *love* is law's keeping. We love to do the things that please Jesus because we love Him. We love to obey His Word because we love Him who IS the Word. We love to walk in the light because the light in which we walk is Him whom we love. The Psalmist cried out, "O how I love thy law! It is my meditation all the day" (Psalm 119:97).

Salvation would be impossible by the keeping of the law. Does ANY man keep the law? Those who know the Bible

117

will readily confess that no mortal has ever kept God's law perfectly, nor will anyone *ever* keep it: "Now we know that what things soever the law saith, it saith to them who are under the law: *that every mouth may be stopped, and all the world may become guilty before God*" (Rom. 3:19). We know that because of the weakness of the flesh we *cannot* keep the law; but thank God, Romans 8:1-4 tells us:

"There is therefore now no condemnation to them which are in Christ Jesus, who walk not after the flesh, but after the Spirit. For the law of the Spirit of life in Christ Jesus hath made me free from the law of sin and death. *For what the law could not do, in that it was weak through the flesh, God* sending His own Son in the likeness of sinful flesh, and for sin, *condemned sin in the flesh: That the righteousness of the law might be fulfilled in us, who walk not after the flesh, but after the Spirit.*"

Our helplessness and our hopelessness drives us to our knees in humble confession to Christ who alone kept the law perfectly and is therefore the END of the law for righteousness. We are *saved* by God's grace through faith, we are *kept* by God's grace through faith, we *overcome* by faith, and *whatsoever is NOT of faith is sin!* When we exercise faith in Jesus, we possess the Christ who fulfilled every jot and tittle of the law and therefore we stand before God justified — not by law, but by faith in Him who *fulfilled* the law.

The Primary Purpose of the Incarnation

Verse 5: "And ye know that He was manifested to take away our sins; and in Him IS no sin."

More words have been spoken and more books written about Christ Jesus than have been said or written about any other hundred men who ever lived. Many and varied are the ideas in the minds of men as to why He came into this world. Even the liberals and modernists say a lot of nice things about Him. They declare that He was a great teacher, an extraordinary man who set a wonderful example as the founder of a great religion; but He was much, much more than all these things combined: "*He was manifested*" for the primary purpose of dealing with the sin-question. Before there was a

world, before there was a man, before there was SIN the
sovereign God knew exactly what would happen and He made
provision for man to be saved from sin:

"Forasmuch as ye know that ye were not redeemed with
corruptible things, as silver and gold, from your vain conversation received by tradition from your fathers; but with the
precious blood of Christ, as of a Lamb without blemish and
without spot: *Who verily was foreordained before the foundation
of the world, but was manifest in these last times for you*"
(I Pet. 1:18-20).

It is true that Jesus was the greatest Teacher and the greatest
Healer who ever lived, He performed the greatest miracles
ever performed on earth; but great as these were, they were
sidelines. His main purpose was to pay the sin-debt. He was
manifested to deal with the sin-question in flesh, to do in flesh
what God's holy law could not do because of the *weakness* of
the flesh.

"He was manifested *to take away our sins*." The precious
blood of Christ Jesus, the sacrificial Lamb foreordained before
the Creation, is God's divine eraser, and when applied to the
unbeliever's heart, that blood forever erases our sins and God
forgets that we have sinned. Through one offering Jesus did
that which all of the Old Testament offerings could never do:
"For it is not possible that the blood of bulls and of goats
should take away sins . . . but this Man, after He had offered
one sacrifice for sins for ever, sat down on the right hand of
God . . . For *by one offering He hath perfected for ever* them
that are sanctified" (Heb. 10:4, 12, 14).

The blood of the Old Testament sacrifices could not remove
sins: it was a *covering* for sin, a shadow between God and sin.
The sacrifices offered by the Old Testament saints covered their
sins until the Lamb of God should give HIS blood — *the one
eternal sacrifice that would TAKE AWAY sin*:

"Being justified freely by His grace through the redemption
that is in Christ Jesus: whom God hath set forth to be a
propitiation through faith in His blood, to declare His righteousness for the remission of sins that are past, through the forbearance of God; to declare, I say, at this time His righteous-

ness: that He might be just, and the Justifier of him which believeth in Jesus" (Rom. 3:24-26).

In this passage, *"sins that are past"* points back to the sins of the Old Testament era, those who brought their sacrifices and offered them according to the law. The blood shed covered their sins until, in the fulness of time, Jesus came: "But when the fulness of the time was come, God sent forth His Son, made of a woman, made under the law, to redeem them that were under the law, that we might receive the adoption of sons" (Gal. 4:4, 5).

If Jesus had never come, not one person could ever have been saved, from Adam until this present hour. Every drop of blood shed from Eden to Calvary pointed to the blood of the Lamb: "And for this cause He is the Mediator of the New Testament, that by means of death, for the redemption of the transgressions that were under the first testament, they which are called might receive the promise of eternal inheritance" (Heb. 9:15).

Christ's death and His shed blood were retrospective in effect as having to do with the Old Testament saints. We could say that Calvary, in the true sense of the word, has no specific date. The Lamb was promised (foreordained) before the foundation of the world, before man was created. It was settled by the eternal council of God, the Trinity agreeing that the Lamb would die for the sins of the world. Abel, Noah, Abraham, Moses, and all other Old Testament saints, will be in heaven because Jesus was "manifested to take away our sins," and His blood cleanses from ALL sin.

"In Him IS no sin." This is much more than just a fact; it was a Divine necessity: *otherwise the entire program of salvation would be void.* It was imperative that the sin-debt be paid by one without sin, and only God could provide such a sacrifice. Therefore, Christ was God in flesh, reconciling the world unto Himself. If Jesus had sinned, He could not have died for sinners. *In HIM is no sin,* but when He died on the cross, God the Father gathered all the sin that ever was, from Eden until the consummation of all things, and laid that sin on Jesus — not only all the sin that HAS been, but all the sin that WILL BE — and He paid the sin-debt in full!

The Holy Spirit has been pleased to give us certain expressions having to do with Christ's all-sufficient sacrifice for sin — expressions which clearly illustrate how completely and fully the healing balm of His atonement covers the ugly cancer of man's transgressions:

He was manifested to take away our sins (I John 3:5).

He offered one sacrifice for sins (Heb. 10:12).

He gave Himself for our sins (Gal. 1:4).

He is the propitiation for our sins (I John 2:2).

He suffered for our sins — the Just for the unjust (I Pet. 3:18).

He was once offered to bear the sins of many (Heb. 9:28).

He bore our sins in His own body on the tree (I Pet. 2:24).

In Matthew 26:28 Jesus said, "For this is my blood of the New Testament, which is shed for many for the remission of sins."

In I Corinthians 15:1-3 Paul said, "Moreover, brethren, I declare unto you the Gospel which I preached unto you, which also ye have received, and wherein ye stand; by which also ye are saved, if ye keep in memory what I preached unto you, unless ye have believed in vain. For I delivered unto you first of all that which I also received, how that Christ died for our sins according to the Scriptures."

In each of these Scriptures we see clearly pointed out — first, the sins of the sinner; second, the sacrifice of the Saviour. Jesus made the one all-sufficient sacrifice for all sins of all sinners of all ages. In the same way the scapegoat on the Day of Atonement in the Old Testament era was separated from the people to take away the sins of Israel (Lev. 16:21), so Christ Jesus our Saviour was manifested to take away OUR sins by His death and shed blood. He not only took away the penalty which sin demanded, He also destroyed the *power* sin gained over man through Adam's transgression. What the first Adam lost by *disobedience,* the last Adam bought back through *perfect* obedience. The sin-question is settled; *Jesus* settled it. The question that will determine your eternal destiny is "What think ye of Christ? Whose Son is He?" If you deny Him, He will deny you. If you confess Him, He will confess you (Matt. 10:32, 33).

The judgment holds no fear for the true believer: "Herein is our love made perfect, that we may have boldness in the day of judgment: because as HE is, so are we in this world" (I John 4:17). The ground of our confidence is that Christ will not in that day condemn those who are like Himself. True believers are righteous even as HE is righteous: "But of Him are ye in Christ Jesus, who of God is made unto us wisdom, and righteousness, and sanctification, and redemption: that, according as it is written, He that glorieth, let him glory in the Lord" (I Cor. 1:30, 31).

When we truly believe on Jesus Christ and trust Him as our Saviour, all that belongs to Him — righteousness, holiness, purity — belongs to US through perfect imputation and progressive impartation. His love is being perfected in us; we are predestined to be conformed to His image (Rom. 8:29; I John 3:2). All believers, born of the Spirit and washed in His blood, are seated with Christ in the heavenlies and therefore we have confidence in the day of judgment.

"Who shall lay anything to the charge of God's elect? It is God that justifieth. Who is he that condemneth? It is Christ that died, yea rather, that is risen again, who is even at the right hand of God, who also maketh intercession for us" (Rom. 8:33, 34).

Who CAN condemn us? Can the Father? It is He who has justified us. We are justified by faith in the shed blood of Jesus and therefore we have peace with God (Rom. 5:1).

Can CHRIST condemn us? It is He who *died* for us. We are members of His body, seated with Him in the heavenlies (Eph. 5:30; 2:6).

Can the Holy Spirit condemn us? He is one with the Father, working in our salvation. He draws us (John 6:44); He "borns" us (John 3:5); He indwells us (Rom. 8:9); He leads us (Rom. 8:14); He assures us (Rom. 8:16); and He seals us (Eph. 4:30).

Can SIN condemn us? Jesus bore our sins (I Pet. 2:24); He was made to be sin for us (II Cor. 5:21); He has taken our sins away (I John 3:5). The sin-question has been settled, and when we are in Jesus sin cannot condemn us. Sin has been atoned for, the sin-debt has been paid. "It is finished!" (John 19:30).

Can SATAN condemn us? No! Christ defeated the devil, took away his power and conquered him (Heb. 2:14, 15; Col. 2:15). Jesus conquered the world, the flesh, the devil, death, hell, and the grave; He has the keys of hell and of death (Rev. 1:18).

Can the LAW condemn us? Christ is the *end* of the law for righteousness to those who believe (Rom. 10:4).

Can DEATH condemn us? Jesus conquered death and removed the sting (I Cor. 15:51-57).

God's holiness, His righteousness, His purity and justice are satisfied in Jesus. There is therefore now *no condemnation* to them which are IN Christ Jesus.

"What shall we then say to these things? If God be for us, who can be against us? He that spared not His own Son, but delivered Him up for us all, how shall He not with Him also freely give us all things? Who shall lay anything to the charge of God's elect? It is God that justifieth. Who is he that condemneth? It is Christ that died, yea rather, that is risen again, who is even at the right hand of God, who also maketh intercession for us.

"Who shall separate us from the love of Christ? Shall tribulation, or distress, or persecution, or famine, or nakedness, or peril, or sword? As it is written, For thy sake we are killed all the day long; we are accounted as sheep for the slaughter. Nay, in all these things we are more than conquerors through Him that loved us. For I am persuaded, that neither death, nor life, nor angels, nor principalities, nor powers nor things present, nor things to come, nor height, nor depth, NOR ANY OTHER CREATURE, shall be able to separate us from the love of God, which is in Christ Jesus our Lord" (Rom. 8:31-39).

Verses 6 and 7: "Whosoever abideth in Him sinneth not: whosoever sinneth hath not seen Him, neither known Him. Little children, let no man deceive you: he that doeth righteousness is righteous, even as HE is righteous."

Here we have deep spiritual truth that needs to be emphasized today as never before, but very few believers are willing to search these verses in the light of other Scriptures and look to the Holy Spirit to guide them into the full meaning of them. Some people are actually afraid to read these verses.

"Whosoever abideth in Him sinneth not." Here we find one of the most precious truths concerning believers that is found in all the Word of God. Notice the two present tenses: "abideth" and "sinneth not." We need to look first at the word "abide" and at some Scriptures that give us information concerning abiding believers:

The Greek word translated "abide" is *meno,* and it means "to be in one specific place all the time." In the New Testament the word is used to describe a dwelling place. In John 1:38 the disciples asked Jesus "Where dwellest thou?" The same word is used in John 4:40 where the Samaritans besought Christ to tarry with them, "and He abode there two days." It is used in John 6:27 when Jesus exhorts believers to labor "for that meat which endureth unto everlasting life." Christ used the same word in John 14:25, speaking of the continued presence of one person with another: "These things have I spoken unto you, being yet present with you." In Acts 27:41 the same word is used referring to the ship on which Paul was being taken to Rome. They ran the ship aground, and it "stuck fast and remained unmoveable." In Romans 9:11 the same word is translated "might stand," speaking of the fixed purpose of God. It is used by Christ when He told His disciples, "If ye continue in my Word, then are ye my disciples indeed" (John 8:31).

In John 15, where Jesus used the Greek word *meno* twelve times, it is translated "abide," "continue," and "remain." In verse 4, He said "Abide in me." (This is a *command* — a call to obedience — not merely a suggestion or an option in choice.) "Abide in me, and I in you." If we do not abide in Him, neither does He abide in us; and He does not take up His abode within us until we exercise faith in His finished work.

Also in verse 4, we learn that union in and with Christ is a divine necessity for fruitfulness. If we do not abide in and commune with the true Vine, there can be no fruit, for the branch is useless and helpless apart from the Vine. Study Ezekiel 15:1-6.

In verse 5 of John 15 we find the *results* of abiding — *"much fruit."* NO fruit is proof positive of professing but not possessing, confessing with the mouth but not believing with the heart.

There are many who announce that they belong to Jesus, but their works deny what they announce. There cannot be a fruitless Christian: "Ephraim shall say, What have I to do any more with idols? I have heard Him, and observed Him: I am like a green fir tree. From me is thy fruit found" (Hos. 14:8). Any branch that is connected to the True Vine will bear some fruit.

John 15:7 declares the blessing of abiding. If we yield to the Lord in obedience, He answers our prayers with His blessings; but if we do not obey Him we need not hope for answered prayer and blessing. Verse 9 gives the *sphere* of the abiding believer: Jesus said, "*Continue ye in my love.*" The abiding believer lives in the element of God's love, he *inbreathes* God's love to his own comfort, rest, and security, and then *outbreathes* that love to the blessing of others.

Verse 10 of John 15 tells us HOW to abide: *If ye keep my commandments,* ye shall abide in my love." How do we abide? The answer is found in one word: FAITHFULNESS. Notice also in this verse, Christ does not ask us to do anything He has not done before us: "If ye keep my commandments, ye shall abide in my love; *even as I have kept my Father's commandments, and abide in His love.*"

In John 15:11 we learn that abiding brings joy. No believer can enjoy his spiritual birthright unless he is obedient and faithful in abiding. The things of earth will pass away, but the joy of the Lord comes to the believer to remain forever.

John 15:16 tells of the *reward* for abiding believers: "Ye have not chosen me, but I have chosen you, and ordained you, that ye should go and bring forth fruit, and that your fruit should remain: that whatsoever ye shall ask of the Father in my name, He may give it you." Fruit borne by the abiding believer is *eternal* fruit.

Every true believer brings forth fruit. When we allow the Lord to discipline us we bring forth *more* fruit, and when we grow in grace as we should we bring forth *much* fruit. It is when we bring forth *much fruit* that we glorify God.

Abiding in Christ means:

Walking as HE walked (I John 2:6).

Loving the brethren as HE loved them (I John 3:14-17).

Abiding with the Father (I John 2:17).

Fellowship with the Father (I John 1:3).

The truth abiding in us (I John 2:24a).

Continuing in the Father and in the Son (I John 2:24b).

The teaching of the Spirit, the unction, the abiding (I John 2:20, 27).

Preparing for the return of Jesus (I John 2:28).

Not committing sin (I John 3:6).

Recognizing that believers have Divine nature (I John 3:9; II Pet. 1:4).

Eternal life is a present possession. NOW are we the sons of God (I John 1:1, 2).

The Holy Spirit abiding in us, remaining in us in power (I John 3:24; 4:13).

Confessing Christ (I John 4:15).

Living in love, love living in us, and faithfulness to the truth (I John 4:16; II John 2).

"Whosoever abideth in Him *sinneth not.*" Here is our second present tense in verse 6. Does this mean that a born again believer lives above sin — *sinless?* Does it mean that he is untouched by sin from the moment he is born again until he departs this life? No, *not in the flesh.* It is the inner man that has the spiritual birth, and that which is born again does not sin. (For a fuller explanation see notes under verse 9 of this chapter.)

"*Whosoever sinneth hath not seen Him, neither known Him.*" John is not speaking here of the natural eye, he is referring to the eye of faith. He who sins has not looked to Jesus who was manifested to *take away* our sins. The person who sins does not know Him.

"*Little children, let no man deceive you.*" Notice to whom these words are addressed. There is no mistake, John is speaking to the "little born ones."

"*He that doeth righteousness is righteous, even as HE is righteous.*" Righteousness is not attained, merited, or earned through right habits or right living. On the contrary, right habits and right living are the *fruits* of imputed righteousness. Righteous living is the result of salvation through Christ: Christ is made unto us "wisdom, and righteousness, and sanctification, and redemption" (I Cor. 1:30). And "to him that worketh not, but believeth on Him that justifieth the ungodly, *his faith is counted for righteousness.* Even as David also describeth the blessedness of the man, unto whom God imputeth righteousness without works" (Rom. 4:5, 6). Christ is our righteousness, and when we put our faith and trust in Him He abides within our hearts in the Person of the Holy Spirit. Therefore we are righteous because HE is righteous.

Most assuredly, the only way a believer dwelling in mortal body *could* be declared righteous as *Christ* is righteous is because God looks upon the *imputed* righteousness — His OWN righteousness. Christ in YOU is the hope of glory (Col. 1:27). "There is therefore now no condemnation to them which are in Christ Jesus . . ." (Rom. 8:1). It will be a happy day in the lives of Christians when they allow the Holy Spirit to reveal to them the real meaning of the new birth.

Verse 8: "He that committeth sin is of the devil; for the devil sinneth from the beginning. For this purpose the Son of God was manifested that He might destroy the works of the devil.

Three definite facts are stated in this verse:

First, *"He that committeth sin is of the devil."* There is no reason for misunderstanding this statement. He who commits sin is of the devil, and a person who is of the devil is certainly not of God!

Second, *"The devil sinneth from the beginning."* This does not refer to "the beginning" in Genesis 1:1; *there was no devil* when God created the heaven and the earth. In his original form Satan was not a devil; he was a created being, originally "the anointed cherub that covereth." We might say that he was the high sheriff who protected the throne of God. The account is found in Ezekiel 28:11-15:

"Moreover the word of the Lord came unto me, saying, Son of man, take up a lamentation upon the king of Tyrus, and say unto him, Thus saith the Lord God: Thou sealest up the sum, *full of wisdom, and perfect in beauty. Thou hast been in Eden the garden of God;* every precious stone was thy covering, the sardius, topaz, and the diamond, the beryl, the onyx, and the jasper, the sapphire, the emerald, and the carbuncle, and gold: the workmanship of thy tabrets and of thy pipes was prepared in thee in the day that thou wast created. *Thou art the anointed cherub that covereth;* and I have set thee so: *thou wast upon the holy mountain of God;* thou hast walked up and down in the midst of the stones of fire. *Thou was perfect in thy ways from the day that thou wast created till iniquity was found in thee.*"

It is easy to see that the things declared about the person described in these verses could not have been said of an earthly king.

Isaiah 14:12-15 gives the account of Lucifer the "shining one," the anointed one who coveted the throne of God and planned to exalt his throne "above the stars of God." Lucifer was a created being, and the Creator is always greater than the ceated. Therefore God cast him out, and the angels whom he brainwashed and led astray were cast out with him. Jude tells us that these angels are "reserved in everlasting chains under darkness unto the judgment of the great day.

Thus we see that "the devil sinneth from the beginning" (v. 8) simply means *the beginning of SATAN* — which was the day iniquity was found in him. "Iniquity" is sin, and the sin Satan committed was the sin of covetousness. He was not satisfied to be subordinate to God, he coveted God's throne and God's power. He attempted to overthrow God, God cast him out of heaven, and he became Satan, the devil about whom we read in the Word of God.

Father, Son, and Holy Spirit were in the beginning, but Satan was NOT in the beginning. We find no record of the *creation of hell* in the beginning — only heaven and earth. There is no mention of hell in connection with the creation, but we do read in Matthew 25:41 that hell was prepared for the devil and his angels — the same angels Lucifer "brainwashed" and led astray when he attempted to overthrow God and take the throne of heaven. The devil *became* a devil when he coveted God's throne, and he has sinned "from (his) beginning." He is a liar, a murderer, the archenemy of God and man.

Third, Jesus was manifested in flesh *"that He might destroy the works of the devil."* In verse 5 He was manifested "to take away our sins," but in our present verse we learn that He was also manifested to destroy the works of Satan.

The devil is a defeated foe and he knows it. He still operates, but God has a program and a plan, and IN that plan Jesus will personally place Satan in the lake of fire. Until that day comes, he will continue to operate. In Genesis 3:15 God spelled out to Satan that his head would be crushed by the seed of the woman, and since that day Satan has been battling against the seed, the Son, and all who are children of God. That battle will continue until the consummation of all things, when the devil will be put into the lake of fire where the beast and the false prophet are, and will be tormented day and night forever and ever (Rev. 20:10).

Bible Sinless Perfection

Verse 9: "Whosoever is born of God doth not commit sin;, for His seed remaineth in him and he cannot sin, because he is born of God."

This is one of the most difficult portions of the Word of God — both Old and New Testaments; but it IS the Word of God and we dare not ignore it. This is part of the verbally-inspired record, just as surely as John 3:16 is part of it, and since ALL Scripture is written for our instruction, we know that God did not put this verse in the Bible simply to fill up space. He means for us to study and rightly divide the Word of Truth.

"WHOSOEVER *is born of God*" — there are no exceptions. There are not *some* "little born ones" who will sin, and some who will not. God has no pets, He shows no partiality, He does not redeem some of His children more fully than others. When God saves He saves perfectly, and we are *complete* in Jesus (Col. 2:9, 10).

Whosoever is born of God "*doth not commit sin.*" Why? Because "*His seed remaineth in him and he cannot sin.*" Whose seed? God's seed. And what IS "God's seed"? In I Peter 1:23 we read, "Being born again, not of *corruptible* seed, but of *incorruptible*, BY THE WORD OF GOD, which liveth and abideth for ever." Thus we learn that the *seed* is the Word of God, incorruptible, eternal. But in John 1:1, 14 we learn, "*In the beginning* was the Word, and the Word was with God, and the Word was God . . . and the Word was made flesh, and dwelt among us. . . ." We know that this Word was none other than Jesus, and in John 1:12, 13 we read, "As many as received (Jesus) to them gave He power to become the sons of God, even to them that believe on His name: which were born . . . of God."

In John 5:24 Jesus said, "Verily, verily, I say unto you, *He that heareth my Word,* and believeth on Him that sent me, hath everlasting life, and shall not come into condemnation; but is passed from death unto life." The only way we can believe on Jesus is to hear the Word. When we hear and *believe* the Word we exercise faith in Jesus and we are saved (born again) by God's grace through faith:

"For by grace are ye saved through faith; and that not of yourselves: it is the gift of God" (Eph. 2:8).

In Romans 10:17 we are told "So then faith cometh by hearing, and hearing by the Word of God." In Romans 1:16 Paul tells us that the Gospel (the Word) is "the power of God unto salvation to every one that believeth. . . ."

We will look at one more passage that is proof positive concerning the seed of God: Paul said to the believers at Corinth, "Moreover, brethren, I declare unto you the Gospel which I preached unto you, which also ye have received, and wherein ye stand; by which also ye are saved, if ye keep in memory what I preached unto you, unless ye have believed in vain. For I delivered unto you first of all that which I also received, how that Christ died for our sins according to the Scriptures; and that He was seen of Cephas, then of the twelve: After that, He was seen of above five hundred brethren at once: of whom the greater part remain unto this present, but some are fallen asleep. After that, He was seen of James; then of all the apostles. And last of all He was seen of me also, as of one born out of due time" (I Cor. 15:1-8).

In Acts 9 we find the account of Paul's conversion. He was born again by hearing the words of Jesus. Read and study that chapter and you will see that Jesus *spoke,* Saul of Tarsus *listened,* he obeyed, he was born again and he preached Christ in the synagogues.

The Bible proves beyond any shadow of doubt that the *seed* of God is the *Word* of God, the Word is *Christ,* and Christ in you is the hope of glory. The believer is in Christ, and Christ is in the believer.

Whosoever is born of God does not commit sin, "for His seed remaineth in him: *AND HE CANNOT SIN.*" Some precious men of God — even born again men — have explained away this verse to their own satisfaction by suggesting it to mean that the believer does not *habitually practice* sin; but the words distinctly tell us that the Word of God abides in his bosom and "he CANNOT sin." Why? The reason is clearly stated: He cannot sin *"because he is BORN OF GOD."*

We know that "the natural man receiveth not the things of the Spirit of God, for they are foolishness unto him: neither can he know them, because they are spiritually discerned" (I Cor. 2:14). When Jesus said to Nicodemus, "Except a man be *born again,* he cannot see the kingdom of God," Nicodemus asked a very sensible question (in the natural sense). He asked, "How CAN a man be born when he is old? Can he enter the second time into his mother's womb, and be born?" Nicodemus was thinking in terms of the physical. Not knowing the spiritual, he asked the only question his knowledge and wisdom allowed him to ask, concerning the new birth. Jesus replied, "Verily, verily, I say unto thee, Except a man be born of water (the Word) and of the (Holy) Spirit, he cannot enter into the kingdom of God. *That which is born of the flesh is FLESH; and that which is born of the Spirit is spirit"* (John 3:1-6 in part).

In other words, Jesus said to Nicodemus, "You are thinking in terms of the birth you received from your mother, you are thinking in terms of the flesh. But I am not talking about a flesh birth, I am talking about a spiritual birth. You must be born of the Word and of the Spirit in the inner man. I did not come to 'born' your flesh, but to 'born' your spirit. That which is born of the flesh is flesh and will *always* be flesh. It is the spirit that must be born again."

When God "borns" one into His family, it is the inner man (the spirit) that is born; and that which is *born of God* does *not* commit sin. God's seed *remains* in the inner man. After the new birth we have Divine nature within us, *and the part of man that is born of God is born to sin no more!* The

Apostle Paul said, "I know that in me (that is, *in my flesh,*) dwelleth no good thing: for to will is present with me; but how to perform that which is good I find not . . . For *I delight in the law of God after the inward man.* . . . So then with the mind I myself serve the law of God; but with the flesh the law of sin" (Rom. 7:18, 22, 25).

It was Paul who said, "There is therefore now no condemnation to them which are in Christ Jesus, who walk not after the flesh, but after the Spirit . . . That the righteousness of the law might be fulfilled in us, who walk not after the flesh, but after the Spirit . . . But ye are not in the flesh, but in the Spirit, if so be that the Spirit of God dwell in you. Now if any man have *not* the Spirit of Christ, *he is none of His*" (Rom. 8:1, 4, 9).

The Apostle Paul was a born again man when he penned the words just quoted, and it is evident that he recognized the existence of the two natures — the spirit and the flesh. Writing to the believers in Galatia he said, "The flesh lusteth against the Spirit, and the Spirit against the flesh: and these are contrary the one to the other: so that ye cannot do the things that ye would" (Gal. 5:17).

Thus we understand that "whosoever is born of God doth not commit sin; for His seed remaineth in him: and *he cannot sin, because he is born of God.*"

Verse 10: "In this the children of God are manifest, and the children of the devil: whosoever doeth not righteousness is not of God, neither he that loveth not his brother."

"The children of God are manifest" because they do righteousness. They live right and do right because they are new creatures in Christ Jesus (II Cor. 5:17). The children of the devil naturally follow the lust of the flesh, the lust of the eyes, and the pride of life because their nature calls for it. So far as *heaven's* record goes, I did not exist until the day I was born again. The man who lived in sin for nineteen years died when the unbeliever became a believer, a new creation with a new heart and a new spirit (Ezek. 36:26). That is what Paul declared when he said, "I am crucified with Christ: nevertheless I live; yet not I, but Christ liveth in me: and the life which I now live in the flesh I live by the faith of the Son of God, who loved me, and gave Himself for me" (Gal. 2:20).

The children of God are manifest because "the grace of God that bringeth salvation" also teaches us to deny ungodliness and worldly lusts, and to live soberly, righteously, and godly in this present world. The God who saves us also has made provision for the purity and holiness of His sons and daughters; and if we walk as He would have us walk our lives make manifest before the world the fact that we are children of God.

"*Whosoever doeth not righteousness is not of God neither he that loveth not His brother.*" Notice how often the Holy Spirit reminds us that true believing automatically produces brotherly love. *God is love,* and when we receive Jesus the love of God comes into our hearts and we love the brethren. If we cannot love our Christian brother whom we have seen, how dare we say we love God whom we have NOT seen? Christianity is practical — "faith without works is dead" (James 2:26). Works are the *result* of salvation, not the *cause* of it. Paul makes this plain in Ephesians 2:8-10 where he tells us that we are saved by grace through faith, the gift of God, "*not of works,* lest any man should boast." But he also tells us that "*we are HIS workmanship, created in Christ Jesus UNTO GOOD WORKS, which God hath before ordained that we should walk in them.*"

True Love Produces Action

Verse 11: "For this is the message that ye heard from the beginning, that we should love one another."

As we study the New Testament we see throughout the books and chapters that there is always divine insistence on the practical. For instance, "As ye have therefore received Christ Jesus the Lord, *so walk ye in Him*" (Col. 2:6). In Romans 1:7 we are "called *to be saints.*" We are to practice in our walk what we declare in our talk. In reality and practicality we are to be what we say we are. "If ye *know* these things, happy are ye if ye *do* them" (John 13:17). Jesus spoke of those who "*say,* and do not":

"Not everyone that saith unto me, Lord, Lord, shall enter into the kingdom of heaven; but he that doeth the will of my Father which is in heaven. Many will say to me in that day, Lord, Lord, have we not prophesied in thy name? and in thy name have cast out devils? and in thy name done many wonderful works? And then will I profess unto them, I never knew you: depart from me, ye that work iniquity" (Matt. 7:21-23). True believers practice what they say.

Verse 10 plainly told us that he who loves not his brother is not of God, and in our present verse John tells us that *"this is the message that ye heard from the beginning."* True love is more than an emotional stir; love is *motional.* True love longs to *do* something, *must* do something. True love must *give*, and many times the giving is costly. Think what it cost God to love the world (John 3:16). True believers do not find it difficult to fellowship with one another, to love one another. Love between brethren is natural. A family where there is no love one for another is not a normal family. If one brother dislikes another, if one sister dislikes another, that is unnatural. For illustration here, John uses Cain and Abel.

Verses 12 and 13: "Not as Cain, who was of that wicked one, and slew his brother. And wherefore slew he him? Because his own works were evil, and his brother's righteous. Marvel not, my brethren, if the world hate you."

Paul tells us that it was *by faith* that Abel "offered unto God a more excellent sacrifice than Cain" (Heb. 11:4). Faith comes by hearing, and hearing by the Word of God. Therefore, Abel was righteous because he heard *and believed* the word of God. *Cain* had the same opportunity — but he hated his brother because *"he was of that wicked one,"* and Abel was righteous. We who are believers should not marvel that the world hates us. It is unnatural for the world to love a Christian because we live in two different spheres. Believers are citizens of heaven, unbelievers are citizens of this world. We have different natures — the unbeliever is of his father the devil (John 8:44) and he is by nature a child of wrath (Eph. 2:3). The believer is a child of God, he possesses Divine nature, and he is dead to the unbeliever insofar as fellowship is concerned. It would be unnatural for the world to love a Christian, but it is natural for believers to love each other. If we do not love our fellow believers we do not love God. Born again people possess the Holy Spirit, the Spirit bears fruit, and "the fruit of the Spirit is love" (Gal. 5:22). Jesus said, "If you love me, keep my commandments" (John 14:15), and He commanded us to love one another.

True Believers Have Assurance

Verse 14: "We know that we have passed from death unto life, because we love the brethren. He that loveth not his brother abideth in death."

There are several ways clearly stated in the Bible whereby we can know that we are saved:

Through the testimony of the *Word* (John 5:24; I John 5:10-13).

Through the testimony of the *Spirit* (Rom. 8:16).

Through the testimony of *our own heart* — the *new* heart God puts within us at the time of the new birth (I John 3:20, 21).

Through our love for the brethren (our present verse).

God is love, Christ is God's love-gift to the sinner, and when we receive *Him*, then certainly when we have Jesus in our hearts we love the brethren. We are not *saved* through loving the brethren; we love the brethren *because we ARE saved.* Thus "*we know that we have passed from death unto life.*"

Greek authorities tell us that in this verse there is a definite article before "death" and before "life." In other words, we know that we have passed from "*THE death*" unto "*THE life*" because we love the brethren. It is not simply *physical* death that we have escaped, but *THE death that is the wages of sin.* All unbelievers are "dead in trespasses and sins" (Eph. 2:1). "She that liveth in pleasure is dead while she liveth" (I Tim. 5:6). The death spoken of here is *eternal* death in the lake of fire, called "the second death" (Rev. 20:14). We know that we have passed from THE death (the wages of sin), and possess THE life (Christ who IS our life). He said, "By this shall all men know that ye are my disciples, if ye have love one to another" (John 13:35).

Not only does love for the brethren bring assurance of salvation to the believer's heart, but the world *also* knows that we are disciples of Jesus when we demonstrate "love in action" toward each other.

Verse 15: "Whosoever hateth his brother is a murderer: and ye know that no murderer hath eternal life abiding in him."

There is little point in taking time and space to comment on this verse, it is so clear. The *"whosoever"* may be minister, deacon, church member in excellent standing — but if he hates his Christian brother he is not saved, he is a murderer. It is not necessary to fire a bullet in order to become a murderer. God's Word plainly says that he who hates his brother is a murderer, and no murderer can enter the kingdom of God (Rev. 21:8; 22:15).

Love at Its Highest

Verse 16: "Hereby perceive we the love of God, because He laid down His life for us: and we ought to lay down our lives for the brethren."

In this verse we see love in action, love at its highest: *Jesus loving a world of sinners!* loving them to such extent that He was willing to lay down His life that those who deserve hell might have life and have it abundantly.

Love is the subject here, *not* proof of the Deity of Christ Jesus. We could never have a part in His supreme sacrifice — the atonement, the expiatory aspect of His death. This has to do with the *exemplary* aspect of the death of the Lord Jesus Christ — love in action: "HE LAID DOWN HIS LIFE FOR US."

The word *"for"* presents an interesting study. Greek authorities tell us that there are two Greek prepositions translated "for," but they have entirely different meanings. For instance, in I Timothy 2:6 we read that Christ "gave Himself *a ransom for ALL.*" Then in Matthew 20:28 we read that He gave His life *"a ransom for MANY."* These two Scriptures seem to be in flat contradiction to each other, but they are not. Paul said "for ALL," Jesus said "for MANY." Which is it? Did Jesus die for ALL? or did He die for MANY? Actually, He died for *both* — He died for all and He died for many. In I Timothy 2:6, "for" in literal translation from the Greek means *"on behalf of."* Thus, Jesus died *on behalf of ALL.* God so loved THE WORLD, Jesus is the propitiation for the sins of the whole WORLD.

In Matthew 20:28 the literal translation of "for" means *"instead of."* Christ died *instead of MANY* — not instead of "all." We know that not *all* will be saved, yet Jesus gave Himself *a ransom for all.* It is not God's will that *any* perish, but that ALL come to repentance. The invitation is to "whosoever," but we know that not all will come to Him. Therefore, Christ died instead of "many" — the many who will accept Him and will not die; they will live because HE lives. He gave Himself for the whole world, He died that *all* might live; but we must receive His finished work in order to have life, and not all will receive it. Those who refuse to receive Him must pay the debt themselves.

We might illustrate the two "for's" in this manner: Suppose a man is travelling along the highway in the wee hours of morning, and sees a house engulfed in flames with a family of mother, father, and five children asleep inside. The traveller rushes up to the house, beats on the door until the mother is awakened; she screams, the traveller rushes in and picking her up bodily carries her from the burning house. He then rushes back into the house, picks up the baby and carries it out to the mother. He then returns to the burning house, rescues another child, then another; but on his fifth trip into the flames he drops, overcome by smoke, and is burned to death along with the rest of the family. He saw the danger, he gave his life *on behalf* of ALL the occupants of the house, but he only gave his life *instead of* the four he managed to save. He died *on behalf* of those who perished in the flames, but he did not die *in their stead.* That is, perhaps, a crude illustration of the verse we are now studying, but it will help us to understand that "hereby perceive we the love of God, because He laid down His life *on our behalf.*"

"*And we ought to lay down our lives for the brethren.*" Does this mean that we should *die* for the brethren as Jesus died on the cross? It does not. It means that we should lay our lives down in *living* for them! The Greek translated "laid down" (as having to do with Jesus' dying on the cross) signifies that the act was done *once,* for *all,* at a definite, specific time and moment, and that it was *finished,* never to be repeated: "This Man, after He had offered *one sacrifice for sins for ever,* sat down on the right hand of God" (Heb. 10:12).

However, the Greek translated "lay down" (concerning believers laying down their lives for the brethren) is in another

tense, signifying — *not* "once for all," but *a continual process.*
Jesus sacrificed His life *once*, never to be sacrificed again. Christians are called upon to present themselves a *living* sacrifice
(Rom. 12:1). We are not to be dead sacrifices; we are to live
for others.

"IF there be therefore any consolation in Christ, if any comfort of love, if any fellowship of the Spirit, if any bowels and
mercies, fulfil ye my joy, that ye be likeminded, having the same
love, being of one accord, of one mind. Let nothing be done
through strife or vainglory; but in lowliness of mind let each
esteem other better than themselves. Look not every man on
his own things, but every man also on the things of others.

"Let this mind be in you, which was also in Christ Jesus: Who,
being in the form of God, thought it not robbery to be equal
with God: but made Himself of no reputation, and took upon
Him the form of a servant, and was made in the likeness of
men: and being found in fashion as a man, He humbled Himself, and became obedient unto death, even the death of the
cross. Wherefore God also hath highly exalted Him, and given
Him a name which is above every name: that at the name of
Jesus every knee should bow, of things in heaven, and things in
earth, and things under the earth; and that every tongue should
confess that Jesus Christ is Lord, to the glory of God the Father.

"Wherefore, my beloved, as ye have always obeyed, not as
in my presence only, but now much more in my absence, work
out your own salvation with fear and trembling. For it is God
which worketh in you both to will and to do of His good pleasure. Do all things without murmurings and disputings: that ye
may be blameless and harmless, the sons of God, without rebuke, in the midst of a crooked and perverse nation, among
whom ye shine as lights in the world; holding forth the word of
life; that I may rejoice in the day of Christ, that I have not run
in vain, neither laboured in vain. Yea, and if I be offered upon
the sacrifice and service of your faith, I joy, and rejoice with you
all. For the same cause also do ye joy, and rejoice with me"
(Phil. 2:1-18).

Jesus said, "Whosoever shall give to drink unto one of these
little ones a cup of cold water only in the name of a disciple,

verily I say unto you, he shall in no wise lose his reward"
(Matt. 10:42).

"And be ye kind one to another, tenderhearted, forgiving one
another, even as God for Christ's sake hath forgiven you" (Eph.
4:32).

Love in Action

Verses 17 and 18: "But whoso hath this world's good, and
seeth his brother have need, and shutteth up his bowels of compassion from him, how dwelleth the love of God in him? My
little children, let us not love in word, neither in tongue; but in
deed and in truth."

The eyes of Jesus never overlooked one in need. Since believers possess Divine nature we should walk in His steps and
see through His eyes. Therefore, a true believer should see the
need of a brother.

Jesus nerver performed one miracle to supply any need of His
own; He had no house in which to live, he had no bed in which
to sleep. He said to His disciples, "The foxes have holes, and
the birds of the air have nests; but the Son of man hath not
where to lay His head" (Matt. 8:20; Luke 9:58). Yet He
stepped over all the laws of nature *when someone else was in
need* (Matt. 14:25; John 20:19). It was the same Jesus who
stepped into the lion's den with Daniel and delivered a brother
in need (Dan. 6:22). This same Jesus walked in the fiery furnace with Shadrach, Meshach, and Abednego, and brought
them forth untouched by the flames. Three brethren were cast
into the furnace, but the king saw *four* walking there, and he
said, "They have no hurt, and the form of the fourth is like the
Son of God!" (Dan. 3:25). Thank God for Hebrews 13:8:
"Jesus Christ the same yesterday, and today, and for ever!"

Jesus was never too busy, never too tired, never too engrossed, to minister to a needy individual. He sat by Jacob's
well, waiting for the disciples to return from the city where
they had gone to buy bread. He was hungry and weary; yet
when they returned from the city He did not eat. He had
bread to eat that they knew nothing of: *He was leading a needy
soul into the door of salvation.* Read the account in John 4:1-42.

As Jesus passed through Jericho, blind Bartimaeus cried out,

"Thou son of David, have mercy on me!" The multitudes surrounding the Lord urged the blind beggar to hold his peace. Surely a busy man like Jesus had no time for such as he. But Jesus stopped and commanded Bartimaeus to be brought to Him, He gave him sight, and immediately he followed Jesus (Mark 10:46-52). How many, many times in His busy life on earth Jesus stopped to help someone in need! And there are so many needy around us today — people with physical needs, spiritual needs, mental needs, people in circumstances which we could make much better — but we are too busy and too unconcerned to help them.

There are many *church members* who are too occupied with their church work to help precious souls in need, souls for whom Jesus died. Often we are too busy to help our Christian brethren, those who are members of the body of Christ. We see their needs — but we have no time to help them.

Luke 10:30-37 records the parable of the Good Samaritan. Read it and study it carefully. It tells of the man who journeyed from Jerusalem to Jericho and fell among thieves. They robbed him, wounded him, and left him by the roadside, half dead. A priest and a Levite, in turn, passed that way, looked at the wounded man, but passed him by. Then came a Samaritan, and seeing the unfortunate one, he had compassion on him, bound up his wounds, put him on his own beast and took him to an inn. There he gave the innkeeper money and instructions to care for the man, and said he, "Whatsoever thou spendest more, when I come again, I will repay thee." That is the Christian spirit. From the way this parable is set forth, it seems likely that the wounded man was a total stranger to the Samaritan — a stranger who was unattractive, bloody, and naked; but his helpless condition touched the heart of the Samaritan and caused him to have compassion for the unfortunate man. We must remember that *Jesus* loved US when we were yet unlovely. God had compassion on us and willingly laid down His life that we might live.

If we profess to be Christian and yet withhold from a needy brother that which we have that would help him, if we do not have compassion toward him, then we dare not profess that the love of God abides in us.

Verse 18 gives the rule for love in action: We are not to love in word, but in deed and in truth. There are occasions when a minister visits widows where there are children in need, and after a pastoral call the minister bows in prayer and asks God to supply the need of that family, when at that time there are hundreds — perhaps thousands — of dollars of God's money in the bank to the credit of the big church with the tall steeple! The parishioners in that church sing, "O, how I love Jesus!" but they love Him in word only — not in deed and in truth. The Bible admonition is, "Be ye *doers* of the Word, and not hearers only, deceiving your own selves" (James 1:22).

Shall we ask ourselves how WE measure up according to the Bible rule of genuine Christianity? Do we love the brethren as we are commanded to love them? Are we ready and willing to help those in need — or are we too self-centered, too occupied with what we are doing, to take the time to render service to others? If we have become so engrossed in our own affairs that we are hardened toward the needs of others, may God pity us and awaken us to our duty as true believers.

The Believer Has Assurance

Verses 19-21: "And hereby we know that we are of the truth, and shall assure our hearts before Him. For if our heart condemn us, God is greater than our heart, and knoweth all things. Beloved, if our heart condemn us not, then have we confidence toward God."

The original here could have been translated, "hereby we know that we are truly HIS." The *"hereby"* points back to what we have just studied. We know that God loved us, because *He laid down His life for us*. If we know that we love the brethren — in deed and not in word only — then we know that we are of the turth; and if we are of the truth we are *truly HIS*, we are truly saved. And thus we "assure our hearts before Him."

"If our heart condemn us. . . ." The Word of God warns, "Keep thy heart with all diligence; for out of it are the issues of life" (Prov. 4:23). If we are born again we have a new heart and Jesus abides within. Our heart then does NOT condemn us, but rather, it *assures* us. If you cannot get *your own heart* to testify to you that you are a child of God, you had better get

alone upon your knees before an open Bible and search the Word until you have assurance.

"*God is greater than our heart, and knoweth all things.*" We find a good example of this in Peter's experience just before the crucifixion. Jesus said to Him, "Simon, Simon, behold, Satan hath desired to have you, that he may sift you as wheat: But I have prayed for thee, that thy faith fail not . . . And (Peter) said unto Him, *Lord, I am ready to go with thee, both into prison, and to death!* And He said, I tell thee, Peter, the cock shall not crow this day, before that thou shalt thrice deny that thou knowest me!" (Luke 22:31-34 in part). You know the sad story: Peter not only *denied* the Lord, he cursed and swore that he had never *known* Him.

After the resurrection, when Peter and the other disciples had fished all night without catching any fish, Jesus prepared breakfast for them; and in that after-breakfast interview between the Lord and Peter, Jesus asked him, "Do you love me?" Peter replied, "Yea, Lord; thou knowest that I love thee." The second time Jesus asked, "Peter, do you love me?" And Peter answered, "Yea, Lord; thou knowest that I love thee." Jesus asked for the *third* time, "Simon, son of Jonah, lovest thou me?" And Peter, grieved that the Lord should ask him the third time, replied, "Lord, *thou knowest ALL things*; thou *knowest* that I love thee!" (John 21:15-17).

Jesus DID know all things, and He knew Peter's heart, just as He had known before the crucifixion that Peter would deny Him; but He was driving home to the impetuous disciple the fact that he was just an ordinary sinner saved by grace, and that he must be on guard at all times, realizing the power of Satan — the same devil who had caused him to thrice deny his Lord.

Beloved, I wonder if *we* really love Jesus? Are we feeding His lambs and His sheep, as He instructed Peter to do? Are we really serving Him as we give our bodies, a living sacrifice? Do our hearts condemn us not? Or do our hearts *condemn* us because of our selfishness and our unconcern?

"*If our heart condemn us not, then have we confidence toward God.*" Let me warn you that the only person who can safely listen to his own heart is the truly born again, blood washed believer. In Acts 23:1, the Apostle Paul gave testimony before his brethren. He said, "Men and brethren, *I have lived in all good conscience before God* until this day" — and yet before his conversion he persecuted the Church and consented to the death of such men as Stephen. In his testimony before King Agrippa he said, "I verily thought with myself, that I ought to do many things contrary to the name of Jesus of Nazareth. Which thing I also did in Jerusalem: and many of the saints did I shut up in prison, having received authority from the chief priests; and when they were put to death, I gave my voice against them. And I punished them oft in every synagogue, and compelled them to blaspheme; and being exceedingly mad against them, I persecuted them even unto strange cities" (Acts 26:9-11).

It is easy to see that before Paul's conversion, his conscience did not guide him aright. It was so seared that he could persecute Jesus in the belief that he was doing God a service. But in Acts 24:16, after he was born again, he said, "Herein do I exercise myself, to have always a conscience void of offence toward God, and toward men." Man can sear his conscience, he can silence it and walk on it until it is no longer sensitive. A born again, dedicated, Spirit-filled believer has a *sensitive* conscience — one of the greatest blessings in a Christian's life; but a senstitive conscience must live in the sunshine of God's love, breathe the breath of the Holy Spirit, bathe in the cleansing Word of God, and walk in the steps of the Saviour.

Dear reader, what about *your* heart? Have you had a conscientious talk with yourself lately? You should. You should ask your heart some very personal questions — such as, "Do I believe with the *heart,* or with the *head?* Do I *love* with the heart — in *deed,* or simply in *words* that are forgotten as soon as they are spoken?" Ask your heart if the Holy Spirit abides there. Is your heart *sealed* by the Holy Spirit? Does your heart *assure* you that you are a child of God? or does your heart condemn you?

It is good practice to ask yourself these questions often. Remember, Man looks on the outward appearance, but God looks on the heart; so "keep thine heart with all diligence; for out of it are the issues of life" (Prov. 4:23).

God Answers Prayer

Verse 22: "And whatsoever we ask, we receive of Him, because we keep His commandments, and do those things that are pleasing in His sight."

James tells us, Ye lust, and have not: ye kill, and desire to have, and cannot obtain: ye fight and war, *yet ye have not, because ye ask not. Ye ask, and receive not, because ye ask amiss, that ye may consume it upon your lusts*" (James 4:2, 3).

Jesus said, "If ye abide in me, and my words abide in you, ye shall ask what ye will, and it shall be done unto you" (John 15:7).

I wonder just how much true praying there is today in the average assembly? God promises to answer our prayers if we keep His words, if His words abide in us and we abide in Him, walking in His steps and doing those things that are pleasing in His sight; but if we ask in order to consume what we receive upon our own lust, to gratify our own desires and satisfy the flesh, then we need not hope to receive an answer to prayer.

We must recognize *the Bible teaching* concerning prayer. Many times we do not know *how* to pray nor what to pray *for*; but every born again believer possesses the Holy Spirit, and the Spirit helps us in prayer:

"Likewise the Spirit also helpeth our infirmities: for we know not what we should pray for as we ought: but the Spirit itself maketh intercession for us with groanings which cannot be uttered. And He that searcheth the hearts knoweth what is the mind of the Spirit, because He maketh intercession for the saints according to the will of God" (Rom. 8:26, 27).

We receive whatsoever we ask if we *"keep His commandments and do those things that are pleasing in His sight."* Does that mean that we must keep the Ten Commandments perfectly or God will not hear our prayers? Verse 23 answers:

Verse 23: "And this is His commandment: That we should believe on the name of His Son Jesus Christ, and love one another, as He gave us commandment."

John 6:1-14 records Jesus' miraculous feeding of the five thousand from the five loaves and two fishes. After that, a great multitude followed Him; but He said to them, "Verily, verily, I say unto you, Ye seek me, not because ye saw the miracles, but because ye did eat of the loaves, and were filled. Labour not for the meat which perisheth, but for that meat which endureth unto everlasting life, which the Son of man shall give unto you: for Him hath God the Father sealed.

"Then said they unto Him, *What shall we do, that we might work the works of God?* Jesus answered and said unto them, *This is the work of God, that ye believe on Him whom He* hath sent" (John 6:26-29).

When we believe on Jesus we are created in Him *unto good works,* and we do good works because He abides within us. Therefore, to work the works of God and do the will of God is to believe on Jesus.

Lest believers suppose that they are to keep the law of Moses (the Ten Commandments) John explains what he means by "*commandment.*" He says, "*THIS is His commandment*: First, that we believe on the name of Jesus Christ; second, that we love one another." Notice that the first part of the commandment is the source for the second part. No one can love as he should love until he believes on the name of the Son of God. The second part of the commandment is the sign in the believer that he has obeyed the first.

Let us notice the answer Jesus gave the Pharisees in Matthew 22:34-40: "When the Pharisees had heard that He had put the Sadducees to silence, they were gathered together. Then one of them, which was a lawyer, asked Him a question, tempting Him, and saying, Master, which is the great commandment in the law? Jesus said unto him, Thou shalt love the Lord thy God with all thy heart, and with all thy soul, and with all thy mind. This is the first and great commandment. And the second is like unto it, Thou shalt love thy neighbour as thyself. On these two commandments hang all the law and the prophets."

According to the verses just quoted, to love the Lord and to love one's neighbor as the Bible *teaches* us to love is to fulfill all the law and the prophets. "Therefore by the deeds of the law there shall no flesh be justified in His sight: for by the law is the knowledge of sin" (Rom. 3:20). "For Christ is the end of the law for righteousness to eve, one that believeth" (Rom. 10:4).

Verse 24: "And he that keepeth His commandments dwelleth in Him, and He in him. And hereby we know that He abideth in us, by the Spirit which He hath given us."

Now see what we have: When we believe on the name of God's Son Jesus Christ, when we love one another as He gave us commandment, we then have the assurance that we dwell in Him, He dwells in us, *we live together with Him.* There is a beautiful picture here, of two dwelling together: We get to know those with whom we live. We know their likes and dislikes. We know the things they enjoy doing, and the things they do not like to do. In like manner, we come to know the Lord as we should know Him through dwelling in Him by faith, by living in His presence as the Holy Spirit abides within our hearts. Through the miracle of God's grace that brought His love down to man, He has allowed us the glorious privilege of intimacy with Him — the believer in God, God in the believer (Rom. 8:1; Col; 1:27; 3:3). We have the mind of Christ (I Cor. 2:16).

"Hereby we KNOW that He abideth in us, by the Spirit which He hath given us." Here again is stated the fact of assurance. There is no such thing as salvation apart from assurance; it is an impossibility to be a born again believer and not know it. We KNOW that God lives in us by the Spirit which He has given us.

Since we live in God and He lives in us, we have the promise, "Whatsoever we ask, we receive of Him." God help us to pray for each other, that we may come to the place where we can understand the things God has made it possible for us to understand, the things He will do for us and give to us if we will only meet the Divine conditions that bring definite answers to prayer.

I JOHN — Chapter 4

1. Beloved, believe not every spirit, but try the spirits whether they are of God; because many false prophets are gone out into the world.

2. Hereby know ye the Spirit of God: Every spirit that confesseth that Jesus Christ is come in the flesh is of God.

3. And every spirit that confesseth not that Jesus Christ is come in the flesh is not of God: and this is that spirit of anti-christ, whereof ye have heard that it should come; and even now already is it in the world.

4. Ye are of God, little children, and have overcome them: because greater is he that is in you, than he that is in the world.

5. They are of the world: therefore speak they of the world, and the world heareth them.

6. We are of God: he that knoweth God heareth us; he that is not of God heareth not us. Hereby know we the spirit of truth, and the spirit of error.

7. Beloved, let us love one another; for love is of God; and everyone that loveth is born of God, and knoweth God.

8. He that loveth not knoweth not God; for God is love.

9. In this was manifested the love of God toward us, because that God sent his only begotten Son into the world, that we might live through him.

10. Herein is love, not that we loved God, but that he loved us, and sent his Son to be the propitiation for our sins.

11. Beloved, if God hath loved us, we ought also to love one another.

12. No man hath seen God at any time. If we love one another, God dwelleth in us, and his love is perfected in us.

13. Hereby know we that we dwell in him, and he in us, because he hath given us of his Spirit.

14. And we have seen and do testify that the Father sent the Son to be the Saviour of the world.

15. Whosoever shall confess that Jesus is the Son of God, God dwelleth in him, and he in God.

16. And we have known and believed the love that God hath to us. God is love; and he that dwelleth in love dwelleth in God, and God in him.

17. Herein is love made perfect, that we may have boldness in the day of judgment: because as he is, so are we in this world.

18. There is no fear in love; but perfect love casteth out fear; because fear hath torment. He that feareth is not made perfect in love.

19.   We love him, because he first loved us.

20.   If a man say, I love God, and hateth his brother, he is a liar: for he that loveth not his brother whom he hath seen, how can he love God whom he hath not seen?

21.   And this commandment have we from him. That he who loveth God love his brother also.

In this chapter, two principal subjects are discussed:

First, the Divine method by which we may determine that we have the Spirit of God and how we may recognize the spirit of delusion. The believer is sure God dwells in him by the Spirit God has given him. John warns that the believer cannot trust every spirit, for even the spirit of Satan and of Antichrist can *profess* to be true to the Word of God. It is important that Christians be able to distinguish between the Spirit of God and the spirit of error, for these ministers of the devil can speak words that will lead many to believe that they truly ARE ministers of the Gospel. Satan can quote more Scripture than most church members, and sad but so, most teachers of error know more about the Bible than many born again believers know. They study to prove their points of error, whereas true believers study to feed the soul.

The evidence John gives of proof that one possesses the Holy Spirit and not the spirit of error is that the Holy Spirit *readily confesses* that Jesus Christ came in the flesh, that He was born of a virgin, and that He was God incarnate. They who deny this cardinal doctrine of Christianity have the spirit of Antichrist. We who are truly born again should praise God for the Holy Spirit within us (ch. 2, vv. 20, 27), the Spirit who recognizes the spirit of Antichrist and directs us so that we will not be led astray, we will not listen to false teachers.

The second principal subject in this chapter is the duty of the believer concerning love, its power and its influence. This subject begins with verse 7 and continues through the rest of the chapter.

One need not read very far in this epistle to discover that love is a favorite subject of the inspired writer, John "the beloved disciple." Love has its origin in God, for God IS love. Therefore, if God is in us, WE love. God did not love in word only; He

148

proved His love by giving His Son to die for us; and since He loved us so much, we ought to love one another. Love in action between believers gives true evidence that God dwells in us. Love will give us boldness and confidence in the day of judgment when we stand before God. Love removes all fear, and those who are afraid to live, afraid to die, afraid to face God, afraid of what the future holds, *are not born again.* God does not dwell in the fearful person, nor does the fearful person dwell in God. Revelation 21:8 gives a list of the inhabitants of hell, and first on the list is "the fearful." *Sin* brings fear, but love and salvation remove fear.

We love God because He first loved us. Had it not been for God's grace that allowed Jesus to taste death for every man, we would never have known true love. Also, a man cannot love God and hate his brother. He who hates his brother has not been born of God. The chapter closes with the commandment that he who loves God must love his brother also. It should not be difficult for believers to love one another.

Warning against False Teachers and False Spirits

Verse 1: "Beloved, believe not every spirit, but try the spirits whether they are of God: because many false prophets are gone out into the world."

There are many false spirits in the world today — surely many more than in the early church. There are more species of religion today than ever before — and please notice I said *"religion."* There is *only ONE true religion,* and that is Christianity; all others are man-made. This country has entirely too many teachers and preachers of false doctrines, those who take great joy in using great swelling words and beautiful phrases to make an impression on the listener and lead him into the way of heresy. There are many precious people who are weak, they have not been fully instructed in the things of God. They are saved, but they have not studied nor been instructed, and were it not for the Holy Spirit within them they would be led into gross error. We thank God for I Peter 2:6: "Wherefore also it is contained in the Scripture, Behold, I lay in Sion a chief corner stone, elect, precious: and he that believeth on Him shall not be confounded."

But we need to hear the solemn warning concerning the spirits, because "*many false prophets are gone out into the world.*" If that was true in John's day, think of today! Beloved, there are literally tens of thousands of false prophets abroad in the land. Jesus declared to His disciples that the outstanding sign of His return would be an abundance of deceivers and false prophets. He said, "Take heed that no man deceive you. For many shall come in my name, saying, I am Christ; and shall deceive many . . . and many false prophets shall rise, and shall deceive many" (Matt. 24:4, 5, 11).

Marks of the False Teacher

Verses 2 and 3: "Hereby know ye the Spirit of God: Every spirit that confesseth that Jesus Christ is come in the flesh is of God: And every spirit that confesseth not that Jesus Christ is come in the flesh is NOT of God: and this is that spirit of antichrist, whereof ye have heard that it should come; and even now already is it in the world."

What is the acid test whereby we may know the true Spirit from the false? How can we recognize the true minister, the true Bible teacher? The Word of God answers: "*Every spirit that confesseth that Jesus Christ is come in the flesh is of God.*" Does that mean every person who confesses that *a person named Jesus Christ* was born, lived and died, a historical figure like Herod, Pilate, or the Caesars? No, that is not the meaning here. There are many historians and scholars who, though unbelievers, teach that such a man as Jesus Christ *lived* — but they do not believe ·in His Deity, His Incarnation.

Great Bible scholars who have spent their lives in the study of the Greek language tell us that this phrase *should* read, "Every spirit that confesseth that JESUS IS CHRIST come in the flesh is of God." Notice the difference? "Jesus Christ *is come*" is not the same as "Jesus is CHRIST come."

In Matthew 1:18-25, we learn that Joseph and Mary were "espoused" (engaged to be married), and Joseph discovered that Mary was to become a mother. Under the Mosaic law (Deut. 22:20, 21) a young woman who was found to have lost her virginity was commanded to be stoned; but Joseph loved Mary, and it was his intention to put her away "privily," that is, with no publicity in the matter. "But while he thought on these things, behold, the angel of the Lord appeared unto him in a dream, saying, Joseph, thou son of David, fear not to take unto thee Mary thy wife: *for that which is conceived in her is of the Holy Ghost.* And she shall bring forth a son, and thou shalt call His name JESUS: for He shall save His people from their sins."

"Jesus" means *Saviour. "Jesus"* is the name of our Saviour in human form; *Christ* is His Divine name, the "Anointed One." He was God's Christ before He became man's Jesus. He was with God in the beginning — Christ, Messiah, Anointed One, Divine One. Thus our present Scripture becomes much clearer: Every spirit that confesses that *Jesus is Christ come in the flesh,* also confesses that Jesus is God, the Divine Son of God, born of a virgin. Every spirit that confesses that Jesus is Christ come in the flesh confesses that God was in Christ, and therefore every spirit that confesses that Jesus is Christ come in the flesh confesses His Deity, His Incarnation — and this is the first and fundamental test of every spirit that claims to be of God. The question is, "What think ye of *Christ?* Whose Son is He?" (Matt. 22:42).

Oh yes, there are many who are considered to be great men — great teachers, great preachers, and even evangelists — who say a lot of nice things about Jesus. They declare that He was unique, extraordinary, the most unusual man who ever lived. They confess that He was a great teacher, a great healer, they even go so far as to confess that He did unusual and inexplainable things; but a person can believe all those things about Jesus and still be lost and eternally damned when he departs this life! To believe that Jesus was a great *man* is not enough. To believe that He was unique in His ministry and indescribably great in His teaching and healing is not enough. In order to be saved, we must confess that Jesus is God's Christ come in the flesh. If He was NOT the Divine Son of God, then He was history's greatest hoax, the world's greatest imposter, the biggest liar who ever lived, and He committed the greatest act of blasphemy ever committed, because He *claimed* to be from God, equal *with* God, yea, the only begotten SON of God. He said "I and my Father are *one.*" Jesus was either God in flesh — or the greatest counterfeit who ever lived. He was either The Truth, or the greatest of lies. The most absurd thing any man can do is to step behind the sacred desk, read the Scriptures concerning Jesus, and then deny His Incarnation and His virgin birth. Our Jesus IS God's Christ come in the flesh, and now there is a Man seated at the right hand of the Majesty on high, and that Man's name is Jesus (I Tim. 2:5).

Verse 3 clearly states that if a spirit does NOT confess that Jesus is Christ come in the flesh, that spirit is not of God but of the devil; it is the spirit of Antichrist. We have been living in "the last days" ever since the crucifixion of the Lord Jesus Christ, and these are truly the *last days* of "the last days." Antichrists (plural) are present, and one day immediately after the Rapture of the Church, THE Antichrist will appear. He has many names. In Daniel 8:23 he is called " a king of fierce countenance." In the New Testament he is "the son of perdition" (John 17:12; II Thess. 2:3), "the man of sin" (II Thess. 2:3), the Antichrist. *His spirit* is already here, and HE will come after the Church is taken out of this world to be with the Lord in the air. There are now *many* antichrists — false teachers, false preachers, men who stand behind the sacred desk but in reality are called of Satan, ordained and commissioned by Satan and they will spend eternity in the lake of fire *with* Satan:

"For such are false apostles, deceitful workers, transforming themselves into the apostles of Christ. And no marvel; for Satan himself is transformed into an angel of light. Therefore it is no great thing if his ministers also be transformed as the ministers of righteousness; whose end shall be according to their works" (II Cor. 11:13-15).

It is dangerous and costly for believers to support a minister who denies the Deity of Christ — His Incarnation and virgin birth. To support such a man is to support God's enemy, and believers who are guilty of so doing will lose their reward. John warns about this in II John 7-11. He tells us to be careful lest we lose "those things which we have wrought." This refers to stewardship, not to salvation; we do not "wrought" *salvation*, it is God's free gift. But our stewardship brings reward, and if we knowingly support a minister or teacher of false doctrine, we will lose our reward.

There is no use to claim ignorance in this respect and say that we do not know whether or not our pastor is a fundamental Bible preacher. If we are born again we DO know whether he preaches the truth or not. The Word of God *declares* that we know, by the Holy Spirit who dwells within the believer.

Believers Are Overcomers

Verse 4: "Ye are of God, little children, and have overcome them: because greater is He that is in you, than he that is in the world."

Beloved, it is a tremendous thing to be a child of God. When one exercises faith in the shed blood and finished work of Jesus Christ, instantaneously that person is born of God, and instantaneously he takes up his dwelling IN God, and God dwells in *him*. That very moment he becomes partaker of Divine nature, possessor of the Holy Ghost, seated in the heavenlies in Christ Jesus, sealed with the Holy Ghost until the day of redemption.

In this verse we have assurance that the relationship between the believer and God guarantees victory. The believer belongs to God, God belongs to the believer. He is our Father, we are His children, and Jesus is our Saviour, our elder brother. We are heirs of God, joint-heirs with Jesus. We may sometimes think that we are standing alone. There may be times when it seems that we are the only person in our community who is truly saved, and therefore we think we face the opposition of the enemy alone; but beloved, be not discouraged, for every believer *together with God* forms a majority over any crowd.

"Ye . . . have overcome them." The Word does not say, "You *will* overcome," or "You *may* overcome IF. . . ." The statement is clear and understandable: "Ye HAVE (already) overcome." We are more than conquerors through Him: "There hath no temptation taken you but such as is common to man: but God is faithful, who will not suffer you to be tempted above that ye are able; but will with the temptation also make a way to escape, that ye may be able to bear it" (I Cor. 10:13).

Guaranteed victory is ours because *"greater is He that is in you than he that is in the world."* The Holy Spirit within us is greater than the spirit of Antichrist in the world around us. God in us is greater than the devil and all the demons of hell combined. The demons have always recognized Jesus as God's Christ, but demons cannot be saved. James tells us that the demons believe and tremble (James 2:19), they knew who He was, they did not deny His virgin birth. The devil has more respect for Jesus Christ than some *preachers* do! We cannot conquer Satan in our own power, but Jesus met him face to face and defeated him. He said "Get thee hence, Satan," and that ended it. Satan obeyed and moved on. Beloved, never go to the door when Satan knocks. Call on Jesus — and He will send Satan away.

World-Marks of False Teachers

Verses 5 and 6: "They are of the world: therefore speak they of the world, and the world heareth them. We are of God: he that knoweth God heareth us; he that is not of God heareth not us. Hereby know we the spirit of truth, and the spirit of error."

False teachers are branded. John passes over from the spirit of Antichrist to the individuals in whom the different spirits are made manifest: *"Hereby know we the Spirit of truth, and the spirit of error."* Bear in mind that *"we"* in this epistle means John the Beloved and all truly born again believers; and true believers are not led about by every wind of doctrine, they are not confounded and confused because they have the Holy Spirit, and He immediately recognizes false doctrine and false teachers. If you cannot tell a true man of God from a preacher of error, my advice to you is that you check up on your salvation experience. The devil may have slipped you a counterfeit, because born again believers are not confused by teachers of false doctrine.

"The world heareth them." The masses have always gone after error, following the line of least resistance and going after things that are most spectacular and entertaining. The only time Jesus ever had thousands following Him was when He fed them with the loaves and fishes, and the very next day He told them that they were following Him for another serving

of fish and bread, *physical food,* and not because of the power demonstrated in the miracle. Certainly great crowds do not mean that a man is false — some of the greatest preachers the world has ever known were popular with crowds; but you cannot say, "Surely this man is *God's* man because thousands go to hear him." You cannot judge a minister, teacher, or evangelist on the basis of the crowds who follow him.

The *world* hears the false preacher because he preaches to *please* the world. He is OF the world, his standards and practices of life are of the world. Some churches in America today should be forced to take down the steeple, take out the stained glass windows, and put a "Club" sign over the door. Many modern churches have dances, parties, bingo games, and some even serve beer and cocktails at their parties! Since they have more of the world than they have of the Bible and things of God, we must conclude that they certainly are OF the world and therefore "the world heareth them."

True believers will not be roped in by these worldlings, these ministers of the devil and synagogues of Satan, because *"we are of God."* True ministers ARE of God. They are called of God, ordained of God, empowered by God, and they preach *the Word of God.*

"He that knoweth God heareth us." True believers listen to God's minister because the Holy Spirit in the heart of the minister witnesses to the heart of the believer, and thus the believer recognizes the true minister as he preaches the Word of God.

"He that is NOT of God heareth not us." Unbelievers do not hear God's minister; that is why we have so many church divisions and fusses in the assemblies today. When God's man preaches God's Word from the pulpit in the average church today, you may rest assured that there will be friction in the pew. Unbelievers and hypocrites cannot endure sound doctrine for more than a short time, and then the demons within them declare war on God's preacher.

I have often said that a church that has been going on for years without any trouble or dissension is a *dead* church and God's Word has not been preached from the pulpit. Wherever Jesus spoke while He was on earth, He divided the people. He was the greatest Divider of men the world has ever known.

Some said, "He is of God." Others said, "He has a devil." Some said, "He works His miracles through the power of God." Others said, "He does it through the power of Beelzebub." Some said, "Surely this Man is the Son of God." Others said "He is the product of fornication!" Some believed and loved Him, others did *not* believe, and hated Him. Jesus said, "If they hated me, they will hate those who follow me." You may rest assured that if HE could not please all the people, God's minister today cannot please them all.

"The Word of God is quick, and powerful, and sharper than any twoedged sword, piercing even to the dividing asunder of soul and spirit, and of the joints and marrow, and is a discerner of the thoughts and intents of the heart" (Heb. 4:12). The Word of God is "like a hammer that breaketh the rock in pieces" (Jer. 23:29). The light of the Word exposes the lives of men, and unbelievers do not like to be exposed. Therefore the world does not hear God's man. The person who rejects Christ will keep quiet for awhile, but eventually he will rebel against the pure Gospel and against the true minister of God.

But the real man of God will not let this cause him to pack up and leave town. He will just tighten up his belt, roll up his sleeves, and in humble submission to God he will pray, "Lord, you load my Gospel guns and I will pull the trigger!" God's Word is a fire (I Cor. 3:13) and when you build a fire around a hypocrite he will either get *right* or get *out*. God's man knows the remedy for hypocrisy and unbelief when trouble starts in the local assembly, and God pity a preacher who will let a deacon board run him out of the church where God put him to serve!

"Hereby know we the Spirit of truth, and the spirit of error." In I Corinthians 2:12-16 Paul said, "Now we have received, not the spirit of the world, but the Spirit which is of God; that we might know the things that are freely given to us of God. Which things also we speak, not in the words which man's wisdom teacheth, but which the Holy Ghost teacheth; comparing spiritual things with spiritual. But the natural man receiveth not the things of the Spirit of God: for they are foolishness unto him: neither can he know them, because they are spiritually discerned. But he that is spiritual judgeth all things, yet he himself is judged of no man. For who hath known the mind of the

Lord, that he may instruct Him? But we have the mind of Christ."

God's preachers are not worldlings. They are godly men, citizens of another world. The Holy Spirit is their Guide, God's holy Word is their textbook, and God empowers their message; but the world laughs at them. Paul said, "We are fools for Christ's sake . . . we are despised . . . we are made as the filth of the world, and are the offscouring of all things . . " (I Cor. 4:10-13 in part).

The minister who does not go along with the crowd, fill the church with amusements and put a cookstove and cafeteria in the basement, is classified as "old-fashioned," preaching a "butcher house" religion, but the Bible message is the *only* message that will save souls and make men ready for heaven. God's men preach the Word, they are instant in season, out of season, reproving, rebuking, exhorting (II Tim. 4:2). And "he that knoweth God" hears God's preacher.

When you hear a minister or an evangelist invite the converts in a meeting to unite with "the church of their choice," you may rest assured that he knows neither the Scriptures nor the power of God. True Bible preachers urge those whom they win for Christ to join a church where God's man preaches God's Word. Some ministers today give this invitation: "Join the church of your choice. We are all striving for the same place, working to the same end." Such statements will never fall from the lips of born again, God-ordained ministers of the Word. We are NOT all striving for the same place, we are not all *going* to the same place. Believers are going to heaven, but we are not "striving" to go there; we are going there because we are *trusting*, not because we are striving. We are not all working toward the same end. *Salvation* is not of works; it is by grace through faith — the gift of God.

True Believers Are Born of God

Verses 7-10: "Beloved, let us love one another: for love is of God; and every one that loveth is born of God, and knoweth God. He that loveth not knoweth not God; for God is love. In this was manifested the love of God toward us, because that God sent His only begotten Son into the world, that we might live through Him. Herein is love, not that we loved God, but that He loved us, and sent His Son to be the propitiation for our sins."

Here is introduced the subject of *love*, a subject which occupies the rest of our present chapter. Certainly the Holy Spirit could have found no one through whom to speak on this subject who could have known more about it (insofar as man's knowledge is concerned) then John the beloved disciple. We know from the Scriptures that John displayed a remarkable affection for the Lord Jesus Christ (John 13:23; 21:20).

"Beloved, let us (true believers) *love one another."* Notice the opening word here — *"beloved,"* speaking of the family of God, the true Church. Why should Christians love one another? *"For love is of God."* True love originates in God. No person except a born again child of God knows true love in its fulness, because all true love has its origin in God. When we manifest true love, we show that we have truly been born of the Spirit, for "the *fruit* of the Spirit is love."

"Love is of God," and the more we love in truth, the more like God we become. Envy, strife, wrath, hatred, malice, selfishness — these are fruits that find their source in the devil, not in God. God is love; He is not the originator of hatred, strife, or envy.

"Every one that loveth is born of God." Everyone who loves in truth and purity is a born again person. Many people display love for children, love for the needy, love for their family and friends; but this does not necessarily mean that they are born again. The natural eye cannot differentiate between love that proceeds from the heart of God, and love displayed by man toward others for various reasons. It is altogether possible for unbelievers to so nearly simulate the love of God that *only* God can detect the difference. A person can be kind and generous toward his friends, benevolent in dealing with his family or with others who are in need, and still not be born again. He may have a great deal of natural affection toward others, a great deal of benevolence in character toward the poor and the needy — and yet not love God.

"He that loveth not knoweth not God." The person who does not have a heart of love need not pretend that he is a believer,

for *God is love* and if a man knows God, then God abides in his heart; and the person with God in his heart will love in deed and in truth, not just in word. When God abides in the heart, love automatically issues *from* the heart. Never has so much meaning, so much truth, been crowded into three short words: "God is love." In this age of hatred, strife, animosity, greed, distrust and selfishness when the majority of people seem to think only of self, when most of the wealth seems to be in the hands of only a few and in this land of plenty many go to bed hungry at night, how refreshing it is to know that *"GOD is love!"* It is also refreshing to meet those who have met God, and who, *because* they have met God, love as God loves. In this dark world of sin, sorrow, and heartache there are many precious souls who are truly children of God, possessors of the Holy Spirit, who bear the fruit of love.

In verse 9, John says the same thing Paul said in Romans 5:1-11, but in different words:

"Therefore being justified by faith, we have peace with God through our Lord Jesus Christ: By whom also we have access by faith into this grace wherein we stand, and rejoice in hope of the glory of God. And not only so, but we glory in tribulations also: knowing that tribulation worketh patience; and patience, experience; and experience, hope; and hope maketh not ashamed; because the love of God is shed abroad in our hearts by the Holy Ghost which is given unto us. For when we were yet without strength, in due time Christ died for the ungodly. For scarcely for a righteous man will one die; yet peradventure for a good man some would even dare to die. But God commendeth His love toward us, in that, while we were yet sinners, Christ died for us. Much more then, being now justified by His blood, we shall be saved from wrath through Him. For if, when we were enemies, we were reconciled to God by the death of His Son, much more, being reconciled, we shall be saved by His life. And not only so, but we also joy in God through our Lord Jesus Christ, by whom we have now received the atonement."

It is not difficult to love someone who loves you, someone who is always doing things for you, saying kind things about you; but God commended HIS love toward us while we were yet sinners

4:7-10 The First Epistle of John

— hopeless, strengthless, enemies to God and alienated from Him. Jesus on Calvary was God's love displayed in action. God manifested His love — not by giving something that was *secondary*, but by giving *His only begotten SON*. God gave His best for our worst, that we might have life. We live because JESUS lives. He is alive forevermore, and has the keys to death and hell. Therefore, believers do not fear yesterday, today, nor tomorrow because the Holy Spirit abides in us and we have peace with God through our Lord Jesus Christ. Our sins are forgiven for His name's sake, and "we shall be saved from wrath through Him."

"Herein is love" — that is, God sending His only Son into the world to die for His enemies, that we who deserve death and hell might have life. Because of the sacrifice of God's only begotten Son, His love is manifested in the things that He has done, is doing, and will do for those who trust in Jesus.

"Not that we loved God, but that He loved us." We did not love God. John 1:10-13 tells us that Jesus "was in the world, and the world was made by Him, and the world knew Him not." He came unto His own, and even *His own* rejected Him. Dearly beloved, no *natural man* from Adam until now has been willing to give God first place in soul, spirit, and body, first place in love and service. God gave Adam everything that humanity could want or hope for; yet the one thing God forbade, Adam went after! He openly rebelled against God, He sinned and broke the law of God; and no man *since* Adam has loved God until God first put a new heart within his bosom. Luke 19:10 tells us that the Son of man came to seek and to save *"that which was lost."* When Jesus came into the world, the world was not seeking Jesus — and the world is not seeking Him today.

Jesus came to *give,* not to receive. He came to pay the ransom by giving His life a ransom for many. God's beloved Son came into the world to pay a debt He did not owe, and He paid that debt — the debt of the first Adam and of all the *sons* of Adam.

"Not that we loved God" — no: the night God saved me I did not go to the house of God seeking Him. I did not go there because I loved Him. I went because due to certain circum-

stances I was forced to go. But even though I went to God's house against my will, Jesus was seeking my poor, lost soul, and the Gospel which is "the power of God unto salvation" reached my heart and convicted me of sin. I trusted Jesus that night — but not because I was seeking Him. I came under the hearing of the Word, God sought me through the Word, the Holy Spirit troubled my heart and I was saved. I love God now, I love the Church, I love the Bible, and I love my fellow Christians, but that was not true until God gave me a new heart in which the Holy Spirit dwells.

God loved us, "*and sent His Son to be the propitiation for our sins.*" You will appreciate God the Father as you have never before appreciated Him if you will carefully study the part He had in providing our salvation. *All sin is against God.* The prodigal said, "Against thee, and thee only, have I sinned." God provided the sacrifice for sin because what God demanded only God could provide. He foreordained and purposed the death of Christ to make atonement for the sin of the world, and set Him forth to be a propitiation through faith in His blood.

In the death of Jesus on the cross we see on display the unfolding of the secret purpose of God, the purpose that was settled before the foundation of the world. God who was the Lawgiver is also the *Christ*-giver. In HIM was provided the sacrifice that completely satisfied the law, the holiness, and the righteousness of God. God's law is holy, but because of the weakness of the flesh man could not be justified by the law:

"Therefore by the deeds of the law there shall no flesh be justified in His sight, for by the law is the knowledge of sin. But now the righteousness of God without the law is manifested, being witnessed by the law and the prophets; even the righteousness of God which is by faith of Jesus Christ unto all and upon all of them that believe . . . being justified freely by His grace through the redemption that is in Christ Jesus: Whom God hath set forth to be a propitiation through faith in His blood, to declare His righteousness for the remission of sins that are past, through the forbearance of God; to declare, I say, at this time His righteousness: that He might be just, and the Justifier of him which believeth in Jesus" (Rom. 3:20-26 in part).

Greek scholars tell us that the word translated "commended"

in Romans 5:8 means "to place together; of persons, to introduce to one's acquaintance and favorable notice; hence, to commend, to represent as worthy." The same Greek word is translated "stood with" in the account of Moses and Elijah appearing with Christ on the Mount of Transfiguration (Luke 9:32). It is translated "make" in Galatians 2:18 when Paul said he would make himself a transgressor if he went back to the law of Moses after having accepted the grace of God. In Romans 14:1, 2, in II Corinthians 7:11 and 10:18 the same word is used in the sense of approving another in commending to favorable notice. In all of these instances the meaning is, "they stand together" — the same meaning found in I Samuel 22:23 when David guaranteed Abiathar that his life was secure and safe so long as he abode with him.

Therefore, when God commended His love toward us in setting forth Jesus to be a propitiation for our sins, God the Father associated *Himself* with the death of Christ Jesus on the cross for sinners. The marvelous Gospel of the grace of God is a glorious fact about a glorious act by a glorious God who is love. Christ Jesus our Saviour dying on the cross commends the fact of God's love. The arms of Jesus outstretched on the cross were the arms of Divine love. Only GOD could stretch out His arms on the cross for men who should rightfully spend eternity in hell.

It was God the Father who commended His love toward us in the death of His Son, it was God the Father who sent His Son that "what the law could not do, in that it was weak through the flesh, God sending His own Son in the likeness of sinful flesh, and for sin, condemned sin in the flesh: that the righteousness of the law might be fulfilled in us, who walk not after the flesh, but after the Spirit" (Rom. 8:3, 4).

The atonement explains the Incarnation. The Incarnation of Christ was a Divine necessity if the sin of the world were to be taken away. The blood of bulls and goats could not take away sin, but God gave Jesus a body and in that body He offered the one eternal sacrifice that takes away sin (Heb. 10:1-14); and in obedience to the Divine will of the sovereign God, Christ Jesus the Incarnate One, the Redeemer, took upon Himself *in death* the total responsibility of all the sin of all the world (John 1:29; 3:16; I John 2:1, 2).

Greek scholars tell us that the Greek word translated "sending" in Romans 8:3 means not only to let one go, but to send one forth on a specific mission and fully equip him for that mission. God sent Jesus into the world to be condemned for us. He who knew no sin was made to be sin for us (II Cor. 5:22); and He sent Him equipped — not to condemn us, but to *save* us. The Just came to suffer for the unjust, that He might reconcile us to God. It is through the death of His Son that we are reconciled to God, it is through His blood that we have redemption.

God sent Jesus into the world in a body of flesh for the specific purpose of *condemning sin IN the flesh.* The word translated "condemn" is a tremendous word of force in the Greek language. It points out three things: (1) a crime has been committed; (2) a verdict has been passed; (3) punishment has been meted out. In Hebrews 11:7 we read that Noah built the ark by faith, and in so doing he saved his house; but the Word also says that in saving his house, Noah *"condemned the world."* Concerning Sodom and God's act of judgment upon that wicked city, II Peter 2:6 tells us that Sodom was "condemned with an overthrow." In these instances there was sin which called forth God's sentence of judgment and destruction, and God's execution of that sentence — in the condemnation of the world in Noah's day, and the destruction of Sodom in the day of Abraham.

In the same manner that God condemned the old world in the flood, and as He condemned the cities of Sodom and Gomorrah with fire that fell from heaven, just so, *He condemned His Son to die for us!* (II Cor. 5:21). I confess I cannot comprehend this statement, but though I do not *understand* it, God said it and I believe it. I believe in the finished work of the Lamb without spot or blemish. In the days of the law, the Israelite who stood watching the fire consume the sin-offering could say, "That is myself. There am I, dying for my sin, bearing the wrath of God." In like manner, Jesus was OUR sin-offering — the *perfect and eternal* offering provided by God the Father.

Romans 8:32 tells us that God "spared not His own Son, but delivered Him up for us all. . . ." It was a Divine necessity that Jesus die — not only that He DIE, but that He die a sacrificial death, the death of the cross. If WE were to be spared, God's Son could *not* be spared; He could not save Himself. If He had done as the chief priests suggested (Matt. 27: 42) and had saved Himself, we would all be destined to spend eternity in the lake of fire. Abraham could not find even ten righteous men in Sodom and Gomorrah (Gen. 18:22-23), but thank God, the heavenly Father found ONE righteous Man, and we who believe in His shed blood are spared for the sake of that One, the only begotten Son of God. He was bruised by Jehovah, and because He was bruised, because the blow fell on Him on the cross, we are spared (Isa. 53:8-10).

God delivered up His Son "for us all." Greek authorities tell us that one of the strongest words used to describe God's love and His act in giving Jesus for the sin of the world is the word here translated "delivered." It means to give over into the hands of another. In Romans 1:24, 26, and 28 the same word is translated "gave up" and "gave over," where God gave over to sin and the consequences of sin those who had previously given *themselves* over to sin. In Ephesians 4:19, 5:2, 25, and in Galatians 2:20 the same word is translated "gave" or "given." In I Peter 2:23 it is used when Jesus committed Himself to the Father.

In Romans 4:25 Paul clearly states WHY God delivered up His sinless, spotless, only begotten Son: He was *"delivered for our offences, and was raised again for our justification."* The eternal God, Creator of heaven and earth, delivered up His beloved Son for strengthless, worthless, ungodly sinners, enemies and aliens.

In Isaiah we read of the Saviour, "He is despised and rejected of men; a man of sorrows, and acquainted with grief: and we hid as it were our faces from Him; He was despised, and we esteemed Him not. Surely He hath borne our griefs, and carried our sorrows: yet we did esteem Him stricken, smitten of God, and afflicted. But He was wounded for OUR transgressions, He was bruised for OUR iniquities: the chastisement of OUR peace was upon Him; and with HIS stripes we are healed. All we like sheep have gone astray; we have turned every one to his own way; *and the Lord hath laid on Him the iniquity of us all"* (Isa. 53:3-6).

Christian, think on these words: Our Saviour was "SMITTEN OF GOD . . . and the Lord (JEHOVAH GOD) hath laid on Him THE INIQUITY OF US ALL!" Listen to the cry of Jesus: "My God! My God! WHY hast thou forsaken me?" Then bow your head and thank God the Father that He so loved us that He permitted Jesus to taste death, take away sin, pay the ransom, purchase redemption, *that WE might escape the damnation of hell.*

Believers Ought to Love One Another

Verse 11: "Beloved, if God so loved us, we ought also to love one another."

Since God — pure, holy, sinless — so loved strengthless, hopeless, ungodly sinners, WE certainly ought to love others who, like ourselves, are redeemed by the blood of Jesus, saved by the grace of God. All believers are blood kin — *saved by the blood.* All believers belong to the body of Christ, the true Church. All believers are born of the Spirit and indwelt by Him. The *fruit* of the Spirit is love, and men will know that we belong to Jesus if we love one another. Love is unselfish. Jesus did not think of self, He came to live for others, to serve others, and to die for others. Believers should think of the happiness and success of others. Selfishness has no place in the life of a born again Christian.

Verse 12: "No man hath seen God at any time. If we love one another, God dwelleth in us, and His love is perfected in us."

This same declaration is found in John 1:18: "No man hath seen God at any time; the only begotten Son, which is in the bosom of the Father, He hath declared Him."

In the beginning, Jesus was in the bosom of the Father — the place of protection, love, comfort, rest, and security. This denotes the close relationship, communion, and deep love between Father and Son. God has never been seen by mortal eyes, we cannot become acquainted with Him through the eye-gate; but there is a way through which we are assured that He is near us, even *within* us: we can become acquainted with Him through love. We know He dwells within by the outflow of love from our hearts.

If we love one another, God dwells in us *"and His love is perfected in us."* This does not mean that we are sinless — absolutely perfect; nor does it mean that *our love* is absolute perfection. It means that when we love the brethren as we are *commanded* to love them, such love is the proper carrying out of our love toward God. Without love to the brethren, our love to God would not have accomplished what it was designed in the beginning TO accomplish. We received commandment from God to love each other; and to possess God and NOT love each other as He commanded would be a reflection on the *love* of God. If God so loved such wretched creatures as we were before He saved us, certainly when we possess the love of God and are indwelt by the Holy Spirit, we will love those who are filled with the same love, saved by the same grace, and indwelt by the same Spirit.

Verse 13: "Hereby know we that we dwell in Him, and He in us, because He hath given us of His Spirit."

Here is another statement of assurance. We KNOW that we have truly been born again when we love the brethren, and the reason we love the brethren is because God has given us His Spirit to abide within our hearts: and "the fruit of the Spirit is love, joy, peace, longsuffering, gentleness, goodness, faith, meekness, temperance: against such there is no law" (Gal. 5:22, 23).

Precious truth! We know that we have passed from death unto life, we know that God is our Father and Jesus is our Saviour. We have assurance that we will go to be with Him when we depart this life. We know the Holy Spirit abides in us because we bear fruits that He alone could produce — fruits such as love, joy, peace, gentleness, goodness, longsuffering.

Verse 14: "And we have seen and do testify that the Father sent the Son to be the Saviour of the world."

This epistle opens with the same truth that is repeated here — *"we have seen"* — meaning that John and the other apostles saw Jesus in the flesh, they were in His presence, and they testify that *"the Father sent the Son to be the Saviour of the world."* John and the other apostles heard His wonderful words of life, they witnessed His miracles, miracles which no man could do "except God be with Him"; they were convinced in their own hearts that He WAS the Son of God, and now John assures us that what he is writing is what he has seen and experienced.

Verse 15: "Whosoever shall confess that Jesus is the Son of God, God dwelleth in him, and he in God."

"*WHOSOEVER shall confess*" — not just a select, elect few, but *whosoever* — the rich, the poor; the wise, the unwise; the bond, the free — ALL are included. It is not God's will that ANY perish, but that all come to repentance. God has no joy in the death of the wicked. Jesus invited, "Come unto me, ALL ye that labour and are heavy laden, and I will give you rest" (Matt. 11:28). The invitation is to ALL, to "whosoever will."

What are we to confess? "*That Jesus is the Son of God.*" Here are the keys to heaven. It is clearly stated exactly what the unbeliever must do to become a son of God: He must confess that Jesus is the Son of God — and that means that He was conceived of the Holy Ghost, born of the virgin — the Incarnate One, God in flesh. Whosoever shall confess that Jesus is the virgin-born Son of God, God dwells in that person, and he dwells in God. How could it be made more simple?

Verse 16: "And we have known and believed the love that God hath to us. God is love; and he that dwelleth in love dwelleth in God, and God in him."

Here is repetition of truths declared in previous verses, which is not unusual in this epistle. John often repeats important truths and divine facts. The Holy Spirit delights to dwell on truth and love (God is *love*, God is *truth*).

"*We have known and believed the love that God hath to us.*" In our trials, in the dark hours, in the perplexities of life and when we face many things beyond our understanding, how refreshing to know that God loves us! Such certainty and assurance brings peace that cannot be found anywhere else on earth. We know and believe that God loves us, and "if God be for us, who can be against us?" The trusting believer can face all trials, endure all hardships, dare anything and overcome, knowing that all things work together for good to them that love God and are called according to His purpose. When the storms of life surround us, to remind ourselves that God is love, and that He loves US, puts a silver lining in the darkest cloud.

"He that dwelleth in love dwelleth in God, and God in him." The essence of Christianity is love. *God* is Christianity, *Christ* is Christianity, *love* is Christianity. God, Christ, and love cannot be separated. God loved us in the beginning, we love Him because He first loved us, He abides in us and therefore we love one another. We not only love other *believers,* we love *unbelievers* in that we pray for them, witness to them, and do what we can to bring them into the family of heaven.

The number one need of the whole wide world is to know God — with the heart, not with the head. When one knows God in the heart, that heart is filled with love; and love removes things that are of the devil — corruption, lust, passions, crime, envy, strife, hatred, jealousy — and puts within us truth, kindness, generosity, consideration and love for our fellowman.

The Believer in This World

Verse 17: "Herein is our love made perfect, that we may have boldness in the day of judgment: because as He is, so are we in this world.

Believers are IN the world but not OF the world, "Our citizenship is in heaven; from whence also we look for the Saviour, the Lord Jesus Christ" (Phil. 3:20). Jesus told His disciples, "I go to prepare a place for you. And if I go and prepare a place for you, I will come again, and receive you unto myself; that where I am, there ye may be also" (John 14:1-3 in part). Therefore, believers are citizens of another world.

"Herein is our love made perfect." Love is not static, love is forever increasing, broadening, growing as the days go by. The moment we are born again we become partakers of Divine nature, but the Word admonishes us, "As newborn babes, desire the sincere milk of the Word, that ye may grow thereby" (I Pet. 2:2). Paul said to the Corinthian Christians, "And I, brethren, could not speak unto you as unto spiritual, but as unto carnal, even as unto babes in Christ. I have fed you with milk, and not with meat: for hitherto ye were not able to bear it, neither yet now are ye able. For ye are yet carnal . . ." (I Cor. 3:1, 2, 3 in part). God is love, He dwells in our hearts in the Person

of the Holy Spirit, and the more we know about Him, the more we feed on His Word and walk in the light of the Word, the deeper grows our love for Him.

When two people marry in God's will, they love each other more and more as the years go by. The same is true in the spiritual realm. Every day with Jesus is sweeter than the day before. The longer we live for Him, the more we fellowship with Him in prayer and through the Word, the more we serve Him in faithful stewardship, the more we love and appreciate Him.

In previous verses of this chapter we learned that love is of God, everyone that loveth is *born* of God. There is no room in the believer for the spirit of hatred, greed, jealousy, fear, nor for the spirit of *self*. The believer breathes God's love, and as we breathe His love and feed upon His Word our capacity to love Him is increased. This increases our love for the brethren. Truly, the believer "dwelleth in love" (V. 16).

Notice: ". . . *that we may have boldness in the day of judgement.*" I think we preachers have neglected teaching believers concerning the judgment *for* believers. It is true that sin has already been judged, it is true that Christians will not appear at the Great White Throne judgment in Revelation 20; but they *will* appear before the judgment seat of Christ, to account for deeds done in the body: "For we must all appear before the judgment seat of Christ; that every one may receive the things done in his body, according to that he hath done, whether it be good or bad" (II Cor. 5:10). The judgment for believers has to do with *works*, not *sins*. Our sins have been atoned for and they are remembered against us no more (Heb. 10:17); but every work must come into judgment, and the day of judgment will declare every work:

"But I say unto you, That every idle word that men shall speak, they shall give account thereof in the day of judgment" (Matt. 12:36).

"Why dost thou judge thy brother? or why dost thou set at nought thy brother? for we shall all stand before the judgment seat of Christ" (Rom. 14:10).

"Be not deceived; God is not mocked: for whatsoever a man soweth, that shall he also reap" (Gal. 6:7).

"Knowing that whatsoever good thing any man doeth, the same shall he receive of the Lord, whether he be bond or free" (Eph. 6:8).

"Knowing that of the Lord ye shall receive the reward of the inheritance: for ye serve the Lord Christ. But he that doeth wrong shall receive for the wrong which he hath done: and there is no respect of persons" (Col. 3:24, 25).

Believers will be judged according to their stewardship, and the result of that judgment will be reward or *loss* of reward:

"For other foundation can no man lay than that is laid, which is Jesus Christ. Now if any man build upon this foundation gold, silver, precious stones, wood, hay, stubble; every man's work shall be made manifest: for the day shall declare it, because it shall be revealed by fire; and the fire shall try every man's work of what sort it is. If any man's work abide which he hath built thereupon, he shall receive a reward. If any man's work shall be burned, he shall suffer loss: but he himself shall be saved; yet so as by fire" (I Cor. 3:11-15). This has nothing to do with salvation. It applies to works and rewards.

The judgment for believers will occur immediately after the Rapture (Matt. 16:27; Luke 14:14; I Cor. 4:5; II Tim. 4:8; Rev. 22:12).

It is a Bible fact that a believer can lose his reward. In II John 8 we are warned, "Look to yourselves, that we *lose not those things which we have wrought,* but that we receive a full reward." A Christian may receive a *full* reward, *partial* reward, or he may lose ALL of his reward and be saved "so as by fire." Believers who abide in Christ — dedicated, surrendered, Spirit-led — need have no fear of the judgment. If we have been faithful, if we have obeyed His commandment that we love God with all of our heart, soul, and strength, we will stand unafraid in that judgment day.

"As He is, so are we in this world." This world is not our home. We are not OF the world, but we are IN the world as ambassadors for Christ (II Cor. 5:20); and since we are here on business for our Saviour and King we should be careful of our conduct and of the way in which we represent Jesus in this world. You may rest assured that even though sinners do not read the Bible, they read the Christian's life and watch every

move he makes. The unsaved will judge Jesus according to the way His people live in this world — the places we go, the things we do, and the company we keep. "We are made a spectacle unto the world, and to angels, and to men" (I Cor. 4:9).

You will notice the Scripture does not say "as He WAS in this world," but "as He IS." Jesus is in the world right now. In His Divine omnipresence He abides in the heart of every believer — "Christ in you, the hope of glory" (Col. 1:27). No man has seen God at any time, but if we are the kind of believers we *should* be, people will see God in US. It is a glorious privilege to be a Christian, but it is an equally great responsibility to name the name of Jesus and confess that we are followers of Him.

The Sure Cure for Fear

Verse 18: "There is no fear in love; but perfect love casteth out fear: because fear hath torment. He that feareth is not made perfect in love."

Note the outline of this tremendous verse:

1. There is no fear in love.
2. Perfect love casteth out fear.
3. Fear hath torment.
4. He that feareth is not made perfect in love.

What IS perfect love? The answer is found in verse 8 of this chapter: "*GOD is love.*" Jesus was God in flesh, therefore Jesus was *perfect love* in flesh. God set forth perfect love when He set forth Jesus to be a propitiation for our sins through faith in His shed blood. Jesus is perfect love, and when He abides in the heart of the believer He removes fear — the fear of yesterday, the fear of today, the fear of tomorrow. We do not know what tomorrow holds, but *Jesus* knows, and HE holds US. We are hid with Him in God.

Perfect love removes the fear of death. I have faced death more than once since I have been saved, and I can truthfully say that as I walked in the valley of the shadow of death I was not afraid. I do not want to die. I love life, and I want to live just as long as God will allow me to stay on this earth. I want to preach His Word, win souls, fellowship with my family and friends; but if I should die suddenly, even before I finish this series of messages, I want the closing pages of this book to carry the message that Evangelist Oliver Greene died without fear! Christians should not fear death.

Someone may ask if Christians are not afraid of the *physical* part of dying, the pain that will accompany death. In answer to such a question I would say, God's grace is sufficient; and since we are not dying at the moment, we need grace to *live* for Him, Then when the time comes for us to die — if that time comes before the Rapture — God will give us dying grace. Atheists and free-thinkers have never written a book about why the saints of God, when they come down to die, *die unafraid!* I know most of you who have seen saints depart this life have witnessed what I have just said. Many times, whether dear old saints who have lived for Jesus through fifty or sixty years, or a young person who has lived for Him only a few months or years, they die smiling — a smile the undertaker cannot remove. I could give one account after another of saints who have gone on to be with the Lord — smiling, shouting, singing the praises of God. Some have testified, "I see angels!" or "I see a bright, white light!"

I challenge you to read the testimones of dying saints, and then read the testimonies of dying atheists and agnostics; then ask some atheist or free-thinker to explain why a saint of God dies with a smile, rejoicing, while the unbeliever many times dies in awful fear even after the administration of all the sedatives and medications it is possible to give him. If doctors would let atheists, agnostics, ungodly men, die a natural death without the use of strong drugs to dull the senses, their testimonies could be used to write some red-hot books on hell fire and what it means to face hell just before departing this life! But thank God, there is no fear in perfect love. The love of God *delivers* us from fear.

The first three chapters of Genesis record the account of the creation of Adam and Eve, the Garden of Eden, and the first days of their life IN the garden. Everything was wonderful until sin entered there. God paid a visit to the Garden every day and fellowshipped with Adam and Eve, and then Adam disobeyed God, stepped over His law and ate the fruit God had forbidden him to eat. The *next* time God stepped into the

Garden and Adam heard His voice, he was frightened; and with Eve he ran and hid. When God called, "Adam, *where art thou?*" Adam replied, "I heard thy voice in the garden, AND I WAS AFRAID, because I was naked; and I hid myself." *Sin* brings fear. *Guilt* makes men afraid. But for the Christian, Christ has borne the sin and the guilt, and therefore the believer has nothing to fear — in this world, nor in the world to come.

Beloved, if you have been truly born again, and yet there is fear in your heart concerning the future, that fear is a definite sign that you have backslidden. You need to repent and ask Jesus to forgive your sins: "If we confess our sins, He is faithful and just to forgive us our sins, and to cleanse us from all unrighteousness" (I John 1:9). Christ Jesus sits at the right hand of God the Father to make intercession for us, and if we are perfectly yielded to Him we have no fear of the day when we will stand before God, because Jesus has promised to stand with us, confess us to the Father, and receive us unto Himself.

"*Fear hath torment.*" Yes indeed! Many of you know the truth of that statement by experience. Even in the *natural* realm it is torment to be afraid. Fear can make one sick, mentally and physically; and certainly *spiritual* fear can make one sick spiritually. *Love* is a *joyous* emotion, but fear is distressing and painful. *Love* brings rest and peace, but fear brings unrest and torment.

Men suffer from many kinds of fear in the physical realm. They fear sickness, they fear the future, they fear that a depression may come, they fear that they may lose their health or their wealth. Many things in the material world cause men to fear; but concerning those material things Jesus said, "Seek ye first the kingdom of God, and His righteousness; and all these things shall be added unto you" (Matt. 6:33).

Paul assured the Philippian believers, "My God shall supply all your need according to His riches in glory by Christ Jesus" (Phil. 4:19). The individual who has put his trust in Jesus has nothing to fear. He will take care of us, He will supply our every need, He will deliver us from the pitfalls of Satan, and He will walk with us until we are safe with Him in Paradise.

"Fear not, little flock; for it is your Father's good pleasure to give you the kingdom" (Luke 12:32).

"For ye have not received the spirit of bondage again to fear; but ye have received the Spirit of adoption, whereby we cry, Abba, Father" (Rom. 8:15).

". . . He hath said, I will never leave thee, nor forsake thee. So that we may boldly say, The Lord is my helper, and I will not fear what man shall do unto me" (Heb. 13:5, 6).

"The Lord is my light and my salvation; whom shall I fear? The Lord is the strength of my life; of whom shall I be afraid?" (Psalm 27:1).

If you can say with David, "The Lord is my Shepherd, "then you can claim every word in the Twenty-Third Psalm; but if the Lord is NOT your Shepherd, then not one word in that glorious passage is yours:

"The Lord is my Shepherd: I shall not want. He maketh me to lie down in green pastures: He leadeth me beside the still waters. He restoreth my soul: He leadeth me in the paths of righteousness for His name's sake. Yea, though I walk through the valley of the shadow of death, I will fear no evil: for thou art with me; thy rod and thy staff they comfort me. Thou preparest a table before me in the presence of mine enemies: thou anointest my head with oil; my cup runneth over. Surely goodness and mercy shall follow me all the days of my life: and I will dwell in the house of the Lord for ever" (Psalm 23).

If the Lord is NOT your Shepherd, invite Him into your heart, believe on Him, and He will save you (Acts 16:31). Then He will become your Saviour, Shepherd, Keeper, Protector, Mediator, and you will have nothing to fear — in this world, nor in the life to come.

Verse 19: "We love Him, because He first loved us."

I stated earlier in this study that it is not difficult to love someone who loves us, someone who does nice things for us or says nice things about us; but GOD loved us while we were yet unlovely, while we were yet sinners, enemies to Him. We have all sinned and come short of the glory of God, we all deserve to spend eternity in the lake of fire; but God loved us in spite of what we deserved and in spite of our rebellious attitude toward Him. He manifested His love toward us by sending Jesus to die for us, that we might be saved from sin. Had we never known

Jesus, we could never have known the love of God. We love God because He first loved us and sent His Son into the world to die for us.

We also love God because of the excellency of His character. When we are born again, Divine nature comes into our hearts and abides there (II Pet. 1:4; Rom. 8:9); and Divine nature within us automatically loves God because of God's excellent nature. Like attracts like, and the Divine nature of God attracts the Divine nature within the believer. Love originated in God, proceeded from God in Jesus, and Jesus declared God to us. We hear and believe the words of Jesus (John 5:24), we are saved by hearing and believing on Him; but we love God for a much deeper reason: We love Him because He is God, and God is love. He is worthy of all of our love.

Verse 20: "If a man say, I love God, and hateth his brother, he is a liar: for he that loveth not his brother whom he hath seen, how can he love God whom he hath not seen?"

Down through the years, God's preachers have been accused of being too blunt, too harsh, too plain of speech; but my dear fellow believer, how many preachers have you heard speak from the pulpit with such boldness as John uses here? If a man — *any* man — says he loves God, yet that man hates his Christian brother, "HE IS A LIAR!"

This is not the first time such strong language has been used in this epistle. In Chapter 1, verse 6, we read: "If we say that we have fellowship with Him, and walk in darkness, WE LIE, and do not the truth." In chapter 1, verse 8 we read, "If we say that we have no sin, we deceive ourselves, AND THE TRUTH IS NOT IN US." In chapter 1, verse 10, "If we say that we have not sinned, WE MAKE HIM A LIAR, AND HIS WORD IS NOT IN US." In chapter 2, verse 4, "He that saith, I know Him, and keepeth not His commandments, IS A LIAR, AND THE TRUTH IS NOT IN HIM." Then in chapter 5 verse 10 we find this declaration: "He that believeth on the Son of God hath the witness in himself: he that believeth not God HATH MADE HIM A LIAR; because he believeth not the record that God gave of His Son."

The Word of God is plain and understandable. It wears no

frills, no fringe, no sugar-coating. Men are either saved or lost. They tell the truth or they are liars. They live for God or they live for the devil. Therefore the Holy Spirit clearly spells out the fact that if a man professes to love God and yet in his actions he proves that he hates his Christian brother, that man is NOT a believer, no matter what he claims. He is a liar — and then the Holy Spirit explains why: *"For he that loveth not his brother whom he hath seen, how can he love God whom he hath NOT seen?"*

In verse 12 we were told that no man has seen God at any time. God is an eternal Spirit — He does have a form, the Bible speaks of His hands, His feet, His eyes, His ears; but no man has *seen* Him at any time. We do see our brothers in Christ, and certainly it is unreasonable to suppose that a man would love God, whom he has *never* seen, if he cannot love the brethren (*children* of God) whom he has seen and whom he knows personally.

Here the subject is approached from the human standpoint: It is certainly much easier to love our family and those with whom we are well acquainted, those with whom we associate from day to day, than it would be to love someone whom we have never seen. Man is made in the image of God, and if we cannot love those who are made in God's image, then how can we love God? If a person is genuinely born again, hate moves out of the heart immediately. It is a divine impossibility for hate and love to live in the same heart. When God comes in, the devil goes out. When *love* comes in, *hate* goes out. When a man is truly born again he will love all men, especially those of the household of God. He will not love all things that all men do, he may not love all things that some *believers* do; but God is love, and the believer possesses God. Therefore, with God in the heart the Christian will love the brethren. Jesus loved even the unlovely, and Jesus in YOU will love the brethren — yes, even the unlovely; not their ways, not their habits, but their souls.

Verse 21: "And this commandment have we from Him, That He who loveth God love his brother also."

Please notice that this is not a suggestion, it is a command.

Christians are commanded to love their Christian brothers just as they love God; and if we as believers do NOT love other believers, we dare not say that we love God. *"He who loveth God"* must love his brother also. This is His command, and if we love God we will obey that command.

I JOHN — Chapter 5

1. Whosoever believeth that Jesus is the Christ is born of God; and every one that loveth him that begat loveth him also that is begotten of him.

2. By this we know that we love the children of God, when we love God, and keep his commandments.

3. For this is the love of God, that we keep his commandments: and his commandments are not grievous.

4. For whatsover is born of God overcometh the world: and this is the victory that overcometh the world, even our faith.

5. Who is he that overcometh the world, but he that believeth that Jesus is the Son of God?

6. This is he that came by water and blood, even Jesus Christ; not by water only, but by water and blood. And it is the Spirit that beareth witness, because the Spirit is truth.

7. For there are three that bear record in heaven, the Father, the Word, and the Holy Ghost; and these three are one.

8. And there are three that bear witness in earth, the Spirit, and the water, and the blood; and these three agree in one.

9. If we receive the witness of men, the witness of God is greater: for this is the witness of God which he hath testified of his Son.

10. He that believeth on the Son of God hath the witness in himself; he that believeth not God hath made him a liar; because he believeth not the record that God gave of his Son.

11. And this is the record, that God hath given to us eternal life, and this life is in his Son.

12. He that hath the Son hath life; and he that hath not the Son of God hath not life.

13. These things have I written unto you that believe on the name of the Son of God; that ye may know that ye have eternal life, and that ye may believe on the name of the Son of God.

14. And this is the confidence that we have in him, that, if we ask any thing according to his will, he heareth us:

15. And if we know that he hear us, whatsoever we ask, we know that we have the petitions that we desired of him.

16. If any man see his brother sin a sin which is not unto death, he shall ask, and he shall give him life for them that sin not unto death. There is a sin unto death: I do not say that he shall pray for it.

17. All unrighteousness is sin: and there is a sin not unto death.

18. We know that whosoever is born of God sinneth not; but he that is begotten of God keepeth himself, and that wicked one toucheth him not.

19. And we know that we are of God, and the whole world lieth in wickedness.

20. And we know that the Son of God is come, and hath given us an understanding, that we may know him that is true, and we are in him that is true, even in his Son Jesus Christ. This is the true God, and eternal life.

21. Little children, keep yourselves from idols. Amen.

The first three verses of this chapter are a continuation of the discussion from the previous chapter on the subject of love.

In verses 4 and 5 we learn the way of victory for the believer. Verses 6 through 9 again present evidence that Jesus is the Son of God, very God in flesh, a truth Divinely witnessed both in heaven and on earth. Verse 10 declares that the Christian has the witness in himself, and he who *believes NOT* has made God a liar.

Verses 11 and 12 give the record concerning eternal life through God's Son, and verse 13 tells us why all these things are written: "That ye may know that ye have eternal life, and that ye may believe on the name of the Son of God."

Verses 14 and 15 set forth our confidence in Christ, so we may know that if we ask anything in His name, we have the petitions we desire *according to His will*. A true believer will pray in the words of Jesus, "Not my will, but thine, be done."

In verses 16 and 17 we learn the power of prayer, the duty of praying for those who have sinned, the *uselessness* of praying for one who has committed the sin unto death. Verses 18 through 20 climax all that the Holy Spirit has declared through John the Beloved concerning salvation and how we may KNOW that we are saved. These verses tell us that those who are born of God do not sin. The whole world lies in the lap of the Wicked One, but believers know that the Son of God has come, and through HIM we have understanding of the truth, for He IS truth — the true God and eternal life.

Then in the last verse of this love letter from God to His little children we find an exhortation: Believers — yes, blood washed sons of God — are admonished and exhorted to keep themselves from idols. Even the most spiritual saint needs to be on guard lest some interest so absorb both time and thoughts that it becomes an "idol," taking the place that should be occupied by Jesus Christ, the virgin-born Son of God.

Faith Keeps Us from the World and Gives Us Victory

Verse 1: "Whosoever believeth that Jesus is the Christ is born of God: and every one that loveth Him that begat loveth Him also that is begotten of Him."

Faith is the beginning of salvaton, faith is the continuation of salvation, and "whatsoever is *not* of faith is sin." We might say that faith is the heartbeat, the bloodstream, the very *life* of the Christian experience, from start to finish. Faith is the victory that overcomes the world, and "the just shall *live* by faith."

"*WHOSOEVER believeth.* . . ." Again John reminds us that salvation is for all — not just a certain group who are elected to be saved while all others are predestined to be damned. "Whosoever" includes all and excludes none. *God loved the WORLD,* and Jesus is the propitiation for the SIN of the world. Never let anyone tell you that some are predestined to be saved while others are predestined to be damned. Such doctrine is not in the Word of God.

"*Whosoever believeth that Jesus is the Christ IS BORN OF GOD.*" This is not an *intellectual* belief. James 2:19 tells us that the *devils BELIEVE* and tremble — but they are not saved. The meaning here is that whosoever believes that Jesus is the anointed of God, very God in flesh, and receives this truth into his *heart,* is saved — *born of God.* To be born of God, in the deeper sense, means to be *begotten* of God: "Of His own will begat He us with the Word of truth, that we should be a kind of firstfruits of His creatures" (James 1:18). Yes, when we believe that Jesus is the Christ, the Son of God, we believe it because we receive the record God has given us concerning His Son, and that record is, "*This is my beloved Son, in whom I am well pleased*" (Matt. 3:17).

When we believe that Jesus is the Christ, the Son of God, we believe the Word — and Jesus said "He that believeth my Word, and believeth on Him that sent me, hath everlasting life." Everlasting life becomes ours when we are born of God, therefore God has begotten us through the incorruptible seed, *the Word* (I Pet. 1:23).

"And every one that loveth Him that begat, loveth him also that is begotten of Him." Not only do we love "Him that begat" (God the Father); we also love all believers (those who are "begotten of Him"). All born again people possess the Holy Spirit and are filled with the love of God. Divine nature abides in our hearts, and when we love the God who has begotten us we will love our spiritual brothers and sisters. Regardless of denominational differences, all true believers belong to the one Church — the body of Christ; all true believers are baptized *into* that body, all true believers drink of one Spirit. (Study I Corinthians 12:12, 13 and Ephesians 5:25-32.)

All true Christians belong to one family. We are saved by God's grace, we are led by His Spirit, we share the blessings He bestows upon us. Therefore we are all under the same obligation to love God and to love one another.

John the beloved seems unable to leave the subject of love which is of such vital importance to the Christian life. All blessings and Christian excellencies spring from love and rest on love. John and the Apostle Paul — two spiritual giants — agree on love. In Galatians 5:22 Paul tells us that the *fruit of the Spirit* is love, and in I Corinthians 13 he says:

"Though I speak with the tongues of men and of angels, and have not charity (love), I am become as sounding brass, or a tinkling cymbal. And though I have the gift of prophecy, and understand all mysteries, and all knowledge; and though I have all faith, so that I could remove mountains, and have not charity (love), I am nothing. And though I bestow all my goods to feed the poor, and though I give my body to be burned, and have not charity (love), it profiteth me nothing.

"Charity (love) suffereth long, and is kind; charity (love) envieth not; charity (love) vaunteth not itself, is not puffed up, doth not behave itself unseemly, seeketh not her own, is not easily provoked, thinketh no evil; rejoiceth not in iniquity, but rejoiceth in the truth; beareth all things, believeth all things, hopeth all things, endureth all things.

"Charity (love) never faileth: but whether there be prophecies, they shall fail; whether there be tongues, they shall cease; whether there be knowledge, it shall vanish away . . . And now abideth faith, hope, chairty (love), these three: but the greatest of these is charity (love)" (I Cor. 13:1-13 in part).

Do you know of any other one thing in the entire Word of God that is so described? WHAT "beareth all things"? WHAT "endureth all things"? LOVE! ! ! The Christian experience *begins* with love to God the father, and all else springs from the love which is *rightly directed* to God the Father. God is big enough and has enough love to love every individual in the whole wide world; and if He had not so loved us individually we would never have known eternal life. We could never have known God or loved Him if He had not first loved US.

Verse 2: "By this we know that we love the children of God, when we love God, and keep His commandments."

This is not a matter of choice, it is not a suggestion. If we do not love the children of God, our Christian brothers and sisters, then *we do not love GOD.* God IS love, and the reason we love people — especially the brethren — is because God abides within us. WE love because HE loves, and He lives within our hearts if we are born again.

John has already said the same thing in other words previously in this epistle, but God knows our frame. He knows that we are dust, He knows our memories are short and our nature is weak and frail. So He gives us repetition in order to make a deep impression upon our hearts. We need to hear these things over and over and over again. For example, in *the Gospel of John* the word "believe" is used more than one hundred times in one form or another, although we are told in simple words, "He that *believeth* on Him is not condemned: but he that believeth *not* is condemned already, *because* he hath not believed in the name of the only begotten Son of God" (John 3:18).

If we hope to have spiritual power, if we hope to be successful soul winners, if we hope to glorify God by bringing forth much fruit, then our spiritual life must be cradled in love — yes, the love of God. What we do from any other source of inspiration will be hard, formal, cold and self-seeking. To be what we ought to be, to bring glory to God and magnify the name of Jesus as we should, we must be *filled* with His love, *baptized* in His love, and *compelled BY* His love. We have entirely too much "form" today. The Church needs a baptism of the love of God

— the bloodstream of Christian experience and Christian living.

We know that we love the children of God when we love HIM and keep His commandments — but what ARE those commandments? I John 3:23 answers: "THIS is His commandment, *That we should believe on the name of His Son Jesus Christ, and love one another, as He gave us commandment.*"

Verse 3: "For this is the love of God, that we keep His commandments: and His commandments are not grievous."

When we keep God's commandments, when we believe on the name of His Son Jesus Christ, when we love one another — that is the love of God in action. We have too many words and too little action today. In chapter 3, verse 18 of this epistle John says, "My little children, let us not love in word, neither in tongue; but in deed and in truth." The love of God in action is *doing* — not saying.

In John 15:12 Jesus said, "This is my commandment, That ye love one another, *as I have loved you.*" If we love one another as Jesus loved us, we will serve and sacrifice one for another. He *served,* He *gave,* He *sacrificed* even to the giving of His life, that we might be saved; and *we* should be willing to sacrifice for our brethren. Jesus Himself said, "By this shall all men know that ye are my disciples, if ye have love one to another" (John 13:35).

"*His commandments are not grievous.*" Indeed they are not! It is certainly not grievous to love God, for to *know* Him is to love Him, and the better we know Him the *more* we love Him. (And the more we love God, the more capable we are of loving the brethren, the more we will sacrifice and serve in the name of the greatest Servant of all — Jesus, our Saviour.)

Believers Are Overcomers

Verse 4: "For whatsoever is born of God overcometh the world: and this is the victory that overcometh the world, even our faith."

The Greek language here reads, "*Everything which is begotten of God,*" emphasizing the fact that there is no exception: in every instance the regenerated person has victory. When one is truly born of the Spirit, there is victory over the world. This is a Divine fact that all hell cannot overrule or outlaw. JESUS lived on this earth in a body like unto our bodies, sin apart, and He conquered the world, the flesh, the devil, death, hell, and the grave. To His disciples He said, "In the world ye shall have tribulation: but be of good cheer; I HAVE OVERCOME THE WORLD" (John 16:33). And because of this, the believer overcomes the world with its customs, its darkness, and its ungodliness. The Holy Spirit, through the pen of the Apostle Paul, also declared that the believer has — not just *borderline* victory, but MORE than victory: *"We are more than conquerors through Him that loved us.* For I am persuaded, that neither death, nor life, nor angels, nor principalities, nor powers, nor things present, nor things to come, nor height, nor depth, *nor any other creature,* shall be able to separate us from the love of God, which is in Christ Jesus our Lord!" (Rom. 8:37-39).

We who are born again believers know that all things work together for good to those who love God and are called according to His purpose. When all things are added up, we will see that whatever has happened to us from the day we were born again until the day we look into His precious face, was for our good and God's glory. Every true believer is predestined to be conformed to the image of God's dear Son, and therefore whatsoever happens to the believer is *allowed* to happen in order to mold and make him into that image (Rom. 8:29, 30).

We need to realize that God is a million times more concerned than we are about our success in the spiritual life, because when we sin we bring reproach upon the name of Jesus. God does not want His children to sin, but when we DO sin He has made provision through our Advocate, the man Christ Jesus — the Holy One, the Just One, the True One, who was made like unto His brethren in all things, that He might be a faithful and compassionate High Priest on our behalf before God the father. Believers know a PERSON, not a program. Paul said ". . . *I KNOW WHOM I have believed . . ."* (I Tim. 1:12). He also assured the Philippians, "Being confident of this very thing, that He which hath begun a good work in you WILL PERFORM IT until the day of Jesus Christ" (Phil. 1:6). Notice Paul does not say that Jesus is *able* to perform this work, or that He *may* perform it. He says that He WILL perform it until the day when He comes back to receive His own unto Himself and judge the world and ungodliness.

We find an assuring message in I Peter 1:3-5: "Blessed be the God and Father of our Lord Jesus Christ, which according to His abundant mercy hath begotten us again unto a lively hope by the resurrection of Jesus Christ from the dead, *to an inheritance incorruptible, and undefiled, and that fadeth not away, reserved in heaven for you, who are kept by the power of God through faith unto salvation ready to be revealed in the last time.*"

The salvation of which Peter speaks here is not the redemption we received the moment we believed. He is speaking of that glorious and blessed hope when Jesus comes in glory to receive His own unto Himself. In our *present* verse we have a settled maximum of Christianity — settled by God, not by man: *Whosoever* is born of God (everyone, in every case) has victory over the world.

"*And this is the victory that overcometh the world, even our faith.*" Here is the "why" of victory, and its source. We must begin at the beginning: Victory becomes ours because of the spiritual birth. "Except a man be born . . . of the Spirit, he cannot enter into the kingdom of God" (John 3:5). "That which is born of the flesh is flesh; and that which is born of the Spirit is spirit" (John 3:6). From the moment we are born again, the Holy Spirit abides in our heart. But how ARE we born again? Ephesians 2:8 declares, "For *by grace* are ye saved through *faith*; and that not of yourselves: it is the gift of God." Romans 10:17 tells us, "So then *faith cometh by hearing*, and hearing by the Word of God." In John 5:24 Jesus said, "Verily, verily I say unto you, He that heareth my word, and believeth on Him that sent me, hath everlasting life, and shall not come into condemnation; but is passed from death unto life." The Word is the incorruptible seed that brings life (I Pet. 1:23) and the new life puts within us Divine nature that is more powerful than the spirit of the world. Therefore, from the split second we are born into God's family, though we are babes in Christ, we have within us the power to overcome.

I am sure some of you are already asking, "Is it not possible then for a born again person to backslide?" Yes indeed! it is possible for a born again person to backslide *grievously*; but not everyone who professes to be a *backslider* has been born again. One *must be* regenerated before he can backslide. Many people

join the church and in a few weeks or months turn back to the
very things they left in the world. They may *claim* to be
backsliders, but the truth of the matter is that they simply joined
the local church and were baptized in water; they were never
born again and washed in the blood of Jesus.

Peter was a born again person when Jesus said to Him, "When
thou art converted, strengthen thy brethren" (Luke 22:32).
Peter was a Christian, but he grievously strayed from the Lord
when he followed Him afar off, denied Him three times, cursed
and swore that he did not know Him. But from Luke's account
of this incident we learn that in the space of about an hour
Peter went out and wept bitter tears of repentance (Luke 22:
54-62). He was already saved, he did not need to be regenerated. *He needed to turn back to Jesus.* He had broken fellowship with the Lord and he needed to be converted (turned
back) from following Jesus afar off.

True believers may backslide — some do; but as in the case of
Peter, it does not last long because when once one has tasted of
the things of the Spirit, the devil's garbage is no longer palatable.
The most miserable person on earth is the backslidden Christian!

In Hebrews 12:1, 2 Paul gives this admonition: "Wherefore
seeing we also are compassed about with so great a cloud of
witnesses, let us lay aside every weight, and the sin which doth
so easily beset us, and let us run with patience the race that is
set before us, looking unto Jesus the author and finisher of our
faith; who for the joy that was set before Him endured the
cross, despising the shame, and is set down at the right hand
of the throne of God."

Salvation *begins* when we exercise faith in the finished work
of Jesus. Such faith brings saving grace; grace teaches us to deny
ungodliness and worldly lusts, and to live sober, righteous, and
godly in this present world, looking for that glorious day when
Jesus will call us to meet Him in the clouds in the air. We are
to be looking unto Jesus always, because He is the originator, the
continuation, and the climax of saving faith. He *begins* the
work of salvation, and He *finished* the work of salvation.

Redemption (being born again) is just the *beginning* of this
glorious salvation. We are saved by God's grace through faith,
and "the just shall live by faith" (Rom. 1:17). "Behold, his soul

which is lifted up is not upright in him: but the just shall live by his faith" (Hab. 2:4). "But that no man is justified by the law in the sight of God, it is evident: for, The just shall live by faith" (Gal. 3:11). "Now the just shall live by faith: but if any man draw back, my soul shall have no pleasure in him" (Heb. 10:38).

Our Bible begins with the words, "*In the beginning, GOD . . . .*" Since God was in the beginning, and if we believe that *God IS God,* we should have no trouble believing anything with which God is associated. "*Through faith* we understand that the worlds were framed by the Word of God, so that things which are seen were not made of things which do appear" (Heb. 11:3).

The *world* says "*Seeing is believing.*" At the crucifixion the Pharisees said to Jesus, "Come down from the cross and we will *believe!*" But true faith does not ask to see, feel, taste, or handle; true faith believes *without* seeing. There are many things in the Bible that we will never understand, but we can believe them simply because *God said them.* The Christian believes the Word of God simply because it IS the Word of God. The Christian walks by faith, not by sight, and by faith we have victory over the world, the flesh, and the devil.

Verse 5: "Who is he that overcometh the world, but he that believeth that Jesus is the Son of God?"

The reason some professing Christians cannot overcome the world, the flesh, and the devil is because they have never exercised faith in God unto salvation. They joined a church and were baptized, they embraced a "religion," but they were never born again by faith in the finished work of Jesus. They have their names on a church roll, but they do not possess the new nature through the miracle of the new birth by the power of the Holy Spirit and the incorruptible seed of the Word of God.

It is just as natural for the unregenerate man to go after the world as it is for a pig to eat corn or for a sheep to eat tender grass; but it is *unnatural* for a born again *child of God* to love the world. The only person who can possibly live a Christian life and overcome the flesh and the world is the person who is born of God; and the only way to be born of

God is to believe on His Son, Jesus Christ, and have faith in His shed blood and finished work. Therefore John asks the question, "Who is he — what man or woman — who lives above the world and overcomes the flesh except those who believe that Jesus is the Christ, Son of God and Saviour of sinners?" Those are the only ones who overcome this world and live dedicated, consecrated, Christian lives, proving themselves assets to the kingdom of God, rather than bringing reproach upon the name of Jesus.

Evidence That Jesus Is the Son of God

Verse 6: "This is He that came by water and blood, even Jesus Christ; not by water only, but by water and blood. And it is the Spirit that beareth witness, because the Spirit is truth."

There are many and varied ideas about this verse of Scripture; Bible scholars and teachers do not agree as to its meaning. After many years of study and much prayer and searching of the Scriptures, I am convinced that the "water" mentioned here has nothing to do with water baptism. Some outstanding Bible teachers believe that this points to the baptism of Jesus, but I do not agree. Yes, I believe Jesus was immersed in water; but I also believe that the water here goes much deeper than the water in Jordan where John baptized Jesus. But our fellowship should not be determined by whether or not we agree on the water. We may disagree on the interpretation of the "water" here, but if we agree on the blood of Jesus Christ, which cleanses from all sin, we can fellowship together.

Again we must compare Scripture with Scripture, spiritual things with spiritual. Jesus testified on more than one occasion during His public ministry that He did not come to be ministered unto, but to minister, to give His life a ransom for many, to take away the sin of the world, and to seek and to save that which was lost. He came to lay HIS life down that WE might have life. He knew His mission on earth, and every moment of his life up until He said "It is finished!" His one desire was to be about the Father's business.

Now let us begin at the beginning: If He came to take away the sin of the world, if He came to seek and to save that which was lost, if He came to give His life a ransom for many, *then what brings salvation and what does salvation consist of insofar as HIS part is concerned?*

In John 1:11-13 we read, "He came unto His own, and His own received Him not. *But as many as received Him, to them gave He power to become the sons of God, even to them that believe on His name: Which were born, not of blood, nor of the will of the flesh, nor of the will of man, but of God."*

It is clearly stated that the believer is *"born of God."* In His interview with Nicodemus Jesus said, "Except a man be born *of water and of the Spirit,* he cannot enter into the kingdom of God" (John 3:5).

Now let us go a step further: Jesus said, "water *and* Spirit." We know that God is a Spirit (John 4:24), but is God *"water,"* literally speaking? Suppose we look into the Word of God:

Jesus said to His disciples, "Now ye are clean *through the WORD* which I have spoken unto you" (John 15:3). In Ephesians 5:25, 26 Paul said of the Church, ". . . Christ also loved the Church, and gave Himself for it; that He might sanctify and cleanse it *with the washing of water by the WORD."* In Titus 3:5 we read, "Not by works of righteousness which we have done, but according to His mercy He saved us, *by the washing of regeneration,* and renewing of the Holy Ghost." Thus we are born, cleansed, redeemed and sanctified by "washing by water" — always referring to the Word.

The Samaritan woman at the well asked Jesus for the living water of which He had told her — water that would permanently quench her thirst. Jesus gave her the water — but *what did He give her?* He gave her the WORD: "I that speak unto thee am He." When Jesus said that, the woman threw down her waterpots, ran into the town, and told the men that she had found the Messiah! A great revival broke out as a result of her testimony.

So we see that the "water" is the WORD. We are *born* of the Word and of the Spirit. We are *cleansed* by the Word, by "the *washing* of the Word." We are regenerated by "the *washing* of regeneration" — the new birth. The new birth comes by water (the Word) and by the Spirit. So *Jesus* came by water and Spirit — He was the Word of God in flesh. The Word was in the beginning with God, the Word was God, and the

Word became flesh. Jesus came to earth in a body of flesh
to declare the Father — and He DID declare the Father in
words. He said, "He that *heareth my Word,* and believeth
on Him that sent me, hath everlasting life" (John 5:24 in part).

It is true that Jesus was baptized in water — the record is
found in Matthew 3:13-17. Certainly he did not need to be
baptized to take away any *sin,* because in HIM there WAS
no sin; He was "Jesus Christ the righteous." So the water
baptism of Jesus had nothing to do with sin. He was baptized at the *beginning* of His earthly ministry, and at the *close*
of His ministry, at the crucifixion, when the soldier thrust his
spear into the side of Jesus, *"forthwith came there out blood
and WATER"* (John 19:34).

It is true that Jesus was baptized in water at the beginning
of His earthly ministry, and at the close of His ministry, blood
and water ran from His pierced side; and so far as I am concerned I certainly would not break fellowship with anyone who
contends that the water in our present verse is *baptismal*
water, or that it is the water that gushed from the Saviour's
side when He was crucified; but to me, the following verses
prove that the "water" is the Word — and of course we know
that the *blood* is the cleansing blood of Jesus.

*"And it is the Spirit that beareth witness, because the Spirit
is truth."* At Christ's baptism the Holy Spirit (not water) descended and remained upon Him, and John had been instructed
that whosoever the Spirit came and remained upon would be
the Son of God. So the Spirit, as well as God the Father,
testified at the baptism of Jesus that He was the Son of God —
the Messiah, King of kings and Lord of lords, who had come
into the world as Jesus (Saviour) to save His people from
their sins.

The Spirit (not water) testified to John that he was baptizing
the Son of God, and the Spirit also witnesses to US, testifying
to our hearts when we *possess* the Son of God: "The Spirit
(Himself) beareth witness with our spirit, that we are the
children of God" (Rom. 8:16). Also, in chapter 3, verse 24
of our present epistle we read, ". . . hereby we KNOW that
He abideth in us, *by the Spirit which He hath given us."*

In chapter 2, verses 20 and 27 we read, "But ye have an

unction from the Holy One, and ye know all things . . . But the anointing which ye have received of Him abideth in you, and ye need not that any man teach you: but as the same anointing teacheth you of all things, and is truth, and is no lie, and even as it hath taught you, ye shall abide in Him."

Just before His crucifixion, Jesus told His disciples, "I have yet many things to say unto you, but ye cannot bear them now. *Howbeit when HE, the Spirit of truth, is come, HE will guide you into ALL truth*: for He shall not speak of Himself; but whatsoever He shall hear, that shall He speak: and He will shew you things to come. He shall glorify me: for He shall receive of mine, and shall shew it unto you. All things that the Father hath are mine: therefore said I, that He shall take of mine, and shall shew it unto you" (John 16:12-15).

Verses 7 and 8: "For there are three that bear record in heaven, the Father, the Word, and the Holy Ghost: and these three are one. And there are three that bear witness in earth, the Spirit, and the water, and the blood: and these three agree in one."

The three that bear record in heaven are the Father, the Word (Jesus), the Holy Ghost — *and these three are one.* Here is presented the Trinity — Father, Son, and Holy Ghost,

The three that bear witness in earth are the Holy Spirit, the water, and the blood — and *"these three agree in one."*

Now let me point out something which I trust you will see: Father, Son, and Holy Ghost bear record in heaven — and certainly we know that God is not divided. Therefore, since the Trinity — the Father, the Word (Jesus), and the Holy Ghost — bear record in heaven, it is these three who also bear record in earth. Since the *Word* bears record in heaven, then the Word (not *water*) bears record on earth.

The blood mentioned here is the blood of God. Some things are hard to receive because we cannot understand them; but if we have Scripture that declares this truth, we can accept that declaration even though we may not understand it:

"Take heed therefore unto yourselves, and to all the flock, over the which the Holy Ghost hath made you overseers, to feed the Church of God, *which He hath purchased WITH HIS OWN BLOOD"* (Acts 20:28).

Now what do we have in this verse? Here, admonition is given to pastors (overseers) to feed the Church of God, the body of Christ as described in Ephesians 5:23-32. The Church of God was *purchased* — but *WHO purchased it?* According to this passage, *GOD purchased His Church with His own blood.* We may not understand this, we may not be able to explain it; but the Church of God was purchased with God's own blood, and therefore *the blood shed by Jesus on Calvary was the blood of God.* God begat Jesus — He overshadowed Mary in the Person of the Holy Ghost, she conceived, and gave birth to the only begotten Son of God. The life of the flesh is in the blood (Lev. 17:11) and it was through His blood shed for the remission of sins that God purchased His Church.

Therefore we have the Trinity: God's blood; the Word (Jesus); the Holy Spirit. The same three who bear record on earth also bear witness in heaven — one God, manifested in three Persons. We must interpret Scripture in the light of other Scripture; and since God is not divided, we have in these verses not *six* witnesses, but *three* — three in heaven, the same three on earth.

If we need further proof, we find it in John 12:46-48. Jesus said, "I am come a light into the world, that whosoever believeth on me should not abide in darkness. And if any man hear my WORDS, and believe not, I judge him not: for I came not to judge the world, but to save the world. He that rejecteth me, and receiveth not my WORDS, hath one that judgeth him: the WORD that I have spoken, *the same shall judge him in the last day.*"

Now let us compare Scripture with Scripture, spiritual things with spiritual: In II Timothy 4:1 Paul said, "I charge thee therefore before God, and *the Lord Jesus Christ, who shall judge the quick and the dead at His appearing and His kingdom.*" In the passage from John, *the Word* will judge; in the passage from Timothy, *the Lord Jesus Christ* will judge — both the living and the dead. The Word and Jesus are inseparable because Jesus was the Word in flesh (John 1:1, 14). He brought the Word down to man, and now *Jesus the Man* sits at the right hand of the Majesty to plead our case and make intercession to God the Father for us, His children by faith.

Jesus came by water (by the Word) — but not by words alone. He did not come and simply *announce* that God so loved; He *proved* God's love by laying down His life for us. Yes, Jesus came speaking words — wonderful words of life (John 6:63); but He not only spoke words: *He gave His blood.* He came by water and blood, and the Spirit testified that He was the Son of God.

I believe in baptism as much as any minister possibly could; but my precious believer, we must not add anything to the finished work of the Lamb of God. Baptism is right, it is scriptural, and it should be practiced. Every born again believer should be immersed in water in the name of the Father, and of the Son, and of the Holy Ghost. Every born again believer should likewise examine himself and receive the bread and the fruit of the vine. This should be done until Jesus comes again — but baptism and the Lord's Supper have nothing to do with our redemption. Jesus came to redeem us, He came to save sinners, and He completed the work for which He came. Therefore we must not add water, works, or anything else to His finished work. We are the product of HIS work: *"For we are His workmanship,* created in Christ Jesus unto good works, which God hath before ordained that we should walk in them" (Eph. 2:10).

Salvation leads us into good works. We are saved TO work, we are not saved BY works; and works do not add to our redemption. Works determine our reward — yes; but works do not bring redemption.

God's Testimony Concerning the Son

Verse 9: "If we receive the witness of men, the witness of God is greater: for this is the witness of God which He hath testified of His Son."

All of us receive the witness of men — that is, when we are *children* we believe what our parents tell us. As we grow older and begin our education, we believe what our school-teachers tell us. In the courts of justice, witnesses are under oath to tell the truth, and the judge and jury accept their testimony *as truth.* We read our newspapers and periodicals, and accept the testimony of reporters and newsmen. We study history, and believe the accounts laid down in our history books. No one doubts that George Washington was the first president of the United States — but we who are living today certainly did not *see* him! In this astounding day and age we believe what our spacemen have said concerning the great outer space, where until recently no man had ventured. We have not *been* there, but we believe the testimony of those who *have.* As a matter of fact, beloved, *if we did not believe the testimony given by others we simply could not get along in this life!* The affairs of this world would come to a climax if men ceased to believe the witness of other men, and the Holy Spirit uses this illustration here in order to point out that *"the witness of God is greater"* than the witness of men.

Certainly God's report is much more worthy of our trust and faith. We know that God cannot lie (Heb. 6:18; Tit. 1:2). In Romans 3:4 Paul said "Let God be true, but every man a liar." It is possible for men to bear false witness — sometimes unknowingly, sometimes intentionally; but it is impossible for God to lie or bear false witness. Men have been known to bear false witness for the express purpose of hurting others, but God could never do this, because *God is LOVE.* The witness God has given is truth. Whatsoever He has said can be depended upon. We can hear it, believe it, live by it, and die by it!

"For this is the witness of God which He hath testified of His Son." At the trial of Jesus the Jews said, "We have a law, and by our law He ought to die, *because He made Himself the Son of God"* (John 19:7) — but my dear friend, Jesus did not need to *make Himself* the Son of God. His birth was announced by angels (Luke 2:1-14). His entrance into His public ministry was heralded by God the Father as He announced from heaven, "This is my beloved Son, in whom I am well pleased" (Matt. 3:17). Again on the Mount of transfiguration God audibly announced, "This is my beloved Son, in whom I am well pleased; hear ye Him" (Matt. 17:5).

Just before His crucifixion Jesus cried out to the heavenly Father, "Now is my soul troubled; and what shall I say?

Father, save me from this hour: but for this cause came I unto this hour. Father, glorify thy name. Then came there a voice from heaven, saying, *I have both glorified it, and will glorify it again.* The people therefore, that stood by, and heard it, said that it thundered: others said, An angel spake to Him. Jesus answered and said, This voice came not because of me, but for your sakes" (John 12:27-30). So you see, beloved, on four occasions heaven plainly declared that Jesus was truly the Son of God, and the testimony of God concerning His Son continues in the next three verses of our present study.

Verse 10: "He that believeth on the Son of God hath the witness in himself: he that believeth not God hath made Him a liar; because he believeth not the record that God gave of His Son."

This is one of the most significant and tremendously important "assurance" verses in the New Testament. We are saved by believing on Jesus (John 1:12, 13; 3:16, 18, 36; 5:24; 6:47; Acts 16:31); and when God saves a person, He puts *the Witness* within that person's heart. There is no such thing as salvation apart from assurance; we *know* that we have passed from death unto life; we *know* that our names are written in the Lamb's book of life. Because of the Witness within us *we know WHOM we have believed* and we can say with John, "Hereby we know that He abideth in us, by the Spirit which He hath given us" (I John 3:24).

But notice this: "*He that believeth not God hath made Him (God) a liar.*" Seriously now, would *you* be guilty of calling God a liar? I do not believe you would knowingly do that — and yet, my dear friend, if you are not saved, and if after reading these words you close this book and refuse to receive Jesus as your Saviour, you automatically call God a liar. The Word plainly says, "He that *believeth not God* hath made Him a liar!" Have you read John 3:16? or has it been read aloud in your presence? If you have read or heard the message of that verse and then rejected it you have branded God a liar and declared John 3:16 untrue. Think it over. It is a very serious thing to be exposed to the Word of God and turn a deaf ear to its message.

Why is a person calling God a liar if he believeth not? The

last part of our verse answers: *"BECAUSE he believeth not the record that God gave of His Son."*

Let me illustrate:

The Word of God promises eternal life if we will *hear* the Word and believe on the Lord Jesus Christ (John 5:24; I Pet. 1:23). The Word of God also promises that the grace that *saves* us is able to *keep* us (Rom. 8:31-39). We have God's guarantee that if we hear the Word, believe on Jesus and trust in His finished work He will *save* us, He will *never leave us,* He will *keep* us, and we will be *victorious* over the world, the flesh, and the devil (I John 4:4).

Through God's Word we have the assurance that He will supply our every need in this life (Matt. 6:33; Phil. 4:19), and also the assurance and the guarantee of a home in heaven. God has reserved for us a place in the Pearly White City — an inheritance which Peter describes in words that are inspired of God:

"Blessed be the God and Father of our Lord Jesus Christ, which according to His abundant mercy hath begotten us again unto a lively hope by the resurrection of Jesus Christ from the dead, *to an inheritance incorruptible, and undefiled, and that fadeth not away, reserved in heaven for you,* who are kept by the power of God through faith unto salvation ready to be revealed in the last time" (I Pet. 1:3-5).

In John 14:1-3 Jesus promised to prepare a place for His children, and that He would return and receive us unto Himself:

"Let not your heart be troubled: ye believe in God, believe also in me. In my Father's house are many mansions: if it were not so, I would have told you. *I go to prepare a place for you. And if I go and prepare a place for you, I WILL COME AGAIN, and receive you unto myself; that where I am, there ye may be also."*

Now let us sum up what has been said:

When we hear the Word of God and believe on the Lord Jesus Christ, God saves us for Christ's sake and gives us victory over the world, the flesh, and the devil. Then He keeps us by His mighty power, supplies our every need, and reserves a home for us in heaven — a home that will never fade away. He also promises to come for us, and take us where He is, "and so shall we ever be with the Lord" (I Thess. 4:17).

Beloved, in God there is no variableness nor shadow of turning (James 1:17). Chapter 1 of this present epistle told us that God is *light* and in Him is no darkness at all. He is not twilight, in Him is no shadow, no sunset or dawn — just pure, blazing light. God is truth — not partial truth, not *almost* all truth. God is truth and there is no shadow of error, therefore the record He gave of His Son is either pure truth, or it is purely a lie. Jesus could not have been simply "a good man." He claimed to be God, and if He was NOT God then He was not good. If He was not God then He was the greatest impostor the world has ever known. Therefore for one to hear the record God gave of His Son and reject that record is to commit the most insulting sin possible against God the Father. The person who hears and rejects God's record calls Him a common liar.

Have YOU heard John 3:16? Have YOU heard Romans 3:21-28? Have YOU heard Romans 8:31, 32? If you have, and you are still an unbeliever, you have branded God a liar. Why not stop this very moment and ask God to forgive you and save you for Jesus' sake — and He will do it!.

The Record

Verse 11: "And this is the record, that God hath given to us eternal life, and this life is in His Son."

God said many things about His Son. There are many prophecies in the Old Testament that refer to Him, and many statements about Him in the New Testament — all inspired of God; but the record can be summed up in a very short sentence: "God hath given to us eternal life, AND THIS LIFE IS IN HIS SON." Yes, the record given in this verse is short, but many volumes could be written about it.

"God hath given. . . ." Dear friend, before the world was, before God created the foundation of this earth or the axis upon which it turns, before He created one bit of the dust from which He formed man, He thought, planned, and *wrought* our salvation!

In I Peter 1:18-20 we learn that it was foreordained before the foundation of this world that Jesus the spotless Lamb of

God should redeem us with His precious blood. In the eternity behind us God the Father, God the Son, and God the Holy Ghost met and settled the salvation question; and in that council of the Holy Trinity it was agreed that the Lamb, the only begotten Son, would pay the sin-debt with His own precious blood — and He did exactly that.

The Father laid on Him the iniquity of us all (Isa. 53:6).

He was smitten of God, and afflicted (Isa. 53:4).

He bore our sins in His own body on the cross (I Pet. 2:24).

He laid His life down that we might have life (John 10:18).

Yes, *"God hath given."* Salvation is a gift — it cannot be earned, it cannot be merited through good living or sacrificial giving. Salvation is God's gift to hell-deserving sinners — and the only way to come into possession of a gift is to receive it from the Giver. *God* gave, *Jesus* is the gift, and *to as many as receive Him* He gives power to become the sons of God, "even to them that believe on His name." *God* so loved that He gave His only begotten Son; the *Son* so loved that He came to earth to give His life a ransom for many. He invites, "Come unto me and I will give you rest . . . Him that cometh to me I will in no wise cast out."

Some poor sinners have *sought* salvation, they have tarried long in prayer and then have turned away saying, "I cannot be saved! That is just not for me." The truth of the matter is, we are not saved by trying, we are not saved by tarrying long at an altar, we are not saved through weeping and pleading. *We are saved by RECEIVING THE GIFT OF GOD.*

A hungry man may sit at a table which is laden with food — but he will starve unless he *eats.* Jesus said, "Except ye eat the flesh of the Son of man, and drink His blood, ye have no life in you" (John 6:53). The table is set, the Living Bread has been brought down. The invitation is, "Whosoever will — come and dine. *Eat and live!"*

Men make many excuses for not becoming Christian, but actually there IS no excuse. Romans 2:1 plainly declares, "Therefore thou art inexcusable, O man . . . " Some say, "I cannot *understand* salvation." Others say, "I cannot live the Christian life." Still others say, "If I gave my heart to Jesus I would lose all of my friends." And some poor souls declare, "It would cost me too much to become a Christian! *There is too much to give up.*" I ask you , dear friend, How much does it cost NOT to be a Christian? I invite you to visit the city jails, the chaingangs, the state penitentiaries — and especially do I invite you to visit death row. Ask the men and women who fill our penal institutions how much it cost THEM not to be Christian. Jesus asked the soul-searching question, "What is a man profited, if he shall gain the whole world, and lose his own soul? or what shall a man give in exchange for his soul?" (Matt. 16:26).

"*God HATH given*" — past tense. God is not *going* to give us eternal life at the end of our earthly sojourn — when we die or when Jesus comes. He "hath given" -- eternal life is already ours the moment we are born of the Spirit and washed in His blood. *Victory* comes day by day, *rewards* are earned day by day, but eternal life is not progressive: it becomes ours instantaneously, and we are no more fully redeemed at the end of fifty years than we are when we are first born into God's family. Redemption is sudden, sure, and complete. God does not give us eternal life conditionally, He does not give us eternal life in a measure, and then later redeem us more fully, and finally (at the end of life) give us *full* eternal life! That is not God's way of salvation. He has never done anything partially, He leaves nothing incomplete: "*Beloved, NOW are we the sons of God . . .*" (I John 3:2).

What *kind* of life has God given us? *ETERNAL life.* We give gifts to our loved ones and friends, but those gifts perish — they wear out or they become old and out of date. Not so with God's gift; it is everlasting, eternal. Jesus came that we might have life — abundant and everlasting; and regardless of the changes all around us, our everlasting life remains the same. It never changes, it never grows old, it is never out of date.

Eternal life is an *individual* matter — God gives everlasting life to individuals, not to multitudes, as such. Paul said, "*I am crucified with Christ: nevertheless I live; yet not I, but Christ liveth in ME: and the life which I now live in the flesh, I live by the faith of the Son of God, who loved ME, and gave Himself for ME*" (Gal. 2:20).

There is not one soul that God does not love, there is not one person who cannot have God's gift of eternal life through the shed blood of Jesus. God is not "willing that any should perish, but that all should come to repentance" (II Pet. 3:9). All who will come to Jesus can be saved, "whosoever will" may have God's gift of eternal life.

"And this life is in His Son." This is one of the clearest statements anyone will ever read, and yet the masses misunderstand it. They refuse to believe it. Jesus is LIFE, Jesus is salvation. All believers have eternal life because they have Jesus in their hearts. He does not *show* us the way, He IS the way. He does not *open* the door of salvation, He IS the door. He not only has *power* to save us, He is our SAVIOUR. He not only has power to raise us from the dead, He IS the RESURRECTION and the life.

Therefore

Verse 12: "He that hath the Son hath life; and he that hath not the Son of God hath not life."

This verse presses home to our hearts the vital truth that Christ within us is salvation, Christ in us is the hope of glory; and if we do not have Christ in our hearts we do not have life. Salvation is SOMEONE, not *something*. Salvation is Jesus, the one and only Saviour, the only begotten Son of God, dwelling within the heart:

"There is therefore now no condemnatinn to them which are in Christ Jesus, who walk not after the flesh, but after the Spirit" (Rom. 8:1).

"To whom God would make known what is the riches of the glory of this mystery among the Gentiles; which is Christ in you, the hope of glory" (Col. 1:27).

"Giving thanks unto the Father, which hath made us meet to be partakers of the inheritance of the saints in light: who hath delivered us from the power of darkness, and hath translated us into the kingdom of His dear Son: in whom we have redemption through His blood, even the forgiveness of sins" (Col. 1:12-14).

"For ye are dead, and your life is hid with Christ in God" (Col. 3:3).

Those Who Are Saved Know It

Verse 13: "These things have I written unto you that believe on the name of the Son of God; that ye may know that ye have eternal life, and that ye may believe on the name of the Son of God."

Notice the repetition in this verse: ". . . *you that believe on the name of the Son of God . . . that ye may believe on the name of the Son of God.*" God does not need to say anything but once to make it true, and when there is repetition of the same words or phrases in one verse of Scripture we may rest assured of the *Divine importance* of those words or phrases. This verse gives Divine support of the Bible fact that *faith* is the principle of the Christian life. Christianity *begins* in faith, *continues* in faith, *climaxes* in faith — and whatsoever is NOT of faith is sin! Without faith it is impossible to please God. We who are believers do not merely *think* we are saved, we do not simply *hope* we are saved, we do not just *feel* like we are saved, we are not, by good works or holy living, "just trying to make it to heaven." We KNOW that we are saved. The Word of God declares it and we believe it, because GOD CANNOT LIE.

Every good and perfect gift, everything worth giving or receiving — in this life and in the life to come — is from God: "Every good gift and every perfect gift is from above, and cometh down from the Father of lights, with whom is no variableness, neither shadow of turning" (James 1:17). Receiving Jesus is just the beginning of eternal life, for in that gift of God there are many blessings. All those blessings are in CHRIST, every need is met in Him who is our life: "He that spared not His own Son, but delivered Him up for us all, how shall He not with Him also freely give us all things?" (Rom. 8:32).

In Christ We Are Complete

"Beware lest any man spoil you through philosophy and vain deceit, after the tradition of men, after the rudiments of the world, and not after Christ. For in Him dwelleth all the fulness of the Godhead bodily, and ye are complete in Him which is the head of all principality and power" (Col. 2:8-10).

201

We who are in Christ possess all things; *heaven is at our disposal*! If we seek first His kingdom all things are then added — but apart from Christ NOTHING can be ours. Those outside of Christ are hopeless, helpless paupers.

What glorious possessions we have IN Christ! Eternal life is life that *grows*: "Grow in grace, and in the knowledge of our Lord and Saviour Jesus Christ. To Him be glory both now and for ever. Amen" (II Pet. 3:18).

Eternal life is life that *knows*: "Ye have an unction from the Holy One, and ye know all things" (I John 2:20).

When we possess eternal life, the life we live *shows* that we are children of God: "Return to thine own house, and shew how great things God hath done unto thee . . ." (Luke 8:39).

Believers possess life that produces rivers of living water, life that *flows*: "He that believeth on me, as the Scripture hath said, out of his belly shall flow rivers of living water" (John 7:38).

Assurance in Prayer

Verses 14 and 15: "And this is the confidence that we have in Him, that, if we ask any thing according to His will, He heareth us: And if we know that He hear us, whatsoever we ask, we know that we have the petitions that we desired of Him."

"This is the confidence that we have in Him." Here, "confidence" has to do with answered prayer, which is one of the results of believing on the Lord Jesus Christ (v. 13). When we *truly believe*, we have the assurance that our prayers will be answered if we pray in the will of God.

In chapter 3 verse 21 of this epistle we were told, "Beloved, if our heart condemn us not, then have we *confidence toward God*." In chapter 4 verse 17, "Herein is our love made perfect, that we may have boldness (*confidence*) in the day of judgment: because as He is, so are we in this world."

We have confidence (assurance) concerning our *salvation*, we have confidence (assurance, boldness) concerning *the day of judgment*, and we have confidence concerning *prayer*. True believers are assured that God will do what He has promised. *"If we ask anything according to His will He heareth us."*

Here is given the proper and necessary attitude (and limitation) in prayer. God has *not promised* to grant us things contrary to His will. He answers prayer — but sometimes His answer is "no" when we think He should say "yes." We should always pray as JESUS prayed: "Not my will, but thine, be done." The true Christian does not want God to answer any petition contrary to His divine will; we want Him to give whatever is best for us, whatever will glorify HIM. The true believer should always be ready to rest his case in the hands of Him who *knows and does* whatever is best for us — and who could better know our needs than the God who loved us and gave His only begotten Son to die for us?

What is meant by *"according to His will"?* Surely the Holy Spirit means *"in accordance with what God has made known CONCERNING His will."* There are many verses in the New Testament that definitely point out the will of God — for example, I Thessalonians 4:3: *"For this is the will of God,* even your sanctification, that ye should abstain from fornication." It is always God's will to forgive sins and sanctify the believer. It is always His will to comfort us in the hour of sorrow, to supply our every need, to furnish sufficient grace and wisdom for our guidance and direction.

In Philippians 4:13, 19 Paul said, "I can do all things *through Christ* which strengtheneth me . . . My God shall supply all your need according to His riches in glory *by Christ Jesus."*

In John 14:27 Jesus told His disciples, "Peace I leave with you, MY peace I give unto you: not as the world giveth, give I unto you. Let not your heart be troubled, neither let it be afraid."

In James 1:5 we read, "If any of you lack wisdom, let him ask of God, that giveth to all men liberally, and upbraideth not; and it shall be given him."

In II Corinthians 12:7-10 Paul said, "Lest I should be exalted above measure through the abundance of the revelations, there was given to me a thorn in the flesh, the messenger of Satan to buffet me, lest I should be exalted above measure. For this thing I besought the Lord thrice, that it might depart from me. And He said unto me, My grace is sufficient for thee: for my strength is made perfect in weakness. Most gladly therefore will I rather glory in my infirmities, that the power of Christ may rest upon me. Therefore I take pleasure in infirmities, in reproaches, in necessities, in persecutions, in distresses for Christ's sake: for when I am weak, then am I strong."

We should always remember when we pray that we are members of God's *family*, members of the body of Christ, and as we pray for God's will to be done we should not think of our own needs and blessings without taking into consideration *the family of God*. In earthly families a child might ask from the parent something that would interfere with the rights, comforts, and well being of the rest of the family, and in such case the father would withhold such request. The same is true in the family of God: we should never be selfish in our prayers. Our attitude should be, "Lord, let me live from day to day/ In such a self-forgetful way/That even when I kneel to pray,/ My prayer shall be *for others*." When we demonstrate such love and unselfishness, we may rest assured that God will take care of our individual needs.

There are times when we know not *what* we should pray for, and at such times the Holy Spirit intercedes on our behalf:

"Likewise the Spirit also helpeth our infirmities: for we know not what we should pray for as we ought: but the Spirit itself maketh intercession for us with groanings which cannot be uttered. And He that searcheth the hearts knoweth what is the mind of the Spirit, because *He maketh intercession for the saints according to the will of God*" (Rom. 8:26, 27).

If we would have more assurance that God answers prayer when we pray according to His will, we should study the lives of Moses, David, Elijah, Daniel, Nehemiah, the Apostle Paul — and even the life of Christ Himself. Jesus sometimes prayed all night — and if HE needed to pray, how much more should WE realize our need and take advantage of the privilege of prayer!

Prayer works wonders in the life of the believer: "They that wait upon the Lord shall renew their strength; they shall mount up with wings as eagles; they shall run, and not be weary; and they shall walk, and not faint" (Isa. 40:31).

In this marvelous Day of Grace there is no definite place or position for prayer. It seems that Jesus often prayed in the mountains: "And when He had sent the multitudes away, He went up into a mountain apart to pray: and when the evening was come, He was there alone" (Matt. 14:23). He also loved to pray in the Garden of Gethsemane (John 18:2).

Daniel loved to pray before an open window in his room, with his face turned toward Jerusalem: "Now when Daniel knew that the writing was signed, he went into his house; and his windows being open in his chamber toward Jerusalem, he kneeled upon his knees three times a day, and prayed, and gave thanks before his God, as he did aforetime" (Dan. 6:10).

But is not necessary to be in the mountains, in a room, in a garden, or in church. We can pray anywhere, at any time, knowing that if we pray according to the will of God, He hears and answers prayer. The believer should pray about everything he does, everywhere he goes, every change he makes. There is nothing too small and insignificant, nothing too mammoth or complicated, for God to take time to work out for us. When we need pennies, we should ask the Lord for pennies, but when we need hundreds of dollars we should not be afraid to ASK for hundreds of dollars. God is able to supply ALL needs — both small and great. We should pray about our health, we should pray about our family needs and family life, we should pray about the needs of the community, we should pray about anything and all things that have to do with our success in the Christian life or that have to do with glorifying the name of Jesus as we travel this earthly pilgrimage.

James said, "Is any among you afflicted? Let him pray. Is any merry? Let him sing psalms. Is any sick among you? Let him call for the elders of the church; and let them pray over him, anointing him with oil in the name of the Lord: And the prayer of faith shall save the sick, and the Lord shall raise him up; and if he have committed sins, they shall be forgiven him. Confess your faults one to another, and pray one for another, that ye may be healed. The effectual fervent prayer of a righteous man availeth much. Elias was a man subject to like passions as we are, and he prayed earnestly that it might not rain: and it rained not on the earth by the space of three years and six months. And he prayed again, and the heaven gave rain, and the earth brought forth her fruit. Brethren, if any of you do err from the truth, and one convert him; let him know, that he which converteth the sinner from the error of his way shall save a soul from death, and shall hide a multitude of sins" (James 5:13-20).

God has not changed. We serve the God of Elijah, and when we trust and obey as Elijah did, God will answer our prayers.

The objective side of prayer is the theme of our present verses. *"Anything"* in verse 14 is like *"whatsoever"* in chapter 3, verse 22: "Whatsoever we ask, we receive of Him, because we keep His commandments, and do those things that are pleasing in His sight." You will notice that "anything" and "whatsoever" depend upon *conditions* — "according to His will" and "because we keep His commandments."

As we consider these verses, we face the fact that we *must* be born of God, submissive, obedient, keeping His commandments, abiding in Him. We must *know* the will of God, and the only place to learn His will is in His WORD. Knowing that we are born again by believing in the finished work and the shed blood of Jesus, knowing that we obey His Word, keep His commandments and abide in Him, and knowing His divine will, we are ready to *ask* — being assured that "WE HAVE THE PETITIONS THAT WE DESIRED OF HIM."

We need to read James 4:2-10 often: "Ye lust, and have not: ye kill, and desire to have, and cannot obtain: ye fight and war, yet ye have not, because ye ask not. Ye ask, and receive not, because ye ask amiss, that ye may consume it upon your lusts.

"Ye adulterers and adulteresses, know ye not that the friendship of the world is enmity with God? Whosoever therefore will be a friend of the world is the enemy of God. Do ye think that the Scripture saith in vain, The spirit that dwelleth in us lusteth to envy? But He giveth more grace. Wherefore He saith God resisteth the proud, but giveth grace unto the humble. Submit yourselves therefore to God. Resist the devil, and he will flee from you.

"Draw nigh to God, and He will draw nigh to you. Cleanse your hands, ye sinners; and purify your hearts, ye double minded. Be afflicted, and mourn, and weep: let your laughter be turned to mourning, and your joy to heaviness. *Humble yourselves in the sight of the Lord, and He shall lift you up!"*

It is true that God may not grant the specific thing for which we pray (Luke 22:42; II Cor. 12:8, 9); but He never *disre-*

gards the prayers of His children. If it is for our good that God withhold what we ask for, then He *withholds* it. But God is faithful and we know that He will do that which is best for us if we are willing for His will to be wrought in our lives. Therefore *we know that we have the petitions* — perhaps not immediately and not necessarily as we *ask* them; but if we are truly surrendered to His will, God will answer in His own good time as He sees best. He may delay the answer to try our faith, to *strengthen* us in the faith; but the heart's desire and first prayer of every Christian should be, "Lord, grant unto me those things that will be for my good and bring the most glory to your name!"

The believer who finds time to strive in earnest, faithful, believing prayer will thrive in the Christian life and his life will glorify God. Many believers are not eloquent in words — they pray in poor English and broken phrases; but the stammering prayer of *an abiding believer* is music to the ears of God. He does not listen to the *construction* of the prayer, He looks upon the sincerity of the heart — and He hears and answers.

Let us notice a few of the prayers recorded in God's Word: In Luke 18:13 the publican prayed the prayer of the penitent sinner: "God be merciful to me a sinner" — and Jesus tells us that this man "went down to his house justified (saved)."

Psalm 17:8 records the prayer of a feeble saint: "Keep me as the apple of the eye, hide me under the shadow of thy wings."

In humble submission to God we should pray with the psalmist, "Shew me thy ways, O Lord; teach me thy paths. Lead me in thy truth, and teach me: for thou art the God of my salvation; on thee do I wait all the day" (Psalm 25:4, 5).

When we are tempted we should pray, "O my God, I trust in thee . . . let not mine enemies triumph over me" (Psalm 25:2).

The believer should be willing at all time to pray, "*Search me, O God, and know my heart: try me, and know my thoughts: and see if there be any wicked way in me, and lead me in the way everlasting*" (Psalm 139:23, 24).

According to Philippians 4:6, the Christian should pray about *everything*: "Be careful for nothing; but *in every thing by prayer and supplication with thanksgiving let your requests be made known unto God.*"

Moses prayed when the Israelites sinned and were being bitten by the fiery serpents. The Lord answered his prayer — and prescribed a remedy (Numbers 21:9).

Elijah prayed — and God sent the ravens to feed him: "And the Word of the Lord came unto him, saying, Get thee hence, and turn thee eastward, and hide thyself by the brook Cherith, that is before Jordan. And it shall be, that thou shalt drink of the brook; and I have commanded the ravens to feed thee there. So he went and did according unto the word of the Lord: for he went and dwelt by the brook Chedrith, that is before Jordan. And the ravens brought him bread and flesh in the morning, and bread and flesh in the evening: and he drank of the brook" (I Kings 17:1-6). God still has many ravens.

Naaman was a leper, and in answer to prayer he was cleansed. He obeyed the word of God's prophet, he believed, and God healed him (II Kings 5:1-14).

Mark 5:25-29 tells of the woman who had spent all of her living on doctors, but in spite of their care she had grown worse. She had a believing prayer in her heart: she believed that if she could but touch the hem of the Saviour's garment she would be healed. She *touched* His garment, "and straightway . . . she was healed of that plague."

Some people *pray*, others simply *say words*. True praying is petition — in faith making our requests known unto God. "Without faith it is impossible to please (God): for he that cometh to God must believe that He is, and that He is a rewarder of them that diligently seek Him" (Heb. 11:6).

Prayer is perseverance in intercession — we should pray untiringly. Jesus prayed all night. If the answer does not come within the next few seconds, we should keep on interceding and seeking.

Spiritual germs cannot live in an environment of prayer. Spiritually speaking, prayer kills germs that would cause us to be weak, handicapped Christians. Prayer brings spiritual help, strength, and vigor. Intercessory prayer puts roses in the cheeks of our spiritual man. Paul admonished the Thessalonians, *"Pray without ceasing"* (I Thess. 5:17).

To make our supplications unto the Lord concerning our *personal* needs is good, but we should not stop there; we should be intercessors for the needs of others. The Syrophenician woman prayed, "Lord, help ME" — but actually, her *heart cry was for help concerning her daughter* (Mark 7:25-30) — and her prayer was answered.

In Matthew 6:6 Jesus said, "But thou, when thou prayest, enter into thy closet, and when thou hast shut thy door, pray to thy Father which is in secret; and thy Father which seeth in secret shall reward thee openly."

In Matthew 7:7 He said, "Ask, and it shall be given you; seek, and ye shall find; knock, and it shall be opened unto you."

When we pray we must remember that we are speaking to the heavenly Father, Almighty God; and we must approach Him in reverence and humility. (Had it not been for God's love and grace in providing Jesus, we could not approach Him *at all*.) God took the initiative in salvation, and the same is true in prayer. God opened the door of salvation in His Son: Jesus IS the door. God also opened the door of prayer, but we cannot approach Him in prayer except in Jesus' name.

However, Paul tells us in Hebrews 10:19 that in the name of Jesus and through His blood we can approach God with boldness: "Having therefore, brethren, boldness to enter into the holiest by the blood of Jesus, by a new and living way, which He hath consecrated for us through the veil, that is to say, His flesh." And in Hebrews 4:16 we read, "Let us therefore come boldly unto the throne of grace, that we may obtain mercy, and find grace to help in time of need."

The Sin unto Death

Verse 16: "If any man see his brother sin a sin which is not unto death, he shall ask, and he shall give him life for them that sin not unto death. There is a sin unto death: I do not say that he shall pray for it."

There is a difference between the *unpardonable sin* and the *sin unto death*. The *sinner* commits the unpardonable sin, the *believer* commits the sin unto death. The unpardonable sin is blasphemy against the Holy Spirit (Matt. 12:31, 32), and certainly a born again believer — *indwelt* by the Holy Spirit, *led* by the Holy Spirit and *sealed* by the Holy Spirit — would not *blaspheme* the Holy Spirit! A born again believer will never commit *the unpardonable sin,* which has to do with destruction of the soul, but a believer *can* commit "the sin unto death."

"If any man see his brother sin a sin which is not unto death. . . ." Remember, this letter was written to "the little born ones," and thus the brother of a believer would be *another believer.* Therefore, if we who are believers see a born again brother sin a sin which is NOT unto death, we may pray concerning that sin and God will give life *"for them that sin not unto death."*

But *"there IS a sin unto death,"* and when a believer has committed that sin there is no point in praying for him. In the life of Abraham we find an illustration of a time when it was useless to pray. In Genesis 18:20-30 God revealed to Abraham that He was going to destroy Sodom and Gomorrah. Abraham knew that his nephew Lot and his family were living in Sodom, so he drew near to God and asked, "Wilt thou also destroy the righteous with the wicked? Peradventure there be fifty righteous within the city: wilt thou also destroy and not spare the place for the fifty righteous that are therein?" The Lord replied, "If I find in Sodom fifty righteous within the city, then I will spare all the place for their sakes." But there could not be fifty righteous men found in all of Sodom — and Abraham continued to pray until the number was reduced to ten — just *ten righteous people* in the great city of Sodom. And the Lord said, "I will not destroy it for ten's sake." But God knew that ten righteous ones could not be found in the city, and verse 33 tells us that "THE LORD WENT HIS WAY, as soon as He had left communing with Abraham."

With God there is a stopping place, a limit; and Abraham had reached that limit in his intercession for Sodom. God ceased communing with him and left Him. What God actually said in departing was, "Abraham, there is no need to pray any longer. There is no need for you to make further request. Pray no more for Sodom, for that city *must be destroyed!*" When a city or an individual has committed such sin, there is no reason for any Christian to pray for that city or that individual.

There are times when we should no longer pray **for certain** people, there are times when we should no longer *witness* to certain people. Concerning things spiritual Jesus said, "Give not that which is holy unto the dogs, neither cast ye your pearls before swine, lest they trample them under their feet, and turn again and rend you" (Matt. 7:6).

God spoke to Hosea concerning Ephraim who had grievously backslidden: "*Ephraim is joined to idols: LET HIM ALONE*" (Hos. 4:17). In other words, God said "There is no need for further warning, no need for further *praying*. Let him alone! let sin run its course" — and it did! Read Hosea 14:4-8.

What IS "*the sin unto death*"? The best place to find the answer is in Paul's letter to the church at Corinth. If you will study the eleventh chapter of I Corinthians in its entirety, you will find that some of the believers were grievously misbehaving at the Lord's table, making gluttons of themselves and drinking until they became intoxicated. Paul said to them, "When ye come together therefore into one place, this is not to eat the Lord's supper. For in eating every one taketh before other his own supper: and one is hungry, and another is drunken. What? have ye not houses to eat and to drink in? or despise ye the Church of God, and shame them that have not? What shall I say to you? Shall I praise you in this? I praise you not" (I Cor. 11:20-22).

In the following verses of that chapter, Paul instructed the Corinthians to examine themselves, search their hearts, and to eat the bread and drink the fruit of the vine only after such examination; for if they should eat the bread and take the cup unworthily they were guilty of the body and blood of the Lord. He followed those instructions with the observation, "FOR THIS CAUSE many are weak and sickly among you, AND MANY SLEEP (are dead)."

Paul also warned the Corinthian Christians that if they would judge *themselves*, repent of their misbehaving in the house of God and straighten up, God would not be forced to judge them; but if they did *not* judge themselves, God would have no *alternative* but to judge and chasten them, that they should "not be condemned with the world" (I Cor. 11:32).

The "sin unto death" therefore is *continually rebelling* against light. When a believer *knows* what he should do, when he is

211

convicted that he should do it, and yet he refuses to obey the Holy Spirit and the Word of God, he is in danger of committing the sin unto death.

We have another instance of this in I Corinthians 5:1-5, when immorality was found in the church. A young man had taken his father's wife and was guilty of fornication. There are those who will not agree that this young man was saved and had committed the sin unto death, but Paul clearly told the other believers in the church what action they should take in this matter:

"In the name of our Lord Jesus, Christ, when ye are gathered together, and my spirit, with the power of our Lord Jesus Christ, to DELIVER SUCH AN ONE UNTO SATAN, FOR THE DESTRUCTION OF THE FLESH, THAT THE SPIRIT MAY BE SAVED IN THE DAY OF THE LORD JESUS" (I Cor. 5:4, 5).

Beloved, it is clear that the sin unto death has nothing to do with the salvation of the soul; it *has to do* with the destruction of the body. Such a person will "suffer loss, *but he himself shall be saved; yet so as by fire*" (I Cor. 3:12-15). All reward is lost, and such a one will stand before God empty handed. What that will mean, I confess I do not know; but according to the passage from I Corinthians, the person who loses his reward will "*suffer loss*" — not loss of soul and spirit, but loss of eternal reward.

Verse 17: "All unrighteousness is sin: and there is a sin not unto death."

According to the Word of God, "All have sinned and come short of the glory of God . . . there is none righteous, no, not one . . . If we say we have no sin, we deceive ourselves and the truth is not in us . . . If we say we have not sinned, we make God a liar and His Word is not in us." Man can (and DOES) sin; but God saves when we repent of our sin and put our faith in the shed blood and finished work of the Lord Jesus Christ. The "sin unto death" is different: it is fatal, and there is no need to pray for a person who has committed that sin.

"*All unrighteousness is sin.*" Men do not agree on the definition of sin, but the Word of God makes it very clear: "Whosoever committeth sin transgresseth also the law: for *sin is the transgression of the law*" (I John 3:4). God's law is holy; and to break the least of His commandments is to be guilty of all. That is why, of necessity, Jesus paid the sin-debt. No one else *could* pay it. What God demanded, only God could provide. Jesus fulfilled every jot and tittle of the law (Matt. 5:17), and therefore He is *"the end of the law for righteousness to everyone that believeth* (Rom. 10:4).

There are those who will not agree that the sin unto death is *physical* death, and that it always applies to a believer. We know that SIN brings *spiritual* death. In the Garden of Eden God said to Adam, "Of the tree of the knowledge of good and evil, thou shalt not eat of it: for in the day that thou eatest thereof THOU SHALT SURELY DIE" (Gen. 2:17). Adam ate — and he died spiritually that very moment! Ezekiel 18:4 proclaims, "The soul that sinneth, it shall die." Paul declared, "Wherefore, as by one man sin entered into the world, and death by sin; and so death passed upon all men, for that all have sinned" (Rom. 5:12).

BUT — our present verse tells us that *"there is a sin NOT unto death,"* and thus if this verse refers to *spiritual* death, then we have a direct contradiction in God's Word — and that cannot be. There are no contradictions in the Bible. By this we know that the "sin unto death" refers to *physical* death. When a Christian falls into sin and continues to LIVE in known sin, refusing to repent, *such living will bring physical death.* Believers are chastened of the Lord, that we should not be condemned with the world.

In John 5:24 Jesus said, "Verily, verily, I say unto you, He that heareth my Word, and believeth on Him that sent me, hath everlasting life, and shall not come into condemnation; but is passed from death unto life." Please notice: He who believes on Jesus IS passed from death unto life and SHALL NOT come into condemnation!

Moses committed the sin unto death. When he first prayed to God for water for the Israelites on their journey from Egypt to Canaan, God instructed him to *strike* the rock, "and there shall come water. out of it, that the people may drink" (Ex. 17:6). The *second* time Moses prayed for water, God told him to *speak* to the rock (Num. 20:7-12); but instead of *speaking* to the rock

213

as God commanded, Moses lifted up his rod and *smote* it again. The Rock is Jesus, the living water; and having been smitten once, He need not be smitten again. Moses deliberately disobeyed God, and God forbade his entering the Promised Land. God took his life and buried him in a valley in the land of Moab, "but no man knoweth of this sepulchre unto this day" (Deut. 32:48-52; 34:1-6).

Achan committed the sin unto death (read Joshua, chapter 7). He knew God's instruction concerning the Babylonian garments, the silver and gold, but in spite of knowing God's will, Achan coveted (*and took*) the garments and gold, and hid them in his tent.

The daily prayer of the Christian should be, "O Lord, cleanse thou me from secret sins . . . Keep me also from presumptuous sins . . . Let the words of my mouth, and the meditation of my heart, be acceptable in thy sight, O Lord, my strength, and my Redeemer!" (Psalm 19:12-14 in part).

We Know

Verses 18-21: "We know that whosoever is born of God sinneth not; but He that is begotten of God keepeth himself, and that wicked one toucheth him not. And we know that we are of God, and the whole world lieth in wickedness. And we know that the Son of God is come, and hath given us an understanding, that we may know Him that is true, and we are in Him that is true, even in His Son Jesus Christ. This is the true God, and eternal life. *Little children, keep yourselves from idols.* Amen."

The Holy Spirit uses the word "*know*" seven times in this chapter (verses 13 through 20). God gave us John's Gospel that we might have eternal life (John 20:31); and He has given us this glorious epistle that we may KNOW that we have eternal life (I John 5:13). Some people say we should not be dogmatic about this, but Paul said, "*I KNOW* WHOM I have believed." We *should* be dogmatic when such dogmatism is based on the Word of God after we have studied and rightly divided the Word of truth. We are living in an age when the contrary winds are blowing and the boisterous waves are beating hard and strong; but when we are founded and grounded upon the Solid Rock, we will weather the storm. The Lord hath spoken. "Thus saith the Lord!"

"We KNOW that whosoever is born of God sinneth not." All through this epistle the Holy Spirit has carefully pointed out that the life of the believer is a *holy* life. Christianity is entirely different from all other religions, because Christianity is God's holiness, God's righteousness and purity, God's divine nature *within*. All other religions are from *without* — external. Unholy living on the part of a professed Christian is contrary to the New Testament *definition* of a Christian.

Notice the verse does not say that whosoever "sinneth not" is a church member, or that he who "sinneth not" is one who lives the best he knows how or is well meaning in all that he does. It says that whosoever sinneth not is he who is *"born of God!"*

The unbeliever walks "according to the course of this world, according to the prince of the power of the air, the spirit that now worketh in the children of disobedience" (Eph. 2:2). The Christian walks as the Holy Spirit leads: "For as many as are led by the Spirit of God, they are the sons of God" (Rom. 8:14). "There is therefore now no condemnation to them which are in Christ Jesus, who walk not after the flesh, but after the Spirit" (Rom. 8:1). Believers walk NOT after the flesh because they walk IN the Spirit. They live differently because they are new creations in Christ.

What else do we know? We know that "whosoever is born of God . . . *that wicked one toucheth him not"* — (the Greek here reads, "lays no hold on him"). The same Greek word is used in John 20:17 when Jesus commanded Mary, "Touch me not." Every born again believer can rejoice and be exceeding glad, knowing that "the wicked one" (Satan) cannot lay hold on him. We are God's property, we possess Divine nature, we have the Holy Spirit by whom we are sealed until the day of redemption. The devil can tempt us, he can try us and test us, he can put pitfalls and snares in our way — but he cannot lay hold on us!

Why do believers possess this glorious, rejoicing assurance? The reason is clearly stated: *"He that is begotten of God keepeth himself."* Again we look to the Greek scholars, men who have spent their lives in studying the language in which the

New Testament was written. One of the greatest Greek scholars
of all time declares that the *context here* demands that "begotten of God" as used in this verse does not have to do with the
believer; it applies to the *Son of God.* We know that we cannot
keep ourselves anymore than we can *save* ourselves. "Wherefore let him that thinketh he standeth take heed lest he fall"
(I Cor. 10:12). "Ye are of God, little children, and have overcome them, because greater is He that is in you, than he that
is in the world" (I John 4:4). We know that we cannot *keep*
ourselves holy any more than we can *make* ourselves holy;
therefore, the phrase should read, "He (Jesus) that is begotten
of God, keepeth him (the believer)." *Jesus,* the only begotten
Son of God, keeps the *believers,* and will not permit the wicked
one to lay hold on us. We are more than conquerors through
HIM!

   Our salvation begins in Jesus (John 3:16).
   God sent Jesus to save us (I John 4:10).
   Through Jesus we overcome (I John 4:4).
   Jesus is able to keep us from falling (Jude 24).
   We need to pray with the Psalmist, "Hold Thou me up, and
I shall be safe . . . " (Psalm 119:117).
   In verse 19, *"we KNOW that we are of God."* We know God
is our Father, we know we are in His family, we know that our
citizenship is in heaven and that we are but pilgrims and strangers on earth. We know our sins are forgiven, we know we
have fellowship with the Father, with the Son, and with our
Christian brethren. We know that we are IN CHIRST, and
therefore our position is different from that of the unbeliever —
different in provision, in protection, in purpose, in potentiality,
in privilege. God said to Moses, "Behold there is a place by me,
and thou shalt stand upon a rock: and it shall come to pass,
while my glory passeth by, that I will put thee in a clift of the
rock, and will cover thee with my hand while I pass by" (Ex.
33:21, 22). Our God is the God of Moses. Jesus is our Rock,
He is the Rock of Ages; and we can say "Rock of Ages, cleft
for me,/Let me hide myself in thee!" The Christian is hid with
Christ in God (Col. 3:3).
   Also in verse 19 we know *"the whole world lieth in wickedness"* — or, "in the wicked one." There are but two classes of

people on this earth — sons of God and sons of Satan, those who are in the Holy One, and those who are in the wicked one. All unbelievers are the property of Satan. Paul speaks of them as those "in whom the god of this world (Satan) hath blinded the minds of them which believe not, lest the light of the glorious Gospel of Christ who is the image of God, should shine unto them" (II Cor. 4:4).

Satan is the prince of the power of the air, the god of this age, the prince of this world — but we know that the Lord Jesus *conquered* the prince of this world, and that already "*the prince of this world is judged*" (John 16:11).

In verse 20, "*we know that the Son of God is come, and hath given us an understanding.*" Through the new birth we become new creations, we have new understanding and new wisdom — *but only in Jesus.* The natural man cannot receive the things of the Spirit of God because they are spiritually discerned (I Cor. 2:14); but *believers possess* the Spirit of God, we have the anointing, and we know the things of God.

In II Kings 5:1-14 we find a beautiful picture of the unbeliever — and then of the *believer.* Naaman was a great man, but he was a leper — and leprosy is a type of sin. A little captive Israelite maid knew that if her master could get in touch with God's prophet, Elisha, he would be cleansed of his leprosy, and because of her testimony Naaman went in search of Elisha — but he went with the wrong attitude. When he arrived at Elisha's house, the prophet did not rush out to meet him as Naaman had supposed he would; he sent his servant instead, to tell Naaman to go and wash in Jordan seven times. This angered Naaman, and he said, "*Behold, I THOUGHT, He will surely come out to me, and stand, and call on the name of the Lord his God, and strike his hand over the place, and recover the leper.*" Naaman thought he could buy his healing. He followed the wrong plan and approached God's man in the wrong way; but when he realized what he had done, he obeyed the instruction of God's prophet and was completely cleansed of his leprosy; his flesh became like the flesh of a child.

Then "he returned to the man of God, he and all his company . . . and said, *Behold, now I KNOW* there is no God in all the earth, but in Israel!" This man who had previously said, "Behold I THOUGHT" now joyfully said "Behold, *now I KNOW!*" *What* did he know? He knew that there was but one God who could heal a leper — and notice what happened when he believed: "his flesh came again like unto the flesh of a little child" (II Kings 5:14). Jesus said, "Except ye be converted, *and become as little children,* ye shall not enter into the kingdom of heaven" (Matt. 18:3); and this epistle of John was *written* to "the little children," God's little "born ones." After Naaman's cleansing, he had a different understanding. We do not *see* — and then believe. We *believe* — and then God *reveals.* When God saves the sinner, the eyes of his understanding are opened (Eph. 1:18).

Believers know that the Son of God is come — not only into the *world,* but into our *hearts* — and has given us an understanding, "*that we may know Him that is true, and we are IN Him that is true, even in His Son Jesus Christ.*" The Son of God has given us the ability to understand enough of the Gospel to receive salvation as a gift, and the ability to understand the things of God. We do not merit this understanding, nor do we acquire it through studying in colleges or seminaries; it is a gift from God, and it was given to us that we might know Him who is the truth, and that we might know that we are IN HIM.

It is wonderful, beloved, it is marvelous, to face the Bible fact that Jesus is the Alpha, the Omega, the beginning and the ending of saving faith. He is not only the Author of eternal life, *He IS eternal life!* "He that hath the Son hath life, and he that hath not the Son of God hath not life."

"*This is the true God, and eternal life.*" Jesus is the true God (God the Father, God the Son, God the Holy Ghost — one God manifested in three Persons). The true God is eternal life, Christ in US is life, therefore because HE lives, WE live. Apart from God, no man can know *the things of God*; "But God hath revealed them unto us by His Spirit" (I Cor. 2:10). Even the desire to *become* a Christian and the ability to understand *how to BELIEVE* comes as a gift from God, revealed to us by the Holy Spirit. The only way anyone can ever know God is through the Son, through the Word, through the Spirit.

The natural man cannot — and *will not* — receive the things of God. Spiritual things are received "not of blood, nor of the will of the flesh, nor of the will of man, but of God" (John 1:13).

John the Beloved placed much emphasis upon the full Deity of Jesus Christ. To deny His full Deity is to be damned, because if we deny the Son, we do not possess the Father. We *must* believe that Jesus is the virgin born Son of God, Christ the Incarnate One. We *must* believe in His full Deity; otherwise we could not accept Him as *"the true God,"* and without knowing the true God we certainly cannot have eternal life! Throughout John's writings he speaks of Jesus as "THE LIFE" — notice John 1:4; 5:26, 40; 6:33, 35, 48, 51, 53, 63; 10:10; 11:25; 14:6; 20:31; I John 1:1, 2; and 5:12.

"Little children. . . ." Several times previously in this epistle John has used this title when addressing believers, and it is only proper that he use it in his parting counsel and admonition to us. All that has been said to the "little children" has been said in order that our joy may be full. That is the birthright of every child of God, and if we are to *enjoy* that spiritual birthright then we must keep ourselves from idols. We must not allow *anything* to come between us and our love for God.

When John warns us to keep ourselves *from idols,* he means that we are not to worship anything or anyone save God. We are not to put our faith in anything or anyone but God, and we are not to allow anything or anyone to come between us and full surrender *to* God.

During John's lifetime the people were *surrounded* by idolatry — and is it not the same today? Some of the outstanding religions — in this country and around the world — set up idols and images, worship crosses and "religious trinkets." John 4:24 clearly tells us, *"God is a Spirit,"* and they that worship Him must worship Him in spirit and in truth." We do not worship God through idols or images — nor through anything else save the one Mediator between God and men, "the Man, CHRIST JESUS!"

We need to remember also that to have an "idol" does not necessarily mean the setting up of some type of image in one corner of our home, or in our church. A man's idol can be his wife, his baby, his home, his automobile, his business, his farm, his race horses, or anything else that occupies the place in a life that God should occupy, anything upon which a person bestows the love that only God *deserves*. It is true that in apostolic days people *did* set up graven images, they bowed down to these images and worshipped them. John is undoubtedly warning the "little children" against this practice, but we need to be warned today against setting up *anything* — object, person, or interest — that might come between us and the true God.

We must be careful, we must be sober and alert, because our adversary the devil is walking about, seeking to devour our testimony. He would cause us to stand in the way of sinners and sit in the seat of the scornful, thus bringing shame and reproach upon the name of Jesus and upon His Church, instead of our being an asset to the cause of Christ and a blessing to the kingdom of God.

God wants first place in our hearts, in our lives, and in our service. Luke 17:10 tells us, ". . . When ye shall have done all those things which are commanded you, say, *We are unprofitable servants: we have done that which was our duty to do!*" We are saved to bring glory and honor to the God who so loved us that He surrendered His only Son to die for us, that we might have life; and *in Jesus* we are "a chosen generation, a royal priesthood, an holy nation, a peculiar people; that (we) should shew forth the praises of Him who hath called (us) out of darkness into His marvellous light" (I Pet. 2:9).

"Little children, keep yourselves from idols. Amen."

"And these things write we unto you, that your joy may be full."

The Second Epistle
of John

II JOHN

1. The elder unto the elect lady and her children, whom I love in the truth; and not I only, but also they that have known the truth;

2. For the truth's sake, which dwelleth in us, and shall be with us for ever.

3. Grace be with you, mercy, and peace, from God the Father, and from the Lord Jesus Christ, the Son of the Father, in truth and love.

4. I rejoiced greatly that I found of thy children walking in truth, as we have received a commandment from the Father.

5. And now I beseech thee, lady, not as though I wrote a new commandment unto thee, but that which we had from the beginning, that we love one another.

6. And this is love, that we walk after his commandments. This is the commandment, That, as ye have heard from the beginning, ye should walk in it.

7. For many deceivers are entered into the world, who confess not that Jesus Christ is come in the flesh. This is the deceiver and an anti-christ.

8. Look to yourselves, that we lose not those things which we have wrought, but that we receive a full reward.

9. Whosoever transgresseth, and abideth not in the doctrine of Christ, hath not God. He that abideth in the doctrine of Christ, he hath both the Father and the Son.

10. If there come any unto you, and bring not this doctrine, receive him not into your house, neither bid him God speed:

11. For he that biddeth him God speed is partaker of his evil deeds.

12. Having many things to write unto you, I would not write with paper and ink, but I trust to come unto you, and speak face to face, that our joy may be full.

13. The children of thy elect sister greet thee. Amen.

This second epistle lays down the essentials of the personal walk of the believer in this day when "many deceivers are entered into the world" (v. 7). There were "many" deceivers in John's day — and today there are many more.

The key words in II John are *"the truth"* — the *whole* of Divinely revealed truth, the entire Word of God.

The Word of God is the only authority for doctrine and instruction in the believer's life and daily practice. All Scripture is given by inspiration, all Scripture is profitable to us (II Tim. 3:16, 17).

"The Truth"

Verse 1: "The elder unto the elect lady and her children, whom I love in the truth; and not I only, but also all they that have known the truth."

"The truth" and love are inseparable in the Christian life from beginning to end. *Jesus* is truth, *the Word* is truth (John 14:6; 17:17). God is love (I John 4:8). Truth, God, Christ, and love cannot be separated as having to do with Christianity.

In this first verse John the Beloved addresses himself to *"the elect lady and her children."* Some have suggested that this refers to the Church, but it seems evident to me that the "elect lady" was a Christian woman who, along with her children, had received the Lord Jesus Christ, accepted the *doctrine* of Christ, and became a true example of grace. Her home was evidently the kind of home all Christian homes should be. It reminds us of the home of Mary, Martha, and Lazarus, where Jesus loved to visit.

In all probability, the elect lady mentioned here had heard the Gospel and been brought to the saving knowledge of Jesus Christ through John's ministry; and if she had not been *saved* through his ministry she had at least been instructed, enlightened, and strengthened thereby. Possibly this believer had written to John for advice concerning the teachers of error and the anti-christs who were already present in that day, and it seems clear that John's epistle is an answer to her questions.

John speaks of this elect lady as one whom he loved *"in the truth"* — and then he clearly brings out the truth that all genuine believers love all other believers. It is impossible to be a born again Christian and not love other Christians, because we are all members of the same body — the body of Christ, the Church of the living God. There can be no real love between a believer and an unbeliever. There can be love as MEN know it, but not love as GOD is love.

Verse 2: "For the truth's sake, which dwelleth in us, and shall be with us for ever."

This is a continuation of verse 1. In other words, John and

the other believers loved this lady and her children because they loved the truth. All true believers, possessors of the truth and the love of God, rejoice in the presence and the fellowship of *other* believers. Truth draws individuals, families, neighborhoods, and communities together in warm affection one for another. For the truth's sake we love all who are OF the truth. There may be instances where we do not love everything that every individual does, but we love the individual *"for the truth's sake, which dwelleth in us."*

Jesus said, "Ye shall know the truth, and the truth shall make you free (John 8:32). To Thomas He said, "I am the truth (John 14:6). Concerning His disciples He prayed, "Father . . . sanctify them through thy truth. Thy Word is truth" (John 17:17). This same truth abides in the bosom of every believer, *"and shall be with us for ever."* We not only *possess* the truth, but the truth will *abide* with us forever. The believer is born of God, indwelt by the Holy Spirit; Christ is in the believer, the believer is in Christ; therefore truth is in the believer and the believer is in truth. If we are born again, truth abides with us every day, every moment of every hour of our lives here on earth, and will abide with us through eternity — *forever.*

The heart of every born again believer is a permanent home for truth, and truth is welcome there. Jesus is truth, the devil is a lie; and when Jesus comes in, the devil goes out. You may rest assured that where the devil abides, truth does NOT abide. It is impossible for man to serve both truth and a lie, it is impossible to serve both God and the devil.

Verse 3: "Grace be with you, mercy, and peace, from God the Father, and from the Lord Jesus Christ, the Son of the Father, in truth and love."

Grace is the capstone of the pyramid of spiritual blessings which we receive through Jesus Christ. In Hebrews 2:9 the Holy Spirit reveals the divine fact that God's grace permitted Jesus to taste death for every man. The *grace* of God was displayed in the *love* of God, love that allowed Jesus to take a body of flesh, and in that body taste death for every man and bear the sins of the whole wide world. Grace brings mercy, and apart from grace there IS no mercy. Grace is unmerited, unearned favor, and grace bestows mercy where no mercy is due. Grace PRECEDES mercy, and by the grace of God the *love* of God was put on display when Jesus was nailed to the cross. Therefore *through His cross* we find "mercy and peace." Jesus said, "Peace I leave with you, my peace I give unto you: not as the world giveth, give I unto you. Let not your heart be troubled, neither let it be afraid" (John 14:27).

Isaiah said, "Thou wilt keep him in perfect peace, whose mind is stayed on (Jesus) . . ." (Isa. 26:3).

Notice John says "Grace . . ., mercy, and peace, *from God the Father.*" It was God the Father who so loved us that He was willing to send His only begotten Son to die for us. We joy in God (Rom. 5:11) because it was He who foreordained that Jesus pay the sin-debt (I Pet. 1:18-23). Grace, mercy, and peace is ours because God the Father loved us and the Lord Jesus Christ died for us.

John carries over into this second epistle the fundamental truth of the Deity of Christ — "*the Son of the Father.*" He was God's CHRIST, He became man's JESUS, Saviour and Lord — all because of God's grace.

The closing words of verse 3 ("in truth and love") are not connected with the Lord Jesus Christ, Son of the Father, but with "*grace be with you, mercy and peace.*" John is here praying that grace, mercy, and peace "*in truth and love*" will be displayed and made manifest to and through this family to whom he writes, that through their testimony others might come to know the grace, mercy, and peace which are ours from God through Christ Jesus. When we walk in truth and in love we invite others to come to know the truth and receive the love of God.

Verse 4: "I rejoiced greatly that I found of thy children walking in truth, as we have received a commandment from the Father."

Here John expresses his great joy that he had learned about the children of this elect lady walking in truth and in God's love. Undoubtedly the testimony of this extraordinary family had been published throughout that part of the country. John does not tell us how he learned about this mother and her children giving this unusual testimony of truth and love, but such testimony was according to Bible standards of Christianity. John said, "Walking in truth as we have received a commandment from the Father" — and the commandment received from the Father is "that we should believe on the name of His Son Jesus Christ, and love one another" (I John 3:23).

The Philippian jailer was instructed, "Believe on the Lord Jesus Christ, and thou shalt be saved, and thy house" (Acts 16:31). In John 4:46-54 we read of the nobleman who went to Jesus for the healing of his child, he believed and was saved *along with all of his house.* Salvation is a household blessing from the Lord. I am not saying that all homes are one hundred percent Christian, nor that they ever *will* be. I am saying *God wants it that way.* It is sad when children do not walk in the footsteps of godly parents, and it is my belief that if we will follow the admonition of the wise man of the Old Testament and "train up a child in the way he should go," if we bring up our children in the fear and admonition of God, *they will be saved* — perhaps not as early as we *want* them to be, but "household salvation" is of God. John's heart was made happy and he rejoiced greatly that this household was walking in truth, living in truth, and loving as the Father commanded Christians to love each other.

Verse 5: "And now I beseech thee, lady, not as though I wrote a new commandment unto thee, but that which we had from the beginning, that we love one another."

The beloved disciple assumed that this basic commandment of Christianity was understood by those to whom he wrote. True Christianity always brings about love among brethren. John was not writing a new commandment, *"but that which we had from the beginning."* (The "beginning" here points back to the time when the Gospel of the marvelous grace of God was first made known. Study John's Gospel 15:12-17.)

That brethren love one another was (and is) a general commandment having to do with all believers; therefore it applied to this elect lady and her children. John spent much time on this basic commandment of Christianity. He loved to dwell on it, he loved to sound out the exhortation to believers. The commandment of love was given by Jesus, and all believers should obey it.

The Law of Moses *demanded* love (Lev. 19:18; Deut. 6:5; Luke 10:27). The law of Christ IS love: "And hope maketh not ashamed; because the love of God is shed abroad in our hearts by the Holy Ghost which is given unto us" (Rom. 5:5). "Beloved, let us love one another: for love is of God; and every one that loveth is born of God, and knoweth God. He that *loveth not* knoweth not God; for God IS love" (I John 4:7, 8). Therefore the law of Christ takes the place of the Law of Moses because Jesus fulfilled every jot and tittle of that law. Jesus said, "Think not that I am come to destroy the law, or the prophets: I am not come to destroy, but to fulfill" (Màtt. 5:17). In Galatians 5:14 Paul tells us, "For all the law is fulfilled in one word, even in this: Thou shalt love thy neighbour as thyself." The law of Christ (the law of love) is not written on tables of stone, but in the heart of the believer (Heb. 8:8-10).

Verse 6: "And this is love, that we walk after His commandments. This is the commandment, That as ye have heard from the beginning, ye should walk in it."

"This is love." The meaning here is that we prove our love when we walk after the commandments of Jesus, and His commandment is that we believe on His name and love one another. When we walk after His commandments we give forth evidence of our love to God.

"This is the commandment." In other words, this is the *"great* commandment." In Mark 12:28-31, one of the scribes asked Jesus, "Which is the first commandment of all." Jesus replied, "The first of all the commandments is . . . Thou shalt love the Lord thy God with all thy heart, and with all thy soul, and with all thy mind, and with all thy strength: this is the first commandment. And the second is like, namely this: Thou shalt love thy neighbour as thyself. There is none other commandment greater than these."

In John 13:34, 35 Jesus said to His disciples, "A new commandment I give unto you, That ye love one another; as I have loved you, that ye also love one another. By this shall all men know that ye are my disciples, if ye have love one to another."

Deceivers and How to Treat Them

In the first six verses of this second epistle, John points out again that believers should love each other and should fellowship with each other in the truth. This is the law of Christ.

In the last verses of the epistle the beloved disciple clearly points out and emphasizes how believers should treat those who are deceivers, those who teach and preach false doctrine.

Verse 7: "For many deceivers are entered into the world, who confess not that Jesus Christ is come in the flesh. This is a deceiver and an antichrist."

Even in John's day believers had to be on guard at all times, for even then there were many deceivers already operating —deceivers who confess not "that Jesus Christ is come in the flesh." This means that these people taught that Jesus was only a man — a *great* man to be sure, a great teacher, but just a man, not God incarnate, not God in flesh. In I John 4:2, 3 John warned concerning these deceivers — false spirits, false prophets and antichrists. Anyone who denies the Incarnation is a deceiver and an antichrist (I John 2:18; 4:3).

In Matthew 24:4, 5 Jesus said to His disciples, "Take heed that no man deceive you. For many shall come in my name, saying, I am Christ; and shall deceive many."

Paul warned Timothy, "This know also, that in the last days perilous times shall come, for men shall be lovers of their own selves . . . having a form of godliness, but denying the power thereof . . . ever learning, and never able to come to the knowledge of the truth" (II Tim. 3:1-7 in part). Today as never before deceivers and false teachers have attacked the Incarnation and the virgin birth. There were false teachers in the days of John, there were false teachers in the days of Paul, and they have been here ever since that time; but today we have a more subtle brand of the spirit of antichrist than we have ever had in ages past. Many men who profess to be ministers of the Gospel stand behind the sacred desk and put together words that lead astray poor, innocent, sometimes ignorant people. These men have theological degrees, they have completed courses of study at outstanding universities, and they mix enough pure Gospel with their error to camouflage their deceitfulness. Thus many of their hearers will devour enough such poison to destroy them, not knowing that they are listening to the enemies of Jesus. Such ministers of Satan will proclaim Christ as a great man, a great teacher, a great healer, the founder of a great "religion."

But Jesus did not come into the world to found a great religion; He came to seek and to save the lost. Jesus did not "found" Christianity — He IS Christianity. There is at the present time a great revival of "church joining" in America, but this is not necessarily a revival of Christianity. One may join a church, support that church and attend upon its services, and be just as sadly lost as the heathen who has never heard the name of Jesus: Actually, the heathen who has never heard the name of Jesus is not guilty of such terrible blasphemy as is the man who *hears* the Gospel, and yet makes that Gospel fit his ideas and ideologies, instead of fitting his life into the Gospel by believing pure Bible doctrine.

Verse 8: "Look to yourselves, that we lose not those things which we have wrought, but that we receive a full reward."

The admonition here is addressed to "the elect lady and her children" but it is also for *our* admonition — as is all Scripture, given by inspiration and profitable to us. The believer should examine his own heart, take stock of his own spiritual status. We should never attack error until we are sure that we are *equipped in the inner man* to wage war against error, and against those ministers of Satan who come to us in sheep's clothing, but inwardly are "ravening wolves" (Matt. 7:15). We should let God turn the searchlight of the Holy Spirit and His Word upon our hearts and see if we have embraced the truth. We should make sure of our calling and election, and be able to say with Paul, "I KNOW WHOM I have believed, and am persuaded that He is able to *keep* that which I have committed unto Him against that day" (II Tim. 1:12). We should never attack the teachers of error in our own strength nor in our own words. When Jesus met Satan (Matt. 4:1-11) He quoted the Word of God, Scriptures from the Old Testament, and Satan took flight. We are no match for the devil, but Jesus and His Word are *more* than a match for him. So we should look to ourselves (individually) *"that we lose not those things which we have wrought."*

This has nothing to do with the believer losing his salvation, because we did not "wrought" our salvation! Salvation is God's gift to the believer — "not by works of righteousness which we have done, but according to His mercy He saved us, by the washing of regeneration, and renewing of the Holy Ghost" (Tit. 3:5). Salvation is "the gift of God: not of works, lest any man should boast" (Eph. 2:8, 9). "For we are His workmanship, created in Christ Jesus unto good works, which God hath before ordained that we should walk in them" (Eph. 2:10).

When the Holy Spirit speaks of *"things which we have wrought"* He is referring to *stewardship,* not to redemption. It will be a happy, victorious day in the lives of many believers when they study the Word and learn the difference between redemption and rewards. We are *redeemed by the BLOOD;* we are *rewarded for our WORKS.* Redemption is a *gift,* rewards are *earned* by faithful stewardship. It is not how *much* we do, but the *sort* of stewardship we render:

"For other foundation can no man lay than that is laid, which is Jesus Christ. Now if any man build upon this foundation gold, silver, precious stones, wood, hay, stubble; every man's work shall be made manifest: for the day shall declare it, because it shall be revealed by fire; and the fire shall try every man's work *of what sort it is.* If any man's work abide which he hath built thereupon, he shall receive a reward. If any man's work shall be burned, he shall suffer loss: but he himself shall be saved; yet so as by fire" (I Cor. 3:11-15).

"For we must all appear before the judgment seat of Christ; that every one may receive the things done in his body, according to that he hath done, whether it be good or bad" (II Cor. 5:10).

The reward of the believer in heaven will be in accordance with services rendered in the name of the Redeemer, to the glory of God and to the edifying of the brethren — the New Testament Church. As a believer, you can rest assured that you will receive all that is coming to you in the day when Jesus rewards His servants for their stewardship; and you may also rest assured that you will not get one thing you do not earn!

Jesus judges and rewards in righteousness; He cannot do wrong. Even a cup of cold water given in His name is not overlooked — but if you have *opportunity* to give a cup of cold water and you do not give it, neither will *that* be overlooked. "Therefore to him that knoweth to do good, and doeth it not, TO HIM IT IS SIN" (James 4:17).

If we would stop and really take stock of ourselves, most of us would give the Lord's work much more of our time than we do. One day we will realize how much we have lost by using time, strength, energy and talents for ourselves that should have been used to the glory of God! Paul said, "Whether therefore ye eat, or drink, or whatsoever ye do, do all to the glory of God . . . And whatsoever ye do in word or deed, do all in the name of the Lord Jesus, giving thanks to God and the Father by Him" (I Cor. 10:31; Col. 3:17).

Revelation 2:4 tells us that the church at Ephesus lost its first love. It is a sad, painful sight to behold a man or woman who begins the spiritual life with a burning zeal for souls, they never miss a service in church, they are witnessing consistently — and then, after awhile, they begin to grow cool toward the things of God, their zeal begins to wane, and in the spiritual life they become dull and careless. Such a person will not receive a full reward. There are many things that account for loss of zeal on the part of a believer, and listening to teachers of error is one of the outstanding ways by which Satan dampens the Christian's zeal to win souls for Jesus. We are saved to serve. God wants us to go out after unbelievers.

Jesus instructed the disciples to tarry in Jerusalem until they were endowed with power from on high — power to witness at home and abroad, to the ends of the earth (Acts 1:4-8). In John 4:35 He said to them, "Lift up your eyes, and look on the fields; for they are white already to harvest!" And in the great commission (found in Matthew 28:19, 20) He said to them, "Go ye therefore, and teach all nations, baptizing them in the name of the Father, and of the Son, and of the Holy Ghost: teaching them to observe all things whatsoever I have commanded you: and lo, I am with you alway, even unto the end of the world. Amen." May we say with Isaiah, "Lord, here am I. Send ME!"

John warns believers to be careful of both testimony and

stewardship, those things which we have wrought, that we may receive "A FULL REWARD." There is such a thing as receiving a partial reward — or no reward at all. This is evident in the passage just quoted from I Corinthians 3. He whose works are wood, hay, and stubble will suffer loss — his works will be burned, "but he himself shall be saved; yet so as by fire." In other words, the *spirit* will be saved, but the individual will lose his reward. This might be illustrated by considering a family fast asleep in their home, and in the wee hours of the morning that home catches fire and burns to the ground, the family escaping with only their nightclothes, everything in the home being consumed. They could be said to be saved "so as by fire," losing everything but their lives. It is possible to stand before God empty handed, and there will be many Christians who will do just that.

In Jude 20-23 we read, "But ye, beloved, building up yourselves on your most holy faith, praying in the Holy Ghost, keep yourselves in the love of God, looking for the mercy of our Lord Jesus Christ unto eternal life. And of some have compassion, making a difference: and others save with fear, pulling them out of the fire; hating even the garment spotted by the flesh."

There will be some who will receive *a FULL reward*. These will be Christians who have lived consistent, consecrated, fruitful lives, loving God with a full heart, serving faithfully, witnessing and bringing in the sheaves. Some will bring forth a hundredfold, some will bring forth sixty, and others only thirty. Therefore some will receive a full reward, some will receive a partial reward, and some will *lose* their reward because of unfaithful stewardship.

God wants our heart yielded unreservedly to Him. He wants our love — all of it. He wants our talents, He wants our body yielded as a living sacrifice, He wants our members as instruments of righteousness (Rom. 12:1; 6:11-13); and "when ye shall have done all those things which are commanded you, say, We are unprofitable servants: *we have done that which was our duty to do*" (Luke 17:10). In Matthew 20:26-28 Jesus said, ". . . Whosoever will be great among you, let him be your minister; and whosoever will be chief among you, let him be your servant: even as the Son of man came not to be ministered unto, but to minister, and to give His life a ransom for many."

I repeat for emphasis, *salvation* is God's gift to hell-deserving sinners, rewards are earned by faithful stewardship, and God's Word clearly distinguishes between the two. Study John 1:11-13; 3:16; 4:10; 5:24; 6:47; Luke 7:50; Romans 6:23; 10:9, 10; Ephesians 2:8, 9; Acts 16:31; and I John 3:1, 2.

Rewards are *future* and will be given to the faithful believers when Jesus comes and we are caught up to meet Him in the clouds in the air. We will be rewarded at the marriage supper of the Lamb. Study Matthew 16:27; II Timothy 4:8; II Corinthians 5:10; and Revelation 22:12. Every Christian should pray daily that the Holy Spirit will lead us into paths of right living, and that He will direct us around the snares of Satan which would ensnare us and cause us to lose part (or *all*) of our reward!

Verses 9 and 10: "Whosoever transgresseth, and abideth not in the doctrine of Christ, hath not God. He that abideth in the doctrine of Christ, he hath both the Father and the Son. If there come any unto you, and bring not this doctrine, receive him not into your house, neither bid him God speed."

"Whosoever transgresseth. . . ." Notice there is no respect of persons here. Whosoever — minister, evangelist, missionary, professor, rich man, poor man, wise man or fool — those who transgress God's law and abide not in the doctrine of Christ do not know God. Such a person may pastor a big church, he may be a professor in a theological seminary, he may be at the head of a great religious organization; but he is lost and on the road to hell. He is one of those to whom Paul refers in II Corinthians 11:13-15:

"For such are false apostles, deceitful workers, transforming themselves into the apostles of Christ. And no marvel; for Satan himself is transformed into an angel of light. Therefore it is no great thing if his ministers also be transformed as the ministers of righteousness; *whose end shall be according to their works!"*

Just what IS *"the doctrine of Christ"?* It is the doctrine which Jesus taught, true doctrine concerning Himself — His pre-existence in the beginning with the Father. Jesus did not come into existence when He was born of the virgin almost two thousand years ago. He was in the beginning with the Father and was equal with the Father. To conform to the doctrine of Christ one must hold to the truth concerning His birth, His precepts, His character, His ministry, His death, His resurrection, His ascension, and His present position at the right hand of God. If we deny any part of the doctrine of Christ, we might as well deny it all because if He lied once, then we cannot believe anything He said about Himself. He left heaven to declare God to man (John 1:18), and if any declaration made by Him *concerning* God is untrue, then we cannot believe *anything* He said. He is either the truth or the lie — and we know that He is TRUTH.

The following statements from the Word of God concern the doctrine of Jesus Christ:

"No man hath seen God at any time; the only begotten Son, which is in the bosom of the Father, He hath declared Him" (John 1:18).

". . . All men should honour the Son, even as they honour the Father. He that honoureth not the Son honoureth not the Father which hath sent Him" (John 5:23).

Jesus said, "My sheep hear my voice, and I know them, and they follow me: and I give unto them eternal life; and they shall never perish, neither shall any man pluck them out of my hand. My Father, which gave them me, is greater than all; and no man is able to pluck them out of my Father's hand. I and my Father are one" (John 10:27-30).

In John 15:23 He said, "He that hateth me hateth my Father also"

In John 17:3 He said, "And this is life eternal, that they might know thee the only true God, and Jesus Christ, whom thou hast sent."

"And many other signs truly did Jesus in the presence of His disciples, which are not written in this book: but these are written, that ye might believe that Jesus is the Christ, the Son of God; and that believing ye might have life through His name" (John 20:30, 31).

"Whosoever denieth the Son, the same hath not the Father:

but he that acknowledgeth the Son hath the Father also" (I John 2:23).

"*He that abideth in the doctrine of Christ*" (he who has received the Word of God concerning Jesus) "*hath both the Father and the Son.*" We believe in one God manifested in three Persons — Father, Son, and Holy Ghost. There is such intimate union between the Father, Son, and Holy Ghost that it is impossible to possess one without the other. If we receive the Son we receive the Father, and all who receive the Son possess the Holy Spirit — the One who "borns" us, baptizes us into the body of Christ, indwells us, leads us, assures us, fills us, and seals us (John 3:5; Rom. 8:9, 14, 16; I Cor. 12:12, 13; Eph. 4:30).

Antichrists, deceivers, and false prophets cannot agree on the Trinity. One group receives Jehovah God but denies Jesus the Son. They say He was an illegitimate, an imposter, born out of wedlock. Another group claims that Jesus is God, and that the Father, Son, and Holy Ghost are simply His titles. They maintain that Jesus is the only Person in the Godhead. The Trinity is plainly seen in the account of the baptism of Jesus in Matthew 3 — Jesus the Son in the water, God the Father speaking from heaven, the Holy Ghost in the form of a dove descending upon Jesus. We believe in God the Father, God the Son, and God the Holy Ghost; and if we possess Jesus we possess the fulness of the Godhead (Col. 2:9, 10).

I cannot *explain* the Trinity, but I believe it because God's Word says it. When we read the Word of God, we should let the Word speak and we should listen. Paul said "Let God be true, but every man a liar" (Rom. 3:4). We may not understand everything in God's Word, but we can *believe* it because it IS God's Word. We are not saved by understanding, we do not live by understanding. We are saved by God's grace through faith, and "*the just shall LIVE by faith!*" (Eph. 2:8; Rom. 1:17).

"*If there come any unto you. . . .*" That takes in the "whosoever" in verse 9. Regardless of who a person is or what he claims, if he comes to your door, to your church, or to your community and denies any part of the doctrine of Christ, here is our Scriptural instruction concerning that person:

"*RECEIVE HIM NOT INTO YOUR HOUSE. . . .*" What

does that mean? Does it mean that I am not to allow any person who is not a believer, a consecrated Christian, to come into my house? No, it does not mean that. Jesus is our example, and HE went into the homes of sinners, sat at table, and ate with them. The meaning in our present verse is simply this:

When someone peddling false doctrine comes to your door, do not invite him in, do not listen to his teaching, do not buy nor accept books and literature from him. To do so is to encourage him and help to support his false religion. It also means that when someone comes to your church preaching error, you should not attend the meetings, you should not support him. It is not enough to be *against* error — we must sever relations with it. Born again Christians should withdraw from a church that allows error to be preached from its pulpit. God's Word commands, "Have no fellowship with the unfruitful works of darkness, but rather reprove them" (Eph. 5:11). In II Corinthians 6:17 we are commanded, "Come out from among them, and be ye separate, saith the Lord, and touch not the unclean thing; and I will receive you."

Hear the testimony of the Apostle Paul concerning preachers or teachers who deny the Gospel of the grace of God:

"I marvel that ye are so soon removed from Him that called you into the grace of Christ unto another gospel: which is NOT another; but there be some that trouble you, and would pervert the Gospel of Christ. *But though we, or an angel from heaven, preach any other gospel unto you than that which we have preached unto you, LET HIM BE ACCURSED. As we said before, so say I now again, If any man preach any other gospel unto you than that ye have received, LET HIM BE ACCURSED"* (Gal. 1:6-9).

Not once, but *twice* in these short verses Paul makes the declaration that if anyone preaches anything except the Gospel of the grace of God, whether that person be man or angel, "let him be accursed" — and to be accursed means *to be damned in the lake of fire!* In other words, if any preach any gospel save that of the Lord Jesus Christ, let him burn in hell for doing it! That is strong language, but it is also *Holy Ghost inspired* language. Thus, we are instructed that if anyone comes to us bringing anything except the pure doctrine of Jesus Christ, we are not to receive him into our home, we are not to allow him to leave his books or his false literature in our home.

Christian friend, never expose yourself to unbelief. Most assuredly I would feed any hungry person or clothe any needy person who came to my home. I would help anyone who needed help, regardless of his nationality or the color of his skin; but I will not allow false teachers or false prophets to enter my home just out of courtesy. I do not allow them to bring their books and false literature into my home nor do they stand on my porch and argue their false religions. I do not argue the Bible. God did not call me to argue the Scriptures, but to preach the Word — to be instant in season, out of season, to reprove, rebuke, exhort. I do not invite false religionists into my home to tell me what they believe. Satan is more subtle than we realize. Never listen to teachers of error, do not stay in their presence.

Some of you may be asking, "Brother Greene, should we not witness to them and try to win them? Should we not tell them about our wonderful Saviour and give them the Gospel of God's grace?" Jesus answered that question long ago. In Matthew 7:6 He said, *"Give not that which is holy unto the dogs, neither cast ye your pearls before swine, lest they trample them under their feet, and turn again and rend you!"* These false religionists are blinded by Satan, steeped in their false beliefs, and more versed in the Scriptures supporting their unbelief than most Christians are. They are not open to reason, and therefore it is utterly useless to witness to them. Thus to give them the precious truths of salvation by grace through faith is to cast pearls before swine.

You will notice that the Lord did not hesitate to speak of the Pharisees, Sadducees, and false prophets as "dogs" and "hogs." You may rest assured that if you spend much time around hogs, the stench of the pigpen will contaminate you. You cannot afford to expose yourself to teachers of error, nor listen to their damnable doctrine. Study the Word of God, feed on the bread of life, and abstain from any association with false teachers and deceivers. "Cease, my son, to hear the instruction that causeth to err from the words of knowledge" (Prov. 19:27).

"Neither bid him God speed." When you send false teachers

on their way, do not say "God bless you." Do not give them money, do not buy their books or literature in order to be rid of them. When you are visiting in a strange church and you have never before heard the man in the pulpit, do not drop money into the offering plate just to be sociable or lest someone think you are a "tightwad." Never give a dime to anyone — pastor, missionary, teacher, book salesman — until you know that person is God's man, preaching God's Word in its truth and purity. When a false teacher comes to your door and you ask him to leave, do not wish him well. If you say anything at all as you close the door, let it be "God pity you!"

Verse 11: "For he that biddeth him God speed is partaker of his evil deeds."

If a believer prays God's blessings upon a false teacher or gives material support to such a one, that believer is contributing to the enemies of Jesus Christ and helping to further the program of Satan in damning souls! Beloved, the devil can send more souls to hell through *false doctrine, lying teachers, and deceiving preachers* than through bootleggers, nightclubs, and barrooms! Man was created incurably religious — *he worships SOME-THING.* All men everywhere have some sort of religion, all men everywhere have their gods. There is no tribe on the face of this earth, no matter how primitive, that does not worship some god, or *gods.* They *fear,* and they worship. Satan knows this, and he offers the line of least resistance to those who are his own children. He cares not how "religious" people may be, nor how conscientious and sincere in their worship, *so long as they do not put their faith and trust in the virgin born, crucified, risen and ascended Lord and Saviour, Jesus Christ the Son of God!* He cares not how many books a man writes nor how fervently he preaches — just so long as he leaves out the blood and the fundamentals of the faith. So if we bid a false teacher "God speed," if we contribute to his ministry or to his material support, we become partakers of his evil deeds and help to spread his damnable doctrine.

There are those who find it difficult to take this passage literally, but beloved, there is no reason why we should NOT take it literally. These teachers of error would stick a gun in the face of God and steal the blood of the Lamb if it were

239

possible. They would deceive *the very elect of God* if it were possible. Liberals, modernists, free-thinkers, atheists and agnostics will steal the faith of your children, tear down the Word of God, and blaspheme the Christ you love! How could *anyone* have a kind word for those who would rob God of the gift He gave that men might be saved? How could *anyone* lend a helping hand to those who would steal the faith of a child who has been reared to fear God and respect the Bible? The dirtiest thief this side of hell is a man who deliberately teaches error and thereby robs men and women of their right to become children of God through hearing the truth.

You shall know the truth, and the truth shall set you free; and if the Son of God sets you free, you are free indeed! But if you are NOT set free by the truth and by God's Son, then you are in bondage to Satan and one day you will be eternally damned in the lake of fire. May God help us to recognize and repudiate the teachers of error and doctrines of demons, no matter what the guise in which they come to us!

"Lay hands suddenly on no man, neither be partaker of other man's sins: KEEP THYSELF PURE" (I Tim. 5:22).

In I Timothy 4:1-6 Paul instructed Timothy concerning false teachers, and told him how to be a good minister:

"Now the Spirit speaketh expressly, that in the latter times some shall depart from the faith, giving heed to seducing spirits, and doctrines of devils; speaking lies in hypocrisy; having their conscience seared with a hot iron; forbidding to marry, and commanding to abstain from meats, which God hath created to be received with thanksgiving of them which believe and know the truth. For every creature of God is good, and nothing to be refused, if it be received with thanksgiving: for it is sanctified by the Word of God and prayer. If thou put the brethren in remembrance of these things, thou shalt be a good minister of Jesus Christ, nourished up in the words of faith and of good doctrine, whereunto thou hast attained."

Jesus, the greatest of all teachers, said, "Beware of false prophets, which come to you in sheep's clothing, but inwardly they are ravening wolves. Ye shall know them by their fruits. Do men gather grapes of thorns, or figs of thistles? Even so every good tree bringeth forth good fruit; but a corrupt tree bringeth forth evil fruit. A good tree cannot bring forth evil fruit, neither can a corrupt tree bring forth good fruit. Every tree that bringeth not forth good fruit is hewn down, and cast into the fire. Wherefore by their fruits ye shall know them.

"Not everyone that saith unto me, Lord, Lord, shall enter into the kingdom of heaven; but he that doeth the will of my Father which is in heaven. Many will say to me in that day, Lord, Lord, have we not prophesied in thy name? and in thy name have cast out devils, and in thy name done many wonderful works? And then will I profess unto them, I never knew you: depart from me, ye that work iniquity" (Matt. 7:15-23).

Yes, it does make a tremendous difference where we attend church. We need to be careful about the minister to whom we listen, the program we support, the literature we read. God help us to be alert, to be on guard, lest we support the enemies of Jesus Christ — and what could be more evil than to support teachers of error who deny the Deity of Jesus, His virgin birth, His vicarious atonement, and His bodily resurrection?

Verse 12: "Having many things to write unto you, I would not write with paper and ink: but I trust to come unto you, and speak face to face, that our joy may be full."

John had much on his heart about which he wanted to talk with "the elect lady and her children," but he planned to visit them shortly and speak with them "face to face," rather than writing.

"*I would not write with paper and ink.*" In John's day there was no paper as we have it today. Writing was done on Egyptian *papyrus* which was made from the pithy membranes of the *papyrus* plant, a name from which we derive our word "paper." Ink was made of soot and water with a mixture of a type of gum which was added to give body and durability to the ink. A reed served as a pen.

The expression "speak face to face" was a common one in that day, meaning "to have conversation with one another." Probably when John visited this Christian home he planned to give instructions and answer any questions this mother and her children might desire to ask.

"*That our joy may be full.*" This is the spiritual birthright of every believer. In I John 1:4 we learned that that epistle was

written that *believers* might enjoy the fellowship enjoyed by
the disciples, and that our joy might be full. After all, Jesus
came into this world that we might have life and have it
abundantly (John 10:10). John wanted to enjoy the spiritual
blessing of fellowshipping in person with this family, and discussing the things of God.

Verse 13: "The children of thy elect sister greet thee. Amen."
Nothing more is recorded relative to this mother spoken of
here as the "elect sister." Possibly she had died, or was absent
at the time her children sent greetings by John the Beloved.
He mentions her as a believer, one who had heard and received
the Gospel and thus had come to know Jesus as her personal
Saviour.

I repeat, all Scripture is given by inspiration, all Scripture
is profitable to us. Believers can benefit greatly from this
second epistle. First of all, we see that John loved this Christian
home and the members of this unusual family. It is refreshing to
a minister to find such a home and family, in his community,
and I know from personal experience that it is truly refreshing
and encouraging to an *evangelist* to have the privilege of
fellowshipping in such a home. We strengthen each other when
we meet together around the table — Christian brothers and
sisters, all of the same mind, discussing the things of the Lord
and feeding the spirit as we enjoy food and fellowship in a
Christian home.

From John's writing here we also learn that believers must
be on guard — today as never before — against teachers of
error. There are many more such deceivers today than when
John penned this warning, and we need to be sober in mind,
spirit, and soul. We need to examine the spirits and be sure we
are listening to truth, nor error. We need to recognize the fact
that even though we do not lose our soul, it will be tragic indeed
to lose even *part* of our reward — and it is possible for a believer
to suffer *total* loss of reward.

This epistle also tells us how we should treat teachers of error.
We are not to encourage them by saying, doing, or *giving* anything that would contribute to the furtherance of their teaching;
we are to refuse them entrance to our home; we are not to wish
them well. We are to be kind to sinners and unbelievers in

attempting to win them to Jesus, but we are NOT to condone or fellowship with *religious error!*

In Hebrews 13:2 Paul tells us, "Be not forgetful to entertain strangers: for thereby some have entertained angels unawares." But there is a difference between "entertaining strangers" and entertaining one who comes to your door to peddle damnable heresy and doctrines of demons.

Yes, every man has a right to his own religion, a right to believe what he *wants* to believe; but even though men are created free moral agents and have the right to eat what God *forbids* eating, do what God *forbids* doing, or believe what God *forbids* believing, *the CHRISTIAN has no right to support that person or give comfort to him!* If you have manufactured your own religion, if you have made the Bible read as you want it to read, if you are bringing about things that satisfy YOU and you believe in allowing every man to have his own religion and believe as he chooses, you had better take time out to build a *heaven* for yourself because you cannot go to GOD'S heaven unless you go *God's* WAY. Jesus said, "*I* am the Way, *I* am the Truth, *I* am the Door — no man cometh unto the Father but by *me.*" So if you plan to spend eternity in God's house you will enter there through the way God provided — and that way is by receiving His Son, the Lord Jesus Christ. If we have the Son we have *life* if we do not have the Son we do NOT have life — and if any person comes to you with any *other* doctrine, do not hear that person, do not fellowship with him, do not allow him to enter your home, do not give him support or words of comfort. If you do, you have contributed to the enemies of Jesus, you are partaker of their evil deeds and their damnable doctrine that sends souls to hell, and (if you are saved) you will certainly lose your reward! May God help us to be careful in these perilous times when there are so many false teachers abroad in the land!

The Third Epistle
of John

III JOHN

1. The elder unto the wellbeloved Gaius, whom I love in the truth.
2. Beloved, I wish above all things that thou mayest prosper and be in health, even as thy soul prospereth.
3. For I rejoiced greatly, when the brethren came and testified of the truth that is in thee, even as thou walkest in the truth.
4. I have no greater joy than to hear that my children walk in truth.
5. Beloved, thou doest faithfully whatsoever thou doest to the brethren, and to strangers;
6. Which have borne witness of thy charity before the church: whom if thou bring forward on their journey after a godly sort, thou shalt do well:
7. Because that for his name's sake, they went forth, taking nothing of the Gentiles.
8. We therefore ought to receive such, that we might be fellow-helpers to the truth.
9. I wrote unto the church: but Diotrephes, who loveth to have the preeminence among them, receiveth us not.
10. Wherefore, if I come, I will remember his deeds which he doeth, prating against us with malicious words: and not content therewith, neither doth he himself receive the brethren, and forbiddeth them that would, and casteth them out of the church.
11. Beloved, follow not that which is evil, but that which is good. He that doeth good is of God: but he that doeth evil hath not seen God.
12. Demetrius hath good report of all men, and of the truth itself: yea, and we also bear record, and ye know that our record is true.
13. I had many things to write, but I will not with ink and pen write unto thee:
14. But I trust I shall shortly see thee, and we shall speak face to face. Peace be to thee. Our friends salute thee. Greet the friends by name.

This brief third epistle was written to a believer named *Gaius*. All that we know about him is recorded here; he is not mentioned anywhere else in the New Testament. We would suppose that he was a member of some local church, and verse 4 of the epistle might lead us to believe that he was converted under John's ministry.

The time and place of the writing of this third epistle are also unknown.

Personal Greetings

Verse 1: "The elder unto the wellbeloved Gaius, whom I love in the truth."

The New Testament mentions the name *Gaius* four other times:

Paul mentions one in Romans 16:23 and refers to him as his host.

In I Corinthians 1:15 Paul tells us that he baptized one Gaius at Corinth.

In Acts 19:29 he speaks of Gaius of Macedonia, one of his fellow helpers in his journeys, who was arrested by the mob at Ephesus.

In Acts 20:4 Paul speaks of Gaius of Derbe who accompanied Paul and Timothy on their journey into Asia.

There is no way of proving whether or not any one of these men was the person to whom John wrote his third epistle. Gaius was a very common name in those days, and the four references may well represent four different people.

John does not tell us whether or not Gaius held office in the church. It would seem that he was a man of influence, possibly a man of wealth. The beloved disciple greeted him as *"well beloved,"* which certainly points out the fact that they were good friends. John speaks of him as one whom he loved *"in the truth,"* meaning that they were brothers in the faith and John loved him for the truth he had received and proclaimed as a believer.

Verse 2: "Beloved, I wish above all things that thou mayest prosper and be in health, even as thy soul prospereth."

The Greek word here translated "wish" in other places is rendered "pray." Hence we know that John prayed for this beloved brother, as he prayed for *all* believers.

"That thou mayest prosper and be in health, even as thy soul prospereth." John earnestly prayed that this beloved brother would prosper and be as well off physically as he was spiritually — an indication that undoubtedly Gaius was unusual in his spiritual life and testimony, and John prayed that he would prosper in all respects as he had prospered in his soul.

The Greek word here translated "prosper" is also used in Romans 1:10 and in I Corinthians 16:2, and has the meaning that John desired success and happiness for Gaius — success in business, in domestic relations, or in any other transaction in which a Christian might become engaged. Thus we see that we should pray for our friends and desire prosperity for them in all things that are honorable. John was concerned about the *health* of this believing brother — he wanted him to enjoy the blessing of a strong body, and to stay physically fit to be a good soldier in the army of Jesus Christ.

Verse 3: "For I rejoiced greatly, when the brethren came and testified of the truth that is in thee, even as thou walkest in the truth."

Who these brethren were, we do not know. This is one reason why I know the Bible was not written by ordinary men, for if *man* had been its author he would have given names on many occasions where there ARE no names. But names do not matter, because God keeps the record and He will reward justly and in righteousness. We do not need to know the names of these men who made the journey to see John the beloved disciple and gave him the report. It is entirely possible that these same men had delivered an epistle from the hand of John to the church (v. 9). Being shamefully treated by Diotrephes, they were perhaps then received into the home of Gaius and treated so royally that it would be natural for them to give this report on the Christian conduct and unselfish spirit of Gaius when they returned to John the Beloved. They *"testified of the truth"* that was in Gaius, which would mean that he stedfastly contended for the truth, walked in truth in spite of the error that was prevalent around him. John commends this dear believer as he did "the elect lady" in the second epistle.

I am afraid we have too little appreciation today on the part of religious leaders concerning the babes in Christ and the young men who are growing in grace. A well-spoken word of commendation when deserved is always encouraging to a young Christian, and certainly we *should* take advantage of every opportunity to encourage them along the way. A word of sincere praise — not Pharisaical flattery — can cause a young believer to press on, when otherwise that believer might become discouraged and falter in his Christian life.

Verse 4: "I have no greater joy than to hear that my children walk in truth."

Since John here refers to his "children" walking in truth, it is not unreasonable to suppose that Gaius was converted under John's ministry. The apostle was an old man by now, and assuming that Gaius was much younger than he, it would only be natural that he would have looked upon John as his spiritual father.

It is always a joy to any minister to learn that those who have been born again under his ministry are consistently growing in grace, walking in truth, and going forward in the things of the Lord. Personally, after more than a quarter of a century of preaching the Gospel, the joy of my heart is to return to a community or a church where I preached years before, and find the converts of those years going on with the Lord, growing in grace, advancing in spiritual matters. It always refreshes my soul to find that those who *believed* under the influence of my preaching are moving on in the things of God — pastoring a church, directing music in the church, perhaps teaching a Sunday school class, rendering faithful service to God.

A Faithful Servant

Verse 5: "Beloved, thou doest faithfully whatsoever thou doest to the brethren and to strangers."

Here John speaks in a more particular way concerning Gaius' acts of kindness and generosity. He speaks of his hospitality and declares that he faithfully discharged his duties as a believer and fulfilled the law of Christ concerning a brother's treatment of another brother. Whatever this man did, he did well, with all of his heart and with a sincere spirit. John did not practice flattery, but he was "the beloved disciple" and he knew that love begets love. This cold world needs a *baptism* of love — the kind of love that removes unselfishness and fills the heart with service to our fellowman.

Notice that John commends Gaius — not only for his hospitality and kindness to *"the brethren,"* but *"to strangers"* as well, people whom he had never met previously, possibly those who visited his church. Undoubtedly these strangers were believers, and therefore they were brethren in the Lord.

Verse 6: "Which have borne witness of thy charity before the church: whom if thou bring forward on their journey after a godly sort, thou shalt do well."

These brethren who bore witness to the kindness and love manifested by Gaius could have testified only to John, or it could be that they gave their testimony before a local assembly. Some have suggested that it could have been before the church in Ephesus.

". . . *Whom if thou bring forward on their journey . . . thou shalt do well.*" The reading here should be "whom, *having brought* forward on their journey."' Such assistance could have been money, it could have been food and lodging, or it could have been that these brethren were personally accompanied by other brethren to encourage them and give them fellowship on the way. One thing we know: Gaius had helped them in every way he possibly could. Now they were about to make another journey and John again commends them to Gaius. In that day it was the custom for the local churches to take care of fellow believers who journeyed through their community or city; but notice that John commends these brethren to the home of Gaius instead of to the church. The reason for this is given in verses 9 and 10. John knew that Gaius would treat these men as Christian brothers, and would help them again as he had helped them the first time, in every possible way. Thus he would "*do well*" because he would be taking care of God's servants — "*a godly sort,*" those who are worthy of support, love, and fellowship, those who are godly men.

Verse 7: "Because that for His name's sake they went forth, taking nothing of the Gentiles."

"*For His name's sake*" points to God, meaning that these brethren were making this journey in the interest of the Lord's business and in the interest of the church, and not for their own sakes. "*They went forth*" of course indicates that they had already departed and were on their journey in the name of the Lord and for His name's sake.

". . . *Taking nothing of the Gentiles.*" This includes all who were not Jews. The term "Gentile" is often used in the New Testament with reference to sinners — moreso *before* the crucifixion than after, because Jesus broke down the middle wall of partition that separated men. Now Jew and Gentile are alike precious in His sight, and He died to save Gentiles as well as Jews. It seems that these brethren had strong convictions about their support and from whom they should *receive* support and hospitality. When they went out they determined to receive no part of their financial help from unbelievers, but from believing brethren only.

In the early years of Christianity there were those who determined to preach the Gospel "without charge," lest they be accused of preaching simply for what they received by way of money or material things. In the beginning years of Paul's ministry he took nothing from his converts, but supported himself by working at his trade as a tentmaker. In Later years, however, he instructed the churches to take care of the brethren, and gave instructions concerning the collections and how they should be given.

These men of whom John speaks refused to take anything from the Gentiles, lest their testimony be hindered. Thus they could preach the Gospel to one and all impartially, and declare that they were doing it without charge. Our God is able to supply our every need, and WILL do so if we are willing to trust Him. When Jesus sent out the seventy he told them, "The labourer is worthy of his hire" (Luke 10:7). Paul told the Corinthians that the Lord has ordained "that they which preach the Gospel should live of the Gospel" (I Cor. 9:14). It is God's plan and program in this Day of Grace that believers support the work of the Lord. We are instructed to lay by in store as God prospers us. Christians should give from the heart, not according to rules and regulations of denominations. We should give because we love Jesus, and we should give bountifully, knowing that if we give bountifully we will reap a bountiful harvest, and if we give sparingly we shall *reap* sparingly.

Verse 8: "We therefore ought to receive such, that we might be fellowhelpers to the truth."

Believers should be hospitable to *other* believers, we should entertain, provide for, and take care of them in any way that they have need if we have the means to *supply* that need. We are workers together for God, members of the same body, members of the one true Church of which Jesus is the head and the foundation. There should be no selfishness among believers. If we see one of our Christian brethren in need we should count it a peculiar joy, not a duty, to *help* that brother, *"that we might be fellowhelpers to the truth."* When we support a servant of God — teacher, minister, evangelist, missionary, or even a layman who is winning souls — we are "fellowhelpers to the truth." We are helping to *proclaim* the truth, and when we give to God's work we should not feel that we are giving to a man or a program, but to the Lord, for the purpose of spreading the Gospel and getting out the good news that Jesus saves. Also, when we support our church and our pastor we have a part in all the souls that are saved through that ministry.

A Domineering Deacon

Verse 9: "I wrote unto the church: but Diotrephes, who loveth to have the preeminence among them, receiveth us not."

John says *"I wrote unto the church."* This points back to the former visit when these brethren went forth to visit in the community and in the church where Gaius was a member. Since it was customary for the local churches to take care of Christians who traveled to and through their area, it was a natural thing for John to commend these men *to* the church.

"But Diotrephes, who loveth to have the preeminence. . . ." I cannot *prove* that Diotrephes was a deacon in the church, but I personally *believe* that he was. We have some godly, God-fearing, humble, Spirit-filled deacons; but we also have some who are just the opposite. Some deacons think it is their job to hire and fire preachers, and to run the church as they see fit; but if they will read the seventh chapter of Acts they will learn that the ministry of a deacon is quite different from what they practice!

Diotrephes did not recognize the authority of John the Beloved, he did not accept John's recommendation as from one of authority in the Church. The Scripture does not tell us whether or not Diotrephes was an official in the church, but we know that he was undoubtedly a powerful individual in that body. This is evident from the influence he wielded. There are such men in the local churches today, men who, if they would tell the truth when asked if they belong to the church, would reply, "I do not belong to the church — *the church belongs to ME.*" There ARE churches (and to my sorrow I have been in a few of them) that are not run by God or by the pastor — nor even by the board of deacons — but by *one person.* Sometimes that person is a man; occasionally, sad to say, it is a woman; but in such instances, the whole church does what that one person commands. As that person goes, so goes the church, the pastor, the deacon board. Diotrephes was such a church member. He rejected John's request and refused to accept the brethren.

Greek authorities tell us that the phrase here translated "*who loveth to have the preeminence*" is only *one word* in the Greek, and it is not found anywhere else in the New Testament. The meaning is simply "one who loves to be *first,*" one who will rule or ruin. But there ARE no rulers or lords in God's Church. Pastors, deacons, church leaders are not to be "lords over God's heritage" (I Pet. 5:3).

"Diotrephes . . . *receiveth us not.*" This means that Diotrephes did not receive John as God's apostle, a true representative of the Church. He was probably *jealous* of John. We know that *Peter* did not fully appreciate John because Jesus referred to him as the disciple whom He loved (John 21:20-22). It could well be that this man was also envious, jealous of John. If this be true, then we have some "Diotrepheses" living today, because there are some churches where only one jealous-hearted man or woman can tie the hands of God and the church cannot go forward because of such an attitude. There are people in the local churches who simply MUST have the preeminence, they must be recognized and used above all others, they just MUST be *seen,* or they refuse to serve — and if possible, they will keep *others* from serving.

Verse 10: "Wherefore, if I come, I will remember his deeds which he doeth, prating against us with malicious words: and not content therewith, neither doth he himself receive the brethren, and forbiddeth them that would, and casteth them out of the church."

According to this verse (and also verse 14) John planned to visit the beloved Gaius and the church to which he belonged, and in connection with that visit he declares "*I will remember his deeds which he doeth.*" This statement points out the fact that John intended taking measures to deal with this man in the proper Christian manner and through the proper channels, to see that he was dealt with and punished for his selfish, arrogant, domineering spirit in the church. John's statement was not made in the wrong spirit, he held no animosity against this man; but it was his duty to deal with those who demonstrated such a spirit toward fellow believers. How many times in John's Gospel (as well as in these epistles) he emphasizes brotherly love! and if we cannot minister to the needs of our brothers in Christ, "how dwelleth the love of God in us?" (I John 3:17). Church leaders and officials sin when they do not deal with a person like Diotrephes. What he had done was done openly and the entire church knew about it; therefore it needed to be *dealt with openly* and before the entire assembly.

In I Corinthians 5:3-5 we learn that Paul practiced discipline in the church at Corinth, and it *should* be practiced today. It is sorely needed.

John speaks of Diotrephes as *"prating against us with malicious words."* The Greek word here rendered "prating" does not occur anywhere else in the New Testament. Its meaning is to "overflow with talk," one who talks too much without saying anything, continually rattling the tongue with no purpose in what is being said.

I think you will agree that we have *the spirit* of Diotrephes in the church today — both male and female. We need to read again the words of Jesus in Matthew 12:36: "I say unto you, *That every idle word that men shall speak, they shall give account, thereof in the day of judgment."*

We need to hear again the admonition of James: "Behold, we put bits in the horses' mouths, that they may obey us; and we turn about their whole body. Behold also the ships, which though they be so great, and are driven of fierce winds, yet are they turned about with a very small helm, whithersoever the governor listeth. *Even so the tongue is a little member, and boasteth great things. Behold, how great a matter a little fire kindleth! And the tongue is a fire, a world of iniquity: so is the tongue among our members, that it defileth the whole body, and setteth on fire the course of nature; and it is set on fire of hell.* For every kind of beasts, and of birds, and of serpents, and

of things in the sea, is tamed, and hath been tamed of mankind: BUT THE TONGUE CAN NO MAN TAME: IT IS AN
UNRULY EVIL, FULL OF DEADLY POISON" (James 3:3-
8).
There is entirely too much idle, foolish talk, too much unprofitable talk, too much back-biting in the church today. If we
could get church members to talk on their knees to God as
much as they talk on the telephone (or across the back fence to
their neighbors) about their brethren and the church, we would
have a revival that would run the devil out of the United
States!
What Diotrephes did against the brethren, he did openly; and
from the tone of the Greek language it seems that he was still
bragging about it. Not willing to drop it, he was prating against
John "with malicious words." The word "malicious" means evil.
Thus Diotrephes had said many evil words against John, words
designed to do injury to the influence and character of this beloved disciple.
"And not content therewith" (not satisfied with what had
happened) "neither doth he himself receive the brethren, and
forbiddeth them that would, and casteth them out of the
church." It is not God's will for any person in the Church to
carry so much weight and wield so much influence as did Diotrephes, and John intended to see that something was done
about it. From John's comment here, it would seem that some of
the brethren in the church were willing to receive the men
whom John sent, but Diotrephes did not want to receive them,
he did not want the church to receive them, and those in the
church who DID want to receive them were persecuted and
caused to be cast out of the church — all because of the influence of Diotrephes.
Verse 11: "Beloved, follow not that which is evil, but that
which is good. He that doeth good is of God: but he that doeth
evil hath not seen God."
It is clear that John had Diotrephes in mind here. Gaius was a
beloved brother who had a good testimony and John was cautioning him not to let the actions of Diotrephes influence him.
However, Gaius was not to take matters into his own hands
and attempt to deal with this domineering man, but rather,

leave it for John to take care of when he visited the church. Gaius was a man of influence and he had shown a Christian spirit in all things; yet John knew that Satan is no respecter of persons and it would be a great blow to the church if Satan could cause this loyal church member to behave in an unchristian manner.

"*He that doeth good is of God.*" Gaius had been kind, generous, hospitable to the brethren, and his display of kindness and goodness was outward proof that he belonged to God. Jesus said, "Ye shall know them by their fruits. Do men gather grapes of thorns, or figs of thistles? Even so every good tree bringeth forth good fruit; but a corrupt tree bringeth forth evil fruit. A good tree cannot bring forth evil fruit, neither can a corrupt tree bring forth good fruit" (Matt. 7:16-18). Gaius was producing good fruit, showing that he had a righteous heart.

"*He that doeth evil hath not seen God.*" An evil tree brings forth evil fruit; the fruit is evil because the *tree* is evil. Men like Diotrephes may be "religious," they may belong to a local church, but they do not know God. They have not received the *truth* of God, they have not seen God with the eye of understanding. They are children of Satan, and therefore their works are evil.

Verse 12: "Demetrius hath good report of all men, and of the truth itself: yea, and we also bear record; and ye know that our record is true."

There were *good* men in the church, they were not all like Diotrephes. Demetrius was in direct contrast to him. He had a good testimony, "*good report of all men,*" and from this we understand that he was a godly man. John knew this man personally, he said "*we also bear record,*" and he could testify concerning Demetrius — a person who had a good report in the church and in the community, a man who practiced Christian living day by day.

Demetrius also had the testimony "*of the truth itself.*" We may fool men but we cannot fool God. Here was a man who bore the testimony of truth that he was a righteous, godly man. It was not simply his outward reputation; it was his actual, daily living that declared him to be a man of good conduct, a man whose character was above reproach.

"Ye know that our testimony is true." John had that kind of testimony. So far as the Word of God tells us, there was nothing of sin or wrongdoing recorded against him. He stayed with Jesus when the other disciples fled in fear for their lives. He stood with the mother of Jesus while the Saviour hung on the cross. To this beloved disciple God dictated five of the New Testament books — five of the most important books in the entire Bible. Through John the Holy Spirit gave us John's Gospel (the salvation book); the First Epistle of John (the joy book); the Second and Third epistles which speak out for truth and brotherly love; and The Revelation —God's last message to man. John was indeed an extraordinary apostle.

Verse 13: "I had many things to write, but I will not with ink and pen write unto thee."

Here we find almost the same words that closed the second epistle. John had many things on his heart, things he wanted to say, but he preferred to wait and converse face to face with this friend and beloved brother. Some things are better said than written. Some things are better settled face to face. Matters between believers can be discussed and settled much better face to face than by correspondence — or even by calling on the telephone. Therefore, much that John carried in his heart could wait until he should visit Gaius and the church, when these things could be talked out in person.

Verse 14: "But I trust I shall shortly see thee, and we shall speak face to face. Peace be to thee. Our friends salute thee. Greet the friends by name."

John certainly had definite plans to visit this community and church shortly. Such matters as had arisen there should be attended to and settled as quickly as possible. John believed in doing things the Bible way, and the Bible way is to face an issue and settle it quickly, even before we bring our offerings unto the Lord. Jesus said, ". . . If thou bring thy gift to the altar, and there rememberest that thy brother hath ought against thee; leave there thy gift before the altar, and go thy way; first be reconciled to thy brother, and then come and offer thy gift" (Matt. 5:23, 24).

"Our friends salute thee." No doubt John had many close friends, and according to the verses we have just studied, the

same was true of Gaius and Demetrius. Therefore they and John would have had many mutual friends, and it is of these mutual friends that John speaks.

"Greet the friends by name." While John no doubt thought of the church collectively, he remembered his brothers in the Lord *individually.* We have entirely too little of such personal attention today. God loved the world — but He also loved individuals. Jesus died for the sins of the world — but He calls individuals to serve Him; He called His disciples one by one. We should look upon our fellow believers as individuals, we should love them individually, and call them by name.

From this third epistle we learn that Christians cannot live in a small world of selfishness. It is our responsibility to pray for our brothers and sisters in Christ, and wish prosperity and happiness for them. Jesus loved the world, He died for the world, and we should give our best to help those who, like ourselves, are members of the family of God.

John found great joy in learning that his children in the faith were practicing true Christian living, walking in the truth and in godly love, discharging the duties of hospitality toward other Christians.

We also learn from this epistle that it is a Christian duty as well as a privilege to support those who travel in the interest of the Gospel — missionaries, ministers, evangelists, all who preach the Gospel and give out the good news of salvation. We should be liberal in our hospitality to them, giving them food and shelter as they pass our way, remembering that what we do for them we do for the Lord, because they represent Him in truth. We should be glad to contribute to the support of missionaries who carry the Gospel to those who have never heard, whether it be at home or in foreign lands. How we need Christian hospitality today between churches! There is so much selfishness among Christians — if folk are of our own little group we help them, and if not, we turn them away or pass them by. This should not be.

In this third epistle we see an example of the trouble one person can cause in an assembly, and we learn that such a person should not be allowed to remain IN the assembly. He should be dealt with — but this should be done according to

Christian principles and the Word of God. Church discipline
should be practiced according to the rules of Christianity laid
down in the Bible, never in anger or for the purpose of
"getting even."

After the domineering spirit of someone like Diotrephes, how
refreshing to read of Christians like Gaius and Demetrius.
We should follow their examples in doing good. We need
more such men in the Church today — men who are kind,
considerate, loving, hospitable, friends to strangers, helpers of
all who need help. I repeat — this poor, selfish, unkind world
needs a baptism of the love of God. More love and unselfishness between Christians would make this world a much better
place in which to live.

I wonder — if John should write an epistle about you and me,
could he say the kind words and give the glowing testimony
he applied to Gaius and Demetrius? or would he be led to
reprimand us for showing the spirit of Diotrephes? May God
help us to search our hearts, and may He empty us of all that
is ugly, selfish, and worldly, and fill us with His love and His
Spirit. May we be living epistles read of all men, to the
glory of God.

I close this series of studies with this prayer:

> *Lord, let me live from day to day*
> *In such a self-forgetful way,*
> *That even when I kneel to pray*
> *My prayer shall be for others!*